W9-AYF-957

PENGUIN BOOKS

WOMEN REBORN:

AN EXPLORATION OF THE SPIRITUALITY OF URBAN INDIAN WOMEN

Renuka Singh has a doctorate in sociology from Jawaharlal Nehru University, New Delhi. For the last twenty years she has been working in the field of women's studies and has presented papers and participated in workshops both in India and abroad. She has also worked with several non-governmental organizations, and at the Women's Studies and Development Centre, Delhi University.

Renuka Singh is the author of *The Womb of Mind* (1990) and has co-authored *Growing Up in Rural India* (1989). She has also published extensively in journals and newspapers. She has been a Research Fellow at the Centre for Cross-Cultural Research on Women at Oxford University, and is currently UGC Senior Fellow at the Centre for the Study of Social Systems, Jawaharlal Nehru University.

PENGUIN BOOKS

WOMEN REBORN

AN EXPLORATION OF THE SPIRITUALITY OF URBAN INDIAN WOMEN

Renuka Singh has a doctorate in sociology from Jawaharlal Nehru University, New Delhi. For the last twenty years she has been working in the field of women's studies and has presented papers and participated in workshops both in India and abroad. She has also worked with several non-governmental organizations, and at the Women's Studies and Development Centre, Delhi University.

Renuka Singh is the author of *The Womb of Mind* (1990) and has co-authored *Growing Up in Rural India* (1989). She has also published extensively in journals and newspapers. She has been a Research Fellow at the Centre for Cross-Cultural Research on Women at Oxford University, and is currently UGC Senior Fellow at the Centre for the Study of Social Systems, Jawaharlal Nehru University.

# Women Reborn

## An Exploration of the Spirituality of Urban Indian Women

Renuka Singh

PENGUIN BOOKS

Penguin Books India (P) Ltd., 210 Chiranjiv Tower, 43 Nehru Place, New Delhi 110 019, India
Penguin Books Ltd., 27 Wrights Lane, London W8 5TZ, UK
Penguin Books USA Inc., 375 Hudson Street, New York, NY 10014, USA
Penguin Books Australia Ltd., Ringwood, Victoria, Australia
Penguin Books Canada Ltd., 10 Alcorn Avenue, Suite 300, Toronto, Ontario M4V 3B2, Canada
Penguin Books (NZ) Ltd., 182-190 Wairau Road, Auckland 10, New Zealand

First published by Penguin Books India (P) Ltd. 1997

Copyright © Renuka Singh 1997

All rights reserved

10 9 8 7 6 5 4 3 2 1

Typeset in Palatino by Digital Technologies and Printing Solutions, New Delhi

**For my mother**

This book is sold subject to the condition that it shall not, by way of trade or otherwise, be lent, resold, hired out, or otherwise circulated without the publisher's prior written consent in any form of binding or cover other than that in which it is published and without a similar condition including this condition being imposed on the subsequent purchaser and without limiting the rights under copyright reserved above, no part of this publication may be reproduced, stored in or introduced into a retrieval system, or transmitted in any form or by any means (electronic, mechanical, photocopying, recording or otherwise), without the prior written permission of both the copyright owner and the above-mentioned publisher of this book.

# Contents

# Contents

# Acknowledgements

Researching and writing about women's experiences with spirituality, especially through their family relationships, has been a very personal journey, helping me to take stock and re-evaluate many aspects of my own life. I wish to offer a very special thanks to my women subjects, who, during the course of their interviews, revealed both disturbing and empowering stories.

My association with His Holiness the Dalai Lama, revered teacher and friend, has been very meaningful. I am grateful to him for his kindness. Also, to his students, Dharmakirti and Scott who have contributed to my project.

When I was at the Centre for Cross-Cultural Research on Women at Oxford University, Shirley Ardener, Dr Ketaki Kushari Dyson, Dr Soraya Tremayne and Dr Jackie Waldren showed great interest in my work and engaged me in stimulating discussions. I thank them as well as Nami Kaur, Susie Roy, Sheila Agarwal and Dr Jackie Tarter for their piquant insights. For making my stay comfortable and interesting in the UK, I am obliged to our family friends—the Johals, Parbhat and Michael Smith.

The completion of this project would not have been possible without the fellowship from the University Grants Commission and funding provided by the British Council during my stay at Oxford. I would also like to thank the Centre for the Study of

Social Systems, Jawaharlal Nehru University, New Delhi for its cooperation, and in particular, Prof Yogendra Singh and Prof K. L. Sharma for their encouragement.

A paper based on this study has been presented at the School of Oriental and African Studies, London; at the University of Washington, Seattle; at the Evergreen State College, Olympia; and at the University of California, Berkeley. Thanks to Dr Julia Leslie, Dr Margaret Scarborough, Dr Sally Goldman and Prof Robert Goldman for their comments and suggestions.

My deepest gratitude goes to my friends: Dian Olson, for her moral and intellectual support, and Guy E. Olson, for taking up the Herculean task of editing this book. Also to Karthika, my editor at Penguin for her critical input and assistance.

Finally, to my father Pritam Singh and sisters, Jyoti Paul and Ashma Singh for their thoughtfulness and emotional sustenance.

# Introduction

This book explores the lives of contemporary urban Indian women and their experiences with spirituality. Such an undertaking necessarily confronts the challenge of studying an area academically unfashionable, perhaps 'airy-fairy' for many. My own personal experiences in the realm of spirituality obviously have had a bearing on this ongoing intellectual project and have compelled me to steer in this direction. Articulating the phenomenon of inner transformation—how the harsh dry wind changes into a gentle breeze—is a daunting task.

In recent years, new patterns have emerged in the ways in which urban women view and seek to empower themselves. Many women have attempted to develop their lives by drawing power through external sources of financial support, polity and society. Others, however, have tried to sustain strength and confidence by seeking a spiritual path as well.

The spirituality of women today remains a relatively uncharted area. The scholarly literature is confined to religious aspects of women's lives—rules, roles and rituals of women in various religions; superstitious behaviour; myths and symbolic representations in art, sculpture, dance, music, cinema, television, and literature—or to research on religious practitioners such as yoginis, gurus, and renunciants. This book, by contrast, presents a sociologial study of modern, secular women for the purpose of understanding the nature and power of their minds, thoughts, and feelings. It also examines women's inter-personal relationships, especially in families, which hitherto have not been explored in depth.

The objective of this study is to present, describe and understand the preoccupation of women with their spiritual transformation. It examines the spiritual evolution of women through family relationships, with special reference to the mother-daughter bond; education and work; sexuality; and their interaction with gurus. Although dreams form an equally important and inextricable facet of women's spiritual awakening, they lie beyond the scope of this study.

Women often create and belong to a second or 'other' family, one that is based, not on biological and social ties, but on spiritual and social connections. Hence, wherever applicable, this study looks into these 'other' family relationships as well.

Needless to say, if women are to engage seriously with the task of self-development, they must first identify areas of conflict and interest. The Beijing World Conference on Women in 1995 identified twelve critical areas for women's development: elimination of poverty and armed conflict; education; health; access to political and economic rights; career advancement; and the nurturing of the girl child. Ideological, religious and cultural differences have been acknowledged, yet, peace and progress for women remains a common aim. A UN report suggests that empowerment of individual women, a wider range of opportunities for both women and men, and building a basis for action at the family and community level, may be the key to social development in the rest of the century and beyond. Evidence is accumulating that free and equal access to health care, family planning and education is not only desirable in itself but a practical contribution to the success of wider objectives, including environmental protection and economic development.[1]

In India, both governmental and non-governmental efforts have been made to assess women's needs and problems, and enhance their status. Many scholars have also described the imbalances created and resolved by the process of development, urbanization, and modernization. It is generally maintained that the relative status of women has deteriorated in post-independence India.[2] In spite of the constitutional protection for women in India, the drop in their numbers, (the sex ratio fell from 945 in 1951 to 929 in 1991), life-expectancy, literacy rate, and economic participation vis-a-vis men denote a situation deleterious to their welfare. Amniocentesis, female infanticide, widespread harassment of brides, rape, and other forms of increasing violence against women speak all too clearly of women's oppression, deprivation, and suffering.

When academicians and activists highlight the 'scarcity-syndrome' experienced by a majority of the ignored and marginalized rural women in India—their struggle to procure the most basic necessities of life such as food, fuel, and water; their minimal control over the conditions and the products of their labours; their passive role in the decision-making process within the family—one may then wonder about the spirit that keeps these women alive and ticking. To many urban women, the positive realities of rural life and the well-springs of their strength remain hidden.

The empirical facts and information about the lives of women provide useful but incomplete understanding of their true conditions. For this, one needs to look into a different terrain—of spirituality. Tapping the spiritual core can prevent women from being short-changed by history or circumstances. While this study focuses on urban women, their predilection and commitment to the spiritual pursuit has relevance as well to young professionals caught up in the development process.

In the past two decades, studies of religion have dealt with different religious ideologies, teachings and prescriptions that determine to a great extent, the identity, role and status of women. Neglected are the implications that religion has for self-perception and enlightenment. However, feminist thinking, by presenting women as both subjects and agents of change, has triggered, according to King, an important paradigm shift in the contemporary study of religion, both in theology and in religious studies.[3]

'The challenge thrown down,' observes Leslie, 'is the need

to see women not merely as the passive victims of an oppressive ideology but also (perhaps primarily) as the active agents of their own positive constructs. This challenge makes demands on us in two distinct areas of research: in our interpretation of religious and ritual texts, and in our evolution of the religious experiences of women.'[4]

Although postmodernism has been a precoccupation of academia for some years, it is difficult to generalize about the character of the postmodern condition. Nonetheless, there is found everywhere a commitment by society to heterogeneity, fragmentation and difference which has been applied to various conflicting socio-cultural projects. So today, instead of generating insights in terms of universals, postmodernists have been emphasizing the 'difference' in the understanding of gender issues—the linguistic, cultural, socio-economic, political, sexual and psychological. The conventional schools of thought have assumed that women can be agents of change and transformation. However, many postmodernists, through deconstruction of unified subjectivity into fragmented subject positions, have questioned this assumption by suspending all forms of value judgments, such as truth, freedom, and rationality for all emancipatory movements.[5] They have also taught us to view both endings and beginnings with scepticism. Thus, dissolution of the unitary subject facilitates feminism(s) of difference(s): differences in the construction of women within their specific social positions.[6]

In Raschke's words, the term 'postmodern' serves as a kind of clandestine intrusion into the kingdom of signification. It concomitantly baffles, bedazzles and enrages—principally because it neither denotes nor intimates anything other than an incursion across the borderland of sensibility.[7] For some, postmodernism implies the death of God and disappearance of religion, for others, the return of traditional faith, and for still others, the possibility of recasting religious ideas.[8] Nothing is simply itself, and nothing is one thing, in this mode of intellectual wandering. Berry suggests that this changed perspective has revived interest in those once-tabooed aspects of 'otherness' which can broadly be termed spiritual or religious.[9] Wernick too points towards an interest manifest not only in popular fundamentalism, but also, and more paradoxically, in the preoccupation with the mystical, the spiritual and the religious that has surfaced in the works of theoreticians of the secular intelligentsia. "As markers, we may think of Derrida's *Of Spirit*, of the Buddhist conception of (not-) self which can be detected in the works of Foucault and others, as underlying the subjects' 'de-centring', and in a more ecclesiastical mode, of Althusser's crypto-Comteian attempt to turn Marxism-Leninism into the heir of Catholicism."[10]

The connection between the new spiritual concerns of postmodernism and its need for an ethical code, argues Wyscnogrod, can serve as a new normative structure after the dismissal of Marxism.[11] So, according to Finn, experiences of excess, disjuncture, difference, chaos and chance are necessary and indispensable conditions of ecstasy, creativity, change and critique.[12] This process has fundamentally altered the attitude towards religious beliefs, practices and organizations, and the seemingly strange resurfacing of the spiritual imperative in the core of secular thought has become largely a global affair. Recently, *The Times of India* carried a report: 'Many members of the urban middle classes and non-resident Indians, disenchanted with traditional religious beliefs, are gravitating towards sects and reformist movements that cut across communities and established religions and focus on morality, asceticism and self-renewal . . . What people find most appealing is the way they combine hi-tech, eco-friendly management skills and social work with the revival of the celibate, ascetic Guru as priest, psycho-therapist and counsellor.'[13]

Today, even the ordinary people wish to take responsibility for their own self-realization and enlightenment, and acknowledge an underlying cosmic consciousness beneath divergent religious traditions and reality. Therefore, one needs to look into the social circumstances which compel religion to retain its older forms or gain new dimensions and roles, and also decipher the spiritual subtext that has begun to surface in the lives of women.

The existing literature regarding gender and religion touches on the following themes, wherein spirituality has only figured recently:

- The mother or the father or the androgynous model of a godhead is examined in the treatment of a divine. Here male and female aspects are combined to form a whole. Some of the literature presents a monistic idea of metaphysical reality. Other literature deals with gender polarization; androcentrism, which considers men as naturally the superior sex and the normative model for being human; and biological essentialism, which valourizes male-female differences and male dominance.[14]
- Gender relations in cross-cultural and historical contexts have explored women's religious roles and behaviour but paid scant attention to how religious symbols and myths determine genderedness.[15]
- Most of the scholarly work deals with religious thought, practices, language and symbols, without regard to gender.[16]
- Some scholars maintain that the task of reconstructing knowledge involves detailed historical research to uncover the voices, experiences and contributions of women in religious history and the life of humankind. As Buchanun points out, it also implies the reformulation of religious beliefs, ethical thought, celebration of the goddess, and what is called the new religious world linked to women's spiritual quest.[17]
- A new school of theological thought is undertaking scholarly work on the goddess phenomenon.[18]
- New perspectives on women and religion are evolving out of a rereading, reconceiving, and reconstructing of religious traditions. These are concerned with women's presence and absence, with women's words and silences, and with recognition given and denied to women.[19]

- Women who have exercised considerable authority, despite their oppression, are becoming subjects of study. These women—nuns, ascetics, mystics, healers, witches and shamans—however, have had to give up their conventional social roles as mothers, wives, and daughters.[20]
- Another area of research deals with women's experiences of the sacred, and female symbols associated with the sacred. The rich feminine symbolism and its ascendency, especially in Hinduism, often goes hand in hand with women's social denigration and low status in everyday life. [21]
- There is a particularly striking contrast between the representation of women as evil and wise. Body, sexuality, menstruation taboos, death, inauspiciousness and witch-like behaviour are linked with the complex issue of evil, which is the antithesis of the spirit of wisdom and compassion in the representations of the female Bodhisattva.[22]
- A challenging area of current research is concerned with women's spirituality. This incorporates women's contemporary spiritual quest or is even seen in feminist consciousness or goddess spirituality. King has surveyed the explicit and implicit spiritual dimensions of contemporary feminism with reference to different religions and cultures.[23] Martin (1993)[24] and Christ and Plaskow (1992)[25] have studied new patterns and needs for feminist spirituality, and Harris has formulated the familiar seven steps of Awakening, Discovering, Creating, Dwelling, Nourishing, Traditioning, and Transforming (1991).[26]

I would like to see my study as a contribution to the exploration of women's spiritual quest. What does spirituality mean to urban Indian women? How do they describe their spiritual experience? How do they transmit it to others? What sort of social influence or authority do they derive from it? What kind of knowledge do they produce? What are the negative or positive self-images of empowerment that emerge in their lives? Is women's spiritual struggle a private or public matter? Is it an unfolding of an ethical self-knowledge? Is this inner voyage, especially in a family setting, a source of strength or is it a defence mechanism against an aggressive social structure? What relationship does it have with their sexuality? What is the role and significance of the guru in women's awakening? Hence, to what extent are women committed to spiritual freedom and simultaneously engaged in historical and social practice marked by self-critical vigilance?

During fieldwork for my earlier book [27], I interviewed two hundred women in Delhi from diverse backgrounds. They displayed a strong commitment to personal relationships and work, and to social/sexual responsibilities. Spiritual advancement through family relationships and daily struggles, therefore, figures prominently in this work.

Before I elaborate on how I conducted this study, it would be useful to note the ambiguity associated with the notion of spirituality, just as with the term 'religion'. Weber, for instance, nowhere attempts a precise definition of religion, apart from implying the centrality of the concept of the supernatural, identifying religious ideas, attitudes, actors and institutions, and examining the relationship between the religious and the secular domain.[28] Even Durkheim and Dumont, Tillich and Jung only tried to highlight certain aspects or dimensions of religion.[29]

Through temperament, choice or limitation, I too feel inadequate in trying to describe, analyse, and even more, define something as intangible as spirituality. One can only try to point out 'domains' or 'fields' that seem analogous to it. Philosophers have faced a similar dilemma. M. Chatterjee, for example, writes:

'The term spirituality exerts a certain seductiveness among those who write on religion these days. It is often used as if we all knew what it means . . . We all seem to be in favour of spirituality these days. But what are we in favour of? Is it necessarily found in religious life or may some of its strongest manifestations arise in other spheres, especially in our own century? It is surely dangerous to invoke something whose meaning is no longer reasonably clear. Indeed, what are we opting for when we pine for the spiritual (if at all we do)? Can it be opted for anyway, or it is one of those elusive things, like happiness, which dissolves at the merest hint of deliberate pursuit? . . . The spiritual, in whatever ways we may close in on its meanings, to get free of all definitions, breaks out of the religious straitjackets that history may have devised for it. And in this breaking loose may lie, if not the redemption of our condition, at least a powerful factor which could well heal the frightening fragmentation of life.'[30]

The term 'spirituality' fell into disuse primarily after the rise of materialism. To study the 'spirit,' which is not a material thing, and bring it down to the empirical level is undoubtedly a difficult enterprise. Probably, one can only intuit about it. For instance, one of my respondents, a teacher from the upper-middle class stated:

'There was a time in my life when I thought that spirituality had something to do with going to church and sitting still, that it was a function of religious observance. Later in life I came to think that the essence of spirituality was the opposite of material progress because I saw that the problems in the world, and within my own family, were caused by the pursuit of material well-being. Again, I thought spirituality was another type of religious observance, somehow quite different from the first form. Instead of sitting still on a wooden pew, it was to sit still on a cushion.

'Yet none of these are in themselves the essence of what spirituality is or is not. In all of them there is something lacking, and in each of them there is the opportunity for spiritual inquiry. When I think back to my younger days, though I lacked a sense of connectedness with going to church, I understood in my heart that the most important thing was love—how much of it I gave and shared and how much I felt I received. The simplicity of this child-mind, I feel, is the basic simplicity of spirituality. We all are seeking to experience boundless love and compassion, for ourselves and for others.

'Spirituality also has the aspect of deep wisdom. Knowledge and wisdom are not the same thing. Where a botanist may know the names of a thousand plants and a thousand trees, he may not actually know any one tree. He may not know what the tree means in the larger picture, how it fits in as a piece of the large world. I feel this is how science has become separate from the deeper understanding of the world. Because of specialization and a materialistic approach to scientific practices, we fail to see or consider the future for others or ourselves.

'The person who is wise sees how things exist, how things arise, abide, and dissolve, and the interconnectedness of all things and people. The wise person only uses what is necessary with the understanding of their place and of the place of others. There is an understanding that there is more to just this one life—as one person compared with many, and as one life in a series of existences.

'I had an opportunity to hear a well-known teacher. He talked of listening and seeing in a deeper way, of how to look deeply into something to see the whole world in that one thing. There were many people at this talk. Afterwards, people really took care with each other when we were leaving the packed hall. Everyone had a smile of joy or the gaze of meditation. We all had shared the experience of how to look at others and the world simply. The feeling of oneness with others, with the world, the feeling of a 'we' instead of a 'me' . . . a greater love was felt. Childlike love and this wisdom share a deep simplicity that I feel is the essence of spirituality. This simplicity—in our thoughts, in our work, in our approach to living—allows the deeper truths to be seen, the spiritual truths.

'I now am trying to make my life simple. This doesn't mean that I sit in my room and only eat rice. The simplicity I am trying to permeate my life with, is a simplicity of the heart. I still have a very busy schedule and I am often running about the city. My last job was somewhat complicated, but I felt that having a simple outlook and a wish to help others made it easier. Now I try to have a good connection with others.'

As Berry claims, 'today a new understanding of spirit has arisen, not as the opposite term of a binary couple, but rather as facilitating a wholly new mode of awareness, which not only invites the thinker to abandon their residual attachment to dualistic thinking, but also offers a potent challenge to their desire for subjective mastery and knowledge. The result of a recovery—or discovery—of this understanding appears to be the attainment of a new capacity for ethical action—whether this is described in terms of love, compassion, altruism or care.'[31] To corroborate further, His Holiness the Dalai Lama remarks on his conception of spirituality, its relationship with religion, and hope for humanity in the wake of communism, capitalism and religion that have produced alienated human beings:

'Basically, the factor or element which creates happiness or satisfaction is what I consider spiritual. For example, compassion, tolerance and altruism bring us happiness and calmness and, therefore, these are basically spiritual. Religion comes later. Actually religion is meant for satisfaction and the ultimate source of happiness. It simply tries to strengthen the element of mental happiness. Perhaps, therefore, positive mental thought is my conception of spirituality.

'From the Buddhist viewpoint, for example in the case of one individual or person like myself, the practice of compassion and religion coincides, but another individual, without religion, can practice spirituality without being religious. So, a secular person can be spiritual. Compassion is compulsory for everyone to practice, and if I am a dictator I will dictate to everyone to do so. Whereas, religion is an individual right. The academics also make a distinction between religion and spirituality, but some religious-minded people do not think there is a distinction. They feel that without religion, proper love and compassion cannot develop. However, I feel that there can be spirituality without religion. For instance, you can have a very good human being, warm-hearted and altruistic, with no religion at all. I found some communists, who are very much concerned about others' rights due to their ideology of socialism, have the willingness to sacrifice their own lives for the benefit of the community. This clearly demonstrates that through certain mental training it is possible to develop that kind of attitude without religion.

'I think religion, ideology, economy, and political systems are all man's creation. Since these are man's creation, they must relate with human feeling and human spirit. So, religion, Marxist ideology or economic system, for example, if carried out by human beings, are humanized. If they are practiced with some human feeling, they fulfil some basic human aspirations. Then they become truly human activities meant for humanity. Therefore, there is no danger. Sometimes, unfortunately, what happens is that an overly religious person reacts at an emotional level and forgets about the human spirit. Thus, religion becomes alienated from the basic human feeling. In such a case, someone will even sacrifice human life for the benefit of all. Whereas a Marxist, for example, when he goes to an extreme, becomes dogmatic and bigoted and forgets about the real goal, i.e., humanity. Different religions and ideologies are meant for humanity and not the opposite.'

Bannet's story, however, suggests that on a different scene of writing, a certain Marx, a certain God and a certain praxis have always implied and supplied each other.[32] 'Marx's struggle was to overcome in this world the dualism of heaven and earth, of the spirit and the flesh, of mysticism and life, of idea and reality—a dualism which Marx and his contemporaries thought stemmed from Christianity. Even though Marx's language shifts, and the scope contracts from the metaphysical to the social, and from the social to the economic, the project remains essentially the same: to unite spirit and matter.'[33] Scholars are inclined to believe that Marx was obviously influenced by Judaism when he wrote 'Practice alone can transform theory into reality' and that 'only the deeds of man can return the world and men from their exile, from their estrangement in egoism, injustice, false independence and corporeal materialism and reunite them with their true being.'

Religion claims to be true and to be connected with ultimate reality, to be the basis for human well-being and the fulfilment of human destiny. However, it is only through spiritual struggle, perhaps akin to human self-realization, that the unity of the temporal and the eternal, the finite and the infinite, is expressed. Hence, it would be apt to make a distinction between religionists and spiritualists. Religionists can be spiritual, whereas spiritualists do not necessarily have to be religious. In other words, commitment to faith and tradition need not conflict with a humanistic pursuit of compassion and wisdom in a seemingly fragmented, mechanized and specialized urban world. So, the question becomes: What will open up a person and create this infinite capacity for reception and response? Through my data I hope to provide a glimpse of this deeply hidden spiritual capacity which is essentially indescribable but can be felt, intuited, or even self-realized.

Today we live in a world governed by the tension of globalism versus regionalism, encouraging a sense of fragmentation and the end of grand narratives.[34] On the one hand there is a celebration of a heightened awareness about the inner self and the unconscious, and on the other, the dilemma posed by a greater assertion of communal and ethnic identity. The danger lies not in one's cultural preservation but in the emergence of a new orthodoxy seeking to hold on to a clear cultural identity and often using it as a ploy for political purposes.

I felt a bit wary when the noted economist Amartya Sen recently pronounced in Calcutta that we Indians should look at our heritage in terms of its ancient achievements in the sciences and technology and not exclusively at its spiritual dimensions. India's spiritual preoccupation was not merely a counterpoint to the West's perceived superiority, it was also part of the country's confrontation with imperialism.[35] Nonetheless, for me, the question is not one of emphasizing either science or spirituality, but of infusing development with wisdom—and not perceiving spirituality merely as a political weapon or an alternative to scientific and technological advancement.

Also, spirituality can counter the one-sided materialism of modern life, its obsession with scientific rationalism, and its tendency to ego-aggrandisement. I am reminded of the reflexiveness that opened up new ways of thought for Jung when he visited India. He was gripped by an 'unexpected power' and wrote, 'The simplicity pervades the spiritual life of India like a fragrance or a melody. To get to know it, it is sufficient to read an Upanishad or any discourse of the Buddha. What is heard there is heard everywhere, it speaks out of a million eyes, it expresses itself in countless gestures, and there is no village or country road where that broad-branched tree cannot be found in whose shade the ego struggles for its own abolition, drawing the world by multiplicity in the All and All-Oneness of Universal Being. The note rang so insistently in my ears that soon I was no longer able to shake off its spell.'[36]

In the present context, remnants of modernism—autonomization and self-legislation—are juxtaposed with the chaos, instability, and flimsiness of postmodernism. Images become more important than words because they reflect referents to a greater degree than words. The urban world provides opportunities, events, choices, anonymity, and a stimulating, intense atmosphere charged with heterogeneity. It becomes pervaded and hegemonized with such artefacts of modern technology as computers, television, videos, advertisements, CDs, cassette decks and cellular phones—all of which invade personal space and time. Lash rightly makes a distinction between modernism, which conceives of representations as being problematic, and postmodernism, which sees reality itself as a problem.[37] He adds:

'Postmodern culture itself, at its best, could in this way be seen as a problem-solving enterprise and in no way inherently "irrationalist." If our contemporary reality has indeed become destabilized through a number of social and cultural processes, then, though it may seem irrationalist to celebrate this new flimsiness of reality, it would surely be a highly rationalist pursuit, either aesthetically or theoretically, to try to make some sense of it.'[38]

My own research stems from a bewilderment born of a long preoccupation with an aesthetic resolution of tensions in human lives. New theoretical expressions of some time-honoured practices and the process of transmuting conflicts, contradictions and paradoxes will hopefully clarify some issues. I have adopted the phenomenological perspective in studying the involvement of women in spirituality and society.

The founding fathers of sociology—Marx, Durkheim and Weber—were all concerned with the religious domain. There has been a resurgence of interest in the social-scientific study of religion in the past few decades. However, the experiential dimension is still understudied, especially in India. Within the phenomenological circle, examination of experience has remained essential to the understanding of religion.[39]

Centrality of the experience of the holy, for instance, is found in the works of Rudolf Otto (1958),[40] hierophany, or the sacred, in Mercia Eliade (1959)[41], and kretophany—a confrontation with the manifestation of ultimate power—in Leeuv (1986)[42]. This intellectual tradition is present in the works of Luckman (1967)[43] and Berger (1979).[44] Bellah (1970)[45] maintains that focus on the experiential aspect of religion is a useful correction to the predominant theoretical concerns in sociology, which tend toward reductionism. For sociology of spirituality, too, the experiential dimension has a world-wide relevance.

Husserl in the earlier part of this century contributed a great deal to phenomenology, a philosophy asserting that all knowledge about ourselves and about the world must originate from personal experience. Phenomenology incorporates some of the insights of rationalists and some of the intuitions of creative artists and poets. Thus, first-person data and women's descriptions of experiences communicate the mixture of freedom and constraint that characterizes their social interactions and inter-personal relationships, while the descriptions conveying 'mood' and 'feelings' disclose the structure of their experiences in unusually great detail.

Historically speaking, women's grand narrative has been that of silence. Hence it becomes appropriate and imperative to explore women's subjectivities in a manner pertinent to sociological studies. The subjective dimension denotes the internal reality of the mind as reflected in the consciousness of the individual social actors and the meaning they attach to this reality.[46] The experiential thus becomes real.

The experiential approach is designed to discover what spirituality means to women and the assumptions they invest it with. This perspective does not reduce women to objects external to human subjectivity; they become centres of experience, not remote objects observable from a distance as is the case in anthropological and psychological studies. Phenomenological understanding entails 'feelings' and introspective analysis of one's own subjective states.

Since the study of spirituality involves subjectivity and reflexivity, I conducted in-depth interviews using a method that can be called the oral autobiographical narrative. Through personal narrative one can clearly see how the subjectivity of women informs their objective reality. To a large extent, this can be apprehended through the intangible world of their feelings or perceptions.

Each interview maintains the anonymity of those subjects who desired it. At the same time, these autobiographical accounts, at times lengthy and circuitous, they reveal the functioning of narrative itself. Merton describes very aptly: 'Autobiographers are the ultimate participants in a dual participant-observer role, having privileged access—in some respects, monopolistic access—to their own inner experience. Biographers of self can introspect and retrospect in ways that others cannot do for them. That advantage is coupled with disadvantages. As we know, introspection and individual memory (as well as collective memory) are subject to patterned distortions and omissions.'[47] Even though all our subjects may not possess the elaborate theoretical arsenal of contemporary narratology, yet they appear to celebrate the narrative spontaneously.

My fieldwork for this project was spread over a period of almost two years from 1992 to 1994. Through network sampling, eleven women of diverse social backgrounds were selected on the basis of personal achievement, from the middle and upper-middle classes in the city of Delhi. They are uniquely qualified in terms of their educational qualifications and predisposition, to address the selected theme, and are in the age bracket of 40 to 60. In addition, for perspective, I also included in this study an interview with my spiritual teacher and with one of his male students. Personal and professional interests constitute the criteria for clustering the case-studies into separate chapters. Although the sample is a small one, and not necessarily representative or statistically significant, it is my hope that these interviews will be useful constructs—not the absolute truth of any woman's experience—and will also generate insights into the impact that modernization has had on women's lives, while helping us to identify the sources of their spiritual sustenance. The study obviously suffers from biases and omissions, and the reader's experience may not fall directly within its parameters. However, the introspection and retrospection of the autobiographical narrative provides rare access to the inner recesses of our protagonists' minds. Each story has a unique configuration and a complex structure that suggests and shows rather than merely tells, leaving it to the reader to intuit the possibilities and vistas of spirituality. Also, this exploration should be seen as a work-in-progress that tries to pick up and present some spiritual strands in the lives of contemporary urban Indian women.

Importance must be given not only to the nature of knowledge but to the mode of discovery as well; data are the end product of an intersubjective exercise and dialogue. However, I am acutely aware of the limitations involved in the interaction between information given and information received. After establishing a rapport with my subjects and briefing them about the area of my interest, I tape-recorded the interviews. In most of the cases it took several sessions, over a period ranging from one month to one year, to complete each interview. Subsequently, these interviews were transcribed and minimally edited in order not to obscure the creative processes through which the protagonists filtered their objective realities. Each interview can be seen as a collection of linguistic symbols that probably reflect experiential events but cannot be assumed to be direct representations of these events. Consequently, I have tried to show that the power of words that emanates from this method of interviewing matches the emotional intensity in the language of poetry, drama and confessions. This systematic and cumulative inquiry highlights dramatic portrayals of emotional realities and also has a summing-up effect as it draws on the whole experience of the subject, thus redeeming fieldwork from being a mere mechanical collection of cold data.

One needs to keep in mind that the location, gender, age and personal history of the fieldworker affects the process, interaction, and the emergent material. Being a single urban woman, a sociologist, and a Sikh certainly has had a bearing on my research. The facts of one's background demand reflexivity on the part of the researcher as well as the subject. I was variously perceived as a stranger, friend, and confidante, but at times also as intimidating, because the autobiographical exchange basically demolishes the fictional character and forces the historical person to come to terms with his/her own past.[48] It was therefore natural and ethical on my part to also take up a self-exemplifying exercise.

Thus, through narrational self-portraiture (i.e., seeing oneself as both character and author), I have tried to focus on the specificity of the subject, to reveal the power of the individual voice, and to demonstrate the social construction of subjectivity, multiple identities, gendered awareness, and memory and its reinterpretations. It is 'historicity' and 'reflexive distance' that operate here, but only in the context of multiple selves and multiple texts since the text produced cannot be read as definitive and timeless. The text is, rather, selective and historically contingent.[49] I have attempted to generate 'truth' of some kind—probably a continuation of 'here' and 'now' and 'there' and 'then'—by capturing the interplay of experience and ideas and of the personal, the historical, and the socio-cultural. At times, one may also get a glimpse of the confessional because the subject sometimes loses control while sharing personal stories. Thus, by emphasizing gender and the expressive voice, one is not merely moving from the abstract to the relational and from universality to particularity, but also discovering new discourses and areas of silence.

Suffice it here to say that it is not my intention to prescribe a normative reality but rather to provide people with the awareness that their existential reality contains options and possibilities for self-determination.

# Chapter 1

## *Desire to Heal: The Counsellor and the Doctor*

Women's autobiographical accounts point to some of the ways in which they have been influential in family and society. Contributors to this study provide abundant and interesting details on the interplay between individual lives and particular social structures. Considering the range of possibilities our subjects confront, they make particular choices regarding their career, family, and mode of spiritual evolution. Women have always been concerned with caring and curing. Through their compassion and nurturance, the counsellor and the doctor manifest their desire to heal, in modern professional settings.

### The Counsellor

A friend had given me her reference: As I sat in the waiting-room of her wooden-walled and dimly lit clinic, situated in a gigantic business complex of the city, I marvelled at the readiness with which she had agreed to be interviewed. Within moments, I was called in and introduced to her client. He was sitting next to her and seemed rather impressed by the fact that his doctor was going to be interviewed by an academic. In a few minutes he left. Thereafter, we were by ourselves—interrupted only by a few phone calls—for hours at a stretch, to share, compare, and review our lives.

She was dressed in an immaculate silk sari and, even though in her mid-forties, looked young and energetic. She came from a south Indian Brahmin family with an army background, received her degree in medicine, and married a north Indian. She and her husband have one daughter. She relates:

'What's my life story? When I look back I can perhaps try to figure out how it was that I came to take up this particular profession and how it has affected my life. Was it something I wanted for myself? Yes, and perhaps it was the turning point in my life.

'I am a doctor, a general practitioner. I have been doing general practice for over twenty years. And the speciality about my practice is that I do a lot of counselling, marriage counselling, sex education, and also child guidance. All these things have evolved over the years. In the beginning when I set up to be an ordinary GP, I gave most of my patients prescriptions. Now I find that sixty per cent of the people go away without a prescription. They need just my counselling. I also started counselling on a slightly wider basis, writing columns on counselling, like in women's magazines. I've also been going regularly to colleges, conducting workshops on sex. Over the years, in my practice as a family physician, I discovered that sex education was one thing lacking in the social system.

'Parents would spend so much time and money on preparing trousseaus for their girls—getting clothes, getting jewellery, deciding whether the sari should have a yellow border or red or pink or what sort of style. What I found was that though people spent more than two years, sometimes ever since the girl was born, collecting things for her, surprisingly, they didn't think it important enough to tell her about married life—what life was going to be like when she got married. They just seemed not to think at all about what advice they had to give a girl on sex, the man-woman relationship, how she was going to adapt herself to a different family. The maximum concern I found in middle-income and slightly higher-income groups was that they wanted the girl to be a little accomplished. So, they would send her to a school where she would learn how to cook, or sew, or drive a car, or do a few other things which they thought would equip her adequately, but nothing about sex, nothing about family life, and nothing about human relationships.

'I had more and more young people coming to me because their marriages were not working out the way they ought to have worked out. Their parents would say, "In our time they worked out, we were told to do these things and we did them, and now these girls don't want to do the chores." What they forgot was, with education our expectations change, our attitudes change, and somewhere along the line we have also to adapt to that and the entire community has to adapt to that. So, here was a girl, they were educating her in a convent, perhaps they were allowing her to date to some extent and giving her some liberty. Then she got married and they expected that she would touch the feet of her parents-in-law when she got up in the morning, that she would singularly obey what she was told. Specially in a middle-class family, I found, one of their criteria was that they wanted a working girl. They wanted a girl who was earning money which meant that she had gone through a certain bit of education. To some degree, she was expected to be independent in her thinking and yet, once she got married, they would tell her, "You must give all your income to us." The in-laws had to get all the income. The husband would say, "What's wrong with that? After all, I give all my money to my mother and she is not going to touch it, it's for us."

'Many times, these girls used to come back and they would confide in me and say, " . . . all those sisters-in-law to be married off as well." While that may be economically viable or practical for the family into which she has got wedded, it seemed to me a very traumatic experience for the girl. She dreams of setting up a house and then she finds nothing is her own. Everything of hers belongs to the family now. They have scant respect for her feelings. The only person she can talk to is her husband whose loyalty very often seems to be wedded entirely to them.

The girls would say, "Doctor, by the time our children grow up, my in-laws are going to be dead and I haven't saved any money. I just don't understand what the system is. Even when I have to go to the office, my mother-in-law gives me five rupees and I have to explain how I spent it. Or she says, I gave you fifty rupees one week ago, what did you do with it, and I have to tell her spending fifty rupees doesn't take you one week now."

'As a result, directly or indirectly, it would tell on the relationship the girl had with her husband and with the family at large. In the social system that exists in many of the middle-class families, ultimately, either the girl will have to kill herself or her sensibility by not bothering, or she'll have to fight all the time. The consequences of both these were not really good. Her parents, if she were to tell them, would say, "Look, you have to learn to adjust." When I heard about these things, I thought that young people must be made a little more aware of what these responsibilities of marriage are. Not just that they are going to have a partner but so many aspects in which their life gets inevitably changed because their life-style is going to change. They are no longer going to be single. This is what I thought of telling the young people in the colleges, where they had asked me to conduct a workshop for a week.

'First I gave a little talk on the human anatomy, about the problems that could arise which are peculiar to a woman because of her physiology. Then, I talked to them about marriage—the problems that they would face physically and emotionally. What are the inter-personal relationships which are important, whether or not you're getting married . . . because you have to interact with the society around you, you can't live all on your own and say I don't care what society thinks. There are certain rules you set for yourself and follow. There are certain rules set by society, and you follow. What is okay for you is not okay for the public. There is nothing wrong with kissing in public, but one does not do it because our social system doesn't allow it. And different systems of society allow different degrees of openness outside as far as physical intimacy is concerned. I talk about all these aspects and then talk about medical problems, about cancer of the breast, about AIDS, and how we can help ourselves. There are so many problems that a woman is exposed to. Initially when I started out I was shocked, but later on I came to accept it as a way of life that a lot of girls are having multi-partner sex.

'I have been brought up in a very broad-minded family, a very learned family. We were given a lot of liberty, but we never misused it. I was sent always to co-ed schools. I had lots of friends. If I had birthday parties, the boys and the girls in my class would attend. We had a very healthy relationship. There was no physical intimacy. But suddenly I found there were so many young girls coming to me. They were getting pregnant, and they were not married. I could not understand how they did this. They were not living separately on their own. I had no experience of sex when I got married. I was very innocent to the ways of the world. I knew my subject and was good as a doctor but that didn't mean I had physical experience. I didn't have experiences with men because of the way we had been brought up. I never consented to a situation when I could have got myself into a tight spot. I do believe that very often if a girl is physically abused, to some extent it might also be because she hasn't been able to protect herself, for whatever reasons. Sometimes it could be real innocence and sometimes it isn't, and somewhere along that line is often where I've had to deal with rape.

'I found that quite often the girl would allow rape to happen. I would see a fifteen-year-old girl who was pregnant and by the time the parents brought her to me she would be four or five months pregnant. I would speak privately to the girl and find out if she was very trusting. A friend of the family, somebody in the family, somebody she's calling Chachaji or Jijaji or whatever, would come to the home. But how did you do it? Where'd you do this? She would say, "It started during the preparation leave of my tenth standard examination. Chachaji had come in the evening and we were just talking and Mother mentioned that she would be going shopping the next day."

'Whatever the conversation, it was very innocent. And the next morning when the girl is studying, this gentleman comes along. She opens the door, "Chachaji, Mummy is not in."

"Doesn't matter, won't you offer me a cup of tea?" She'll say, "Yes, Uncle." She made a cup of tea. And from there it led to the bed. He left threatening, "If you tell Mummy, I'm going to tell her this." The poor child would be too scared to say anything. The parents are going to be thinking of him as their younger brother. As a result, whenever everyone was out, he would come and she was blackmailed into having sex with him because she was scared. I don't know what she was scared of. In fact she should have told her parents not to leave her alone, but instead she would tell him whenever she would be alone. She was a willing partner, if you come to think of it that way. But I know this girl did not enjoy it, she was petrified and didn't know what to do. During that time, she tried to kill herself but didn't quite know how to. When the parents came to know that she was pregnant they brought her to me. I spoke to the parents. They were touching my feet and saying, "Can't you do something?"

'I said abortion cannot be done at this stage. This was many years ago when we didn't have the techniques of doing it. The only other thing was to go to Safdarjung Hospital where your identity will be kept confidential. We never take the names of these people. Whatever can be done for her will be done in human interest, because she's unmarried.

'Next I would ask the parents whether they were going to let this man go free? And most of the time, in the experience that I've had, the parents are not willing to go to the police station or to court or do anything. They're probably right in their own way; litigation will take a long time. She's five months pregnant. You don't have to say anything to prove that she was raped because she is a minor. So, according to law, it's a rape, even if her consent was there.

He was not a real chacha and someone exploited the relationship. I have friends who are my age. My daughter calls them by their name. I don't encourage her to call them "Uncle". If you don't want to be familiar, if you don't want to call them by their first name, don't say anything. Don't make up a relationship which does not exist. Many men take advantage of the situation. Since most of these people would not go in for litigation, I thought of going to the target group of girls who are in college, because they will get married in the near future. It was a very rewarding experience for me because I felt that in my own small way I was doing something to prepare these girls a little better, to face the world and the life they were going to lead. Frankly speaking, the parents ought to be doing this, but they don't seem to do so, for whatever reason. Over the years I've also tried to explain to the parents to be a little more open with their children. They have to tell them the facts of life. When the girl is big enough she has to be told this is what can happen and she has to protect herself. There's no point in painting a fairy-tale picture of life today. But even today I find that parents are still very hesitant. The only difference is that they've accepted that the world is different today and that children must be prepared.

'I have children brought to me by parents who say, "Doctor, tell my daughter all she needs to know as we're going to get her married." There is an improvement in the attitude of parents who recognize that some things cannot be ignored. The other day I had a parent ring me up, saying, "I'm sending my son to you on the pretext of getting a prescription for cough syrup for his grandmother. He has just finished school, and we'll be sending him to Switzerland to do a course in catering. Although you told us we should be telling our children the facts of life, my husband and I have made several unsuccessful attempts and we're not able to talk about sex to our children. So I'm just sending him to you."

'This was a seventeen-year-old guy, a very shy boy. When he came he said, "Aunty, are you free?" I said, "Yes, why don't you sit down? I heard you are going off to Switzerland? Tell me something about how you feel to be going out of the country to study. Do you feel adequately prepared? What are your fears and inhibitions? Do you have any apprehensions?" I think he felt very much at ease. I first asked him all this in a very innocent way. I told him about Western culture and our own culture, about differences in lifestyles, about different situations to adapt to when one is in a different environment. Only then, I said, will one be accepted and only then can one survive. But to some extent there are certain rules we need never change, not in our own society, not in other societies. We've got to be firm about certain things, and there's nothing wrong with it. Just because a group of people does something which is considered fashionable, it doesn't mean everyone will have to do it without really agreeing to what they're doing. In my family nobody smokes, drinks, or gambles. We don't have any addictive habits. I've always thought that no matter how well we bring up our child, there are certain habits which people start because they think those are fashionable. I've seen so many families going to ruin because the man is getting drunk every day to drown his frustrations.

'So I talked to this boy about drinking, about smoking. These are the changes in the cultural system, for whatever reasons they come about. But remember one thing, I said, our moral views are appreciated everywhere in the world. People might be bedding anybody else, anywhere else, but if there's a small scandal about you, it means they do respect people who don't have multi-party sex, who do not just go around doing things because that's what everyone is doing. There are still vices, there are still virtues, no matter if someone tries to tell you what is fashionable or not fashionable. Ultimately you are respected for what you are. I talked to him about so many things.

'I said, "Look, whether you have extra-marital or pre-marital affairs, whether it is really wrong depends on the society you live in. Who am I to say it's wrong? If you think it's right, go ahead and do it, but I should warn you that there are sexually transmitted diseases. It's not only AIDS. There are sexually transmitted diseases which are viral, it's no fun to have them. You've got to think, is sex worth it if you're going to end up with these problems?" At the end of it he said, "Aunty, I just came to get that prescription. You know, I'm going back knowing so much more. You've made me suddenly feel so much more grown up. I feel so much more equipped to face things where I'm going. Initially I had this apprehension, now I feel I'm all ready to go out of the country. I do have to thank you." I said, "Don't thank me. If you feel that way, it is so rewarding for me." Then he came back on vacation and said,

"Aunty, how much that talk has helped me in life and in taking my own decisions. I always remembered what you told me, about the moral values, about how the world respects you for what you are and you must have the strength to be what you want to be. It's not always easy. When ten people are passing around a fag with smack, it takes a lot to say no. I remember this at every stage of my life. I don't smoke and I don't drink and I'm very happy."

'I have had such feedback from so many young people to whom I spoke. I'm happy that I've been able to give so much to so many lives, not materially, but in many other ways.

'The most rewarding experience has been bringing up my own daughter, because I tried to bring her up the ideal way. I was often asked, "She's not spoilt, a single child?" But she never even threw a tantrum. She was given wide options. She was never told, "Don't touch this". I never had to remove a breakable object from the drawing-room or from my table, because she was told, "You don't touch this until you ask permission." So, she would never touch anything. She would always ask. If she asked, it was never refused. If it was a breakable object she was allowed to experiment with it under supervision. If it was made of glass, I would hold it in my hand and let her touch it. By the time she was two, she knew plastic and metal don't break, she knew rubber takes some impact, but she knew that glass breaks. It was all a learning process. We revelled in the way we could teach her. She was hardly one when I let her run her fingers through a flame and I told her this is what hot means, this is what burning means. Before she would touch anything she would ask, "Can I touch this?" When our little child was two years old and it was time for bed-time stories, I would take out the anatomy book and I would show her how the heart looked, how the kidney looked, how they functioned. Her questions were so innocent: "Mama, how do we urinate?" I would explain exactly how the urine formed in the body. I would tell her how we eat, how the digestive process goes on, and what is the end result. So, she grew up without any shame of the human body, and her one comment to me time and again would be, "How wonderful the human body is!" I would tell her how the heart beats and she would tell me, "Mama, don't people say I love you with all my heart? How does the heart feel?" I wanted to put her into school before she was two years old. I went to the Montessori school and they said, "Doctor, we're not running a creche, I hope you understand." I said, "But there must be some criteria." "Yes, what's her age?" "Age?" I said. "What do you mean?" "Well, we do have an age limit because you do expect the child will communicate and will be toilet-trained by that time." I said, "Baby, tell her your name." She gave her full name, she gave my name, she gave my husband's name, our full address, where we worked, what we did. And the two women who were there were surprised with the way she was talking. She also told them what our qualifications were, where we had qualified, how we met and got married, what we did. And when they asked what she would like to become she answered, "I'd like to be a big doctor like my Daddy, not my Mummy . . . postgraduate." "Look, we admit we haven't seen such a kid, but if something goes wrong, what will we do?" Ultimately they said, "Look doctor, there are certain rules which we have to follow but we'll make an exception. She can start coming to school from tomorrow, but she won't be on the roll because the age limit is two and a half years. On her second birthday we'll take her admission officially." And that was the happiest day for all of us.

'I realized the impact of the family when she went to Harvard. I asked, "What subjects have you taken?" She said, "One course each on mathematics, economics and astronomy." I said, "What on earth would you be doing with astronomy?" But apparently she did so well that by the end of the first term she was taken to the observatory. It was later I came to know that she was good enough to use the observatory at will and also teach one class. Whoever wanted to learn could go to her and learn. So, I guess this is why I tell my patients that you're never too young to learn, or never too old. And she was told all this by her father when she still couldn't speak. When she was eight months old we were never tired of speaking to her. We never questioned whether she was learning anything or if she was understanding anything. Each one of us, whatever our strength was, would communicate it to the child. My mother told her so much about our social structure, about our culture, about the Mahabharata, the Ramayana, the Vedas, Puranas, the Gita, and it had a tremendous impact on her life. She's very bright, very bubbly, hundred per cent vegetarian, a non-smoker and non-drinker. She has the value system ingrained so well within herself.

'There's no point in telling your child, "Don't drink it, it's bad for you," when you're gulping alcohol every day. The child sees the truth. When the child sees that somebody in the family is wanted on the phone and the person is signalling that he is not in or is in the bathroom, the child is a silent witness to this sort of falsehood within the family. It's really quite meaningless to tell the child that honesty is the best policy as the child realizes you yourself do not follow the dictum. I recall once when I said, "May I borrow your pencil." The friend with me asked, "Do you have to ask your kid?" I don't have to ask her, but I ask her because she'll ask me. I'll forfeit my right to command if I don't follow the same commands that I set out for her. Double standards are so common in Indian society. That is why, as a nation, we're not able to come up. The rules have to be for everybody. If the child is not allowed to do something, there must be a reason which must be communicated to the child.

'Another mistake people make is they make their children believe they're infallible and some day the child is going to realize the truth and it will be such a disappointment for the child. I've discovered this in small ways. For example, we were invited to a dinner party. I was inattentive, talking to a neighbour, and along came a paan. I just picked up one and put it into my mouth. A second later my daughter asked, "What are you eating?" I said, "I'm sorry, darling, I'm eating a paan." She was told that it wasn't good for her. I was in the midst of fifteen other people. If I spat it out, it could be considered bad manners. There's not much I could do except swallow it and say "Mummy shouldn't have done it. I'll go back and brush my teeth." And she said, "All your teeth will fall off." "I'm going back home to brush my teeth." The child was satisfied with the explanation. I made sure when I went home that I brushed my teeth and she said, "Mummy, that's all right, it does happen." You don't have to paint a picture of yourself as being perfect. You have to be very realistic and convey to the child certain things.

'Parents of single children pamper them badly. The child wants something, it's brought immediately. When you don't bring it the child throws a tantrum. This way the child becomes very stubborn. For example, when you say, "You can't buy the balloon here," he asks you again and you say "No." He asks you a third time. You're engaged in a conversation and say, "Go to hell, go buy it." So, the child learns a very simple lesson. Once or twice you can be refused. But if you really get persistent and pushy, you're not refused. If you want your child to grow secure in his feelings, you've got to be firm in what you do.

'Hence, the socialization of children is very important. I once had a woman who came to me and said, "Doctor, I don't know how to say this! It's very embarrassing!" I said, "Please tell me. It doesn't matter, I'm also married." She said, "Well, have you ever watched television at seven o'clock?" "No, that's the time I run my clinic." She said, "Well, there's this advertisement for Nirodh." "Is it in any way objectionable?" She said, "No, but I am embarrased to watch it with the children. I stand in front of the TV, make it low, and say I'm going to get you something to eat and I try to raise my voice. The other day, I was not there and my son watched the advertisement. Then he came to me and started asking me about it. First I ignored it but he persisted. So I gave a vague answer of Nirodh being a medicine. But I know he was not satisfied with the reply. And next time he sees the advertisement he will ask me about it again." I said, "Fine, I'll answer him. Just bring him along and we'll talk about it. You come along with him. I promise you I won't embarrass you or him."

'The child was about seven years old. She brought him along. She was visibly embarrassed. I gave him one of the writing-pads and told him, "We'll be doing a bit of house economics. Do you buy milk?" He said, "Yes, I go to the milk booth and I put the coin in." "Do you know how much a milk token costs?" He knew how much milk was bought every day.

Then I said, "Does somebody come to clean the house? Let's ask Mummy what she pays." She said she pays hundred and odd rupees. He kept writing everything. And at the end of it he totalled it up and it came to two hundred rupees or so. Then I said, "Suppose your Daddy has three thousand rupees in his account. Now you know how much is left every month. You don't know how much your car costs, how much a scooter costs, you don't know how much a house costs." I went on, "Suppose you had another brother or sister, then the cost of housing will remain the same but cost of other things like milk and food automatically double." So he just doubled it. Then I said, "Suppose there were three children." So he multiplied by three. "Or suppose there are five." "Aunty, then we'll be broke." I said, "You asked Mummy a question. You asked what Nirodh was." He said, "Yes, how did you know?" "Because your mother told me and that's why she's brought you. I'll tell you what it is. Nirodh is a method by which you can have just as many children as you want. You can decide." He said, "You mean, Aunty, you can actually have as many children as you want?" He was so happy with the lesson he'd learnt. He was not interested in knowing exactly how the Nirodh was used.

'Subsequently, the most rewarding thing about this was that the husband came back and said, "I missed the talk. I could have come but I was scared. There was no way I wanted to have a conversation with my son about Nirodh at the age of seven." "Did your wife tell you what conversation we had?" He said, "Yes, I'm ashamed of myself." Subsequently they were so much more free with their child. He understood how difficult it is for parents to afford luxuries for the children. What you've got to do is educate the child, for that you can buy him books. That's what we should do. This was such a good lesson for them, because they found their son had suddenly become so responsible. To me this was a very rewarding experience because I had influenced the lifestyle of a particular family, taught them how they should bring up their children.

'The turning point in my own life was when I was nine or ten years old. My sister was one year older than me. We were very close, almost like twins. She had an accident which rendered her paraplegic. I think from that point of time, I matured a little more. I slowly began to understand how great my parents were as human beings through the amount they did for her, and the way in which they allowed her to be independent, educated, and to become a chartered accountant. They encouraged her to swim. She's a wonderful swimmer. I was not as brilliant as my sister. She's the brilliant one in the family. But slowly, not suddenly, I felt my life must be more useful.

'I think at that time I decided I wanted to become a doctor. My sister was the one slated to become a doctor. She was intelligent, had a fantastic memory, and we always presumed that she would be the doctor. She faced so many problems because they were saying, you cannot study science, you cannot adjust tables to your length, you cannot do practicals. But she did Chartered Accountancy, in the minimum amount of time. In fact, she cleared the examination six months early. I think she probably was the greatest influence in my life apart from my own parents, because I realize that anything can happen to anybody at any time, and what makes you great is how you come out of the situation. Each one of us has his destiny.

'All this, in my growing years, had a tremendous impact on my life. My sister never feared what would happen to her. She has travelled all over. In fact, my daughter has travelled all over the world with her, not with us, because as doctors we never found time to travel with her. My sister would take her to Kashmir and several other hill stations. They stayed on the first floor—when there was no room on the ground—and didn't seem to mind at all. "Why, somebody will carry me or get me a wheelchair and take me up." She had a tremendous impact on not only my daughter but anyone who crossed her path.

'It was so with my parents. They brought us up in the most ideal way. I do not remember a single traumatic experience in life except my sister's accident. It left them and me shattered, but the way they went about taking care of her was courageous in every sense of the term.

'My parents were not religious in the sense that we have never gone to a place of worship regularly or shown in any way that we are religious. I've hardly ever been to a temple myself. We believe in a value system. We think the best religion is to have a set of convictions and to follow them. You do not harm people. You tell the truth. You are a decent human being. You help others where you can help them. You do whatever you can for anyone, whether they are less disadvantaged or not. It doesn't matter. If somebody needs to be helped, you help them.

'My mother is seventy-five. She asked me if I'd get her some books. She wanted books of class I, because she has been teaching this little girl who's about twelve or thirteen years old—actually a maid, a maid who works in the house. She just told my mother once that she paid money in order to learn somewhere. My mother said, "No, you're not doing that. I'll teach you." And she has been teaching her for the better part of a year. My mother has angina, moves with the help of a walking-stick. She was always willing to do things for people. It was never announced or advertised. Her innate goodness came out through such acts of kindness. And, when you see goodness you imbibe it.

'I admire my father. I love and respect him. I wouldn't like to be like him because he was so overly modest. Till date I can say that I have never quarrelled with my parents. I've never said a harsh word to them nor they have said it to me. I would die for them. I could say that for my sister too. I would not only die for her but also give up anything. These are qualities which you try to imbibe without knowing it, and which you try to spread. You met this young gentleman just when you came in. He has paid me perhaps one of the best compliments. He said, "You know something, Doc, you're the nicest person I've met. I'm sure it's like this with anyone who's met you." And I said, "Look, you're very good for my ego but what do you mean by this?" He said, "I cannot believe that you're capable of doing anything wrong or harmful or not ideally to be done." And I said, "God, you've put a very heavy responsibility on me." I've always thought about the number of people who have told me such things, which make me feel I must never waver.

'I remember when I felt sorely tempted to do so was when I was doing my premedical. I was in the final exam stage.

Chemistry was one of my favourite subjects. By chance I met a very close friend of mine. He said that you have to pay Rs 5 to the lab assistant. I said, I was not interested. "Do it because otherwise they will give you calcium chloride and tell them that they gave you carbonative mixture." I said, "Nobody can do that." "Don't be a fool, I'll pay for you." I said, "You're not paying for it, I'm not paying for it." The next day he says, "Think of it again, if you don't make it to a medical college." I said, "I'll make it. I don't care, I don't need to be a doctor." And in my chemistry practicals I got zero out of twenty. I know that I could never have been that wrong because it was one of my strongest subjects. I got the highest marks in the university in my physics, biology practicals and theory. These just managed to see me through the first year. Because of that I said to myself, am I being practical in what I am doing? But I never did have to compromise on my morals. When my daughter was appearing for her 12th standard examination, somebody told her the same thing. And I told her what happened with me. There's a part of me which says we'll not do it, no matter what. That was the advice my father gave me. He said, "Remember one thing, no matter what the compulsion, even if it means the alternative is death, never compromise on your principles." Ultimately you live with yourself. Everything in life comes and goes, your health comes and goes but I think the message you can spread to others is: I haven't compromised on my principles and I hope I never will. Our country is not doing well because we don't have that kind of integrity. Everybody encourages corruption at our cost.

'I had to wait for eight months before I got a sanction for an air-conditioner in this office. I was told it's illegal to have an air-conditioner in business premises. I said that's crazy. There are no windows, there's no ventilation. How can I stay without an air-conditioner? They said, "Well, you can put it down in writing." I wrote the application and they made me run about. How often I went to the Delhi Electric Supply Undertaking (DESU) office! I was there so often that people thought that I was an employee. I was against bribing. Ultimately my husband met a young IAS officer who sanctioned the order.

'So at every stage I have discovered that there are a lot of decent human beings in our country. If we somehow inculcate our morality in our younger generation maybe we'll have a better life for them.

'Coming back to my marriage, after my MBBS I came back to Delhi to stay with my parents. I joined a government hospital and thought, I'll work a couple of years before I start my postgraduation. I met my husband (to be) and we decided to marry. It was a difficult decision for me. It was not an inter-caste marriage, but he comes from Punjab, I come from Karnataka. The cultural differences are inevitable because of this. My mother bought a white sari as we get married in white. When I told my husband I was going to be in a white sari, he said, "God!" His old grandmother was absolutely shocked.

'We don't cover our heads, the Punjabis do. A woman covering her head in my community meant widowhood. In my husband's house it meant modesty. I didn't realize that being Hindus we could have such confusing meanings to the same custom. They would be wearing bright pink or red. I was in stark white with my head covered. No trace of make-up, as it is against the dictates of what normally I do. So I would not wear it that day. I do not wear jewellery normally. My husband is exactly like me. He also agrees with these things but my sister-in-law said, "There's no way you're going to be like this. You simply have to wear this necklace." My husband said, in their community (this was just after we got married and went to his house), you have to cover your head when you enter. I said, the minute I've left my parents' house, I'll cover my head, but in my family my mother will mind it. For me it makes no difference whether I cover my head or not. But we have to respect everyone's wishes. So the minute I got into the car and left my parents' house, I covered my head. At the wedding reception I had on a little bit of jewellery, because my husband said, "They were specially bought for you and they might feel hurt if you don't wear it." "Okay, I'll wear it," I said, "it's not something I do normally, but I will give in this time."

'My husband has always treated me as an equal partner, helped me in all my pursuits. A year and a half ago I started the first All Women's Rotary Club in the world. My husband encouraged me to do it. He has enjoyed my being in the limelight. He shares it with me. If I had to live life all over again, I'd choose him all over again. We do not squabble, we don't have quarrels, we do not fight, we have an ideal relationship. We have a total understanding, we are appreciative of each other's strengths. We are each other's best friend and each other's critic. If I make a mistake he is there and points it out and I make every effort to see that I never do it again. If I do something nice, he's the first person to congratulate me. We both enjoy the compliments the other receives and I think that's the basis for a good relationship.

'The strong family structure is what has made me strong. Interpersonal relationships, bad or good, do create problems. For instance, when I was very young, I was very close to a teacher of mine. She lived fairly near my house and on weekends I used to spend a lot of time at her place. And I was shocked one day when her husband tried to get physcially close. I was so shocked, so confused, I didn't know how to react. So I stopped going to them and she came after two or three days and said, "What's the matter? You haven't come." I made an excuse of being busy with my studies but in my mind there was a terrible conflict. Do I keep up with this pretence? Should I tell her? What should I tell her? I was very scared of going anywhere near that family. He sent me a note. I didn't know how to respond. So I didn't.

'I was fourteen or fifteen. I was very mature for my age, but I think that was the time in my life when I went through a conflict. I remember two or three days of intense ruminations. Then I came to the conclusion that you cannot run away from a problem, you have to face it. So, one day when he was alone I had a frank talk with him. I said, "I need to tell you that I appreciate the fact that you like me a lot, but I also need to tell you that this will be the end of our friendship because of what you're doing. I cannot continue to come to your house and look you in the face because you feel like this about me." "I cannot believe that the feeling is not reciprocal," he said.

'"I don't feel like that about you at all," I said. "I feel guilty knowing this about you. There must be an end to this feeling.

I'll stop coming. I don't want to be constantly a source of temptation." He could hardly believe that at that age I could have talked like that.

'I think it was at that time a realization came to me that you can never run away from a problem. Certain problems are created. I could think of nothing that I had consciously done—but subconsciously, yes. I always had a very shapely figure and I was at an age when I enjoyed wearing clothes that made me look nice. I never wore anything revealing, but I did wear slacks and I did wear tight skirts, which were in fashion. I knew I looked nice. I wore it more often. I ask myself should one dress in a manner that doesn't look nice? I do not have great looks and am not devastatingly beautiful. I'm just ordinary. I said if this can be happening to me, I wonder what will happen to girls who are pretty. I would normally have said of someone: "Probably she encouraged that fellow. That's why he did that." But I came to the mature realization that we may not do something consciously or subconsciously. And I started wearing khadi.

'My friends started asking me, "Why are you wearing clothes of this kind?" I got a peculiar sense of modesty. I lived with it for a fairly long time. Even today I wear a sari all the time, despite my friends telling me, "You've got a much better figure than any of us has got, such a shapely figure. Why don't you wear some other clothes?" And I say, no, because I'm in this profession.

'That was the beginning of it all, which told me that a girl must never be provocative. I tell all the students of the college I go to, be modest in dress. A man must like you for things other than your physical assets. That alone can be the basis of a good relationship one day. So many college students have come back and said, "After you talked to us, doctor, it made us think twice because it makes sense." When I met my husband, we were working in the hospital. We were always very appreciative of each other, and when I was about to leave that particular ward on rotation he said, "When you go away it's going to be unbearable. Why don't we get married?" I mean, we're talking about marriage and he's just talking as though he's asking me to have a coke? I said I have to ask my parents. When I told them, my mother said, "You didn't tell me that you were in love with somebody. Do you love him?" I said, yes, I respect him terribly as a person and, I think I'd like to marry him. So I brought him home. "When are you getting married?" she asked. "Have you done something?" "Oh we haven't done anything, but when we get married I'd like that no one should raise a finger and say she's going round with this guy. Let it be, she's going around with her husband." My mother said that marriage takes time, but I said we want to get married as soon as possible. My mother was worried because north Indians almost always have dowry demands even though he was saying he had no such demands. Then my mother said that we'd like to go to the south, get a South Indian sari, jewellery, and then do some shopping. He said, "Well, if you're not going to do it in six months, she will get a room in the hostel. Once she's living in the hostel it will be tempting for me to go to her room." He was so frank with my parents. "I'd like that we share a room instead of running to each other's room all the time. We don't really get very much time so if I get fifteen minutes in a day, I'd like to see her, which means I'd have to go to her room. So we'd rather get married." My mother thought it was an extremely sensible way of looking at things. He was being very practical. That's how we got married. He had never in any way tried to get physically bold or do anything which would not appeal to me.

'I enjoy an excellent relationship with my husband. I had no experience of sex outside of marriage, and he was so gentle with me. So many young girls come to me, shocked and ashamed. Some of them had a bad experience because there's so much sexual abuse even in marriage. In fact, now when I talk to young couples, I tell them about how much is okay. If both the parties are willing, then you can do whatever you like. But otherwise there should be a limit.

'There was this girl who had no parents. She lived with her brother, his wife, and her father. The brother's wife made this arrangement for the girl to marry an engineer from IIT, Delhi. He was not good-looking, but very bright. But she married someone else who was earning less than her, and was less qualified. They brought her to me on the fourth day because she had run away. She said, "Doctor, I would rather commit suicide, if I have to, but I'm not going back." She told me certain experiences she had which were awful. The guy was a pervert. I advised, "Why should you take your life? You're qualified, you've got a fantastic job. I mean, why should you? Can't you stay on your own?" "God, I never thought of it," she said, "I only thought of killing myself." We got her a place to stay the next day itself. Fifteen years later she came to tell me, "Doctor, I owe it to you that I didn't commit suicide and I'm having a good life." She later quit her job, started a private consultancy. She is extremely successful and very confident.

Recently my husband and I celebrated our twentieth wedding anniversary. This year, for the first time, he had to go away for two months. In almost twenty years of marriage, I've never been away from my husband for a single day. I found myself remembering him every moment of the day. I felt it was driving me crazy. From the time I dropped him at the airport to the time I picked him up again, I felt miserable. All my friends who saw me said, "What's wrong with you? You've lost weight." I did not miss him sexually as much as I missed his tenderness, care and companionship. But at the same time, the physical side of our relationship is as important as the friendship between us. It is this duality which is indispensable in a man-woman relationship. This is what I tell the couples at my clinic.

'There are various problems faced by the patients who come to me. Most common among them is sexual perversion and sexual abuse. Indian men are so inhibited in the expression of their physical needs that when it comes to love making, they can get quite crude. I find that so many of the women come to me with problems which wouldn't occur if the guys were gentle. When I was in the VD centre, we would do a minor surgery and I would say, "You can't have intercourse for two or three weeks," and they'd say, "That's not possible." I would ask the reason. They would say, "No, doctor, no way he'll listen. It is not my need, but my man cannot stay without it." Mostly these patients are from the very low socio-economic class. They have so many problems and the women in most cases are sexually abused. The guy may be a drunkard, he may be forceful, do what he likes. The woman has to be submissive. She has no say at all.

'I can also tell you about male envy and jealousy in the very high socio-economic class. I faced this when I started the club for women. There were three or four dynamic women but their husbands wouldn't let them come to the forefront. The husbands couldn't stand them doing well, they would forbid them to go for club meetings. This is where the element of male ego would come in. There are many women in the upper class who are earning and are financially independent. In spite of that they are not independent in their minds. My husband said, "Let them spend a lakh of rupees, the man will not mind, but let them spend one rupee for a membership which gives them independence, and the man will put his foot down."

'One of my observations is that the sex drive in men is definitely more than in women. Out of the people who've come to me I've seen thousands—not hundreds, but thousands of women—who do not enjoy sex, unlike men. In professional colleges you find a lot of guys going to red light areas. I come from an army background where officers and jawans are away for years on end. The women certainly don't go out with other men, but I know the men do not think twice about going to a red light area.

'Sex is such a taboo word that many patients have a lot of misconceptions about what sex really means. To most of them it means intercourse. And from what I can make out from young girls and boys who come to me, these days people are much more free. I have girls coming to me asking about contraceptives and abortion. Sometimes I'm surprised that they can be so open. They seem to think there's nothing wrong in having sex, whether or not you intend to marry the guy. And they're not afraid that they might catch VD . . .

'. . . I regard myself as a deeply religious person simply because, to me, religion means a code of conduct I set for myself and follow to the extent that I can. You know the human mind is basically frail, and vulnerable, but I am happy to say there is an inner strength in me. My rules for certain things are absolute.

'I'm afraid I don't have any gurus. I just don't believe in gurus. I have never imagined that I can possibly seek solace from a guru.

'My work is very therapeutic. My relationship with my husband and parents has been completely therapeutic. When I want some professional help, I ask my husband. So my work and my husband's support are the most meaningful things for me.'

**The Doctor**

For more than a year I accompanied my mother (who was being treated for cancer) to the doctor's clinic. Her peaceful presence made her patients feel good about themselves. We established a rapport and she showed some interest in my research work. Eventually we had a very lengthy session at her residence. She is in her early fifties, has three children, and comes from an upper-caste, upper-middle-class family. She relates:

'I was brought up in a very traditional, but not religious, way. My parents were very level-headed, I would say very spiritual and orthodox. My father had this thing about education, mine and my brother's. He sent me to the best school in Dehradun, the Convent of St Mary.

'I had heard about IP College in Lucknow. In spite of being very orthodox and all the girls getting married at the age of nineteen, my parents agreed to send me to IP at the age of fifteen after Senior Cambridge. I always wanted to be a doctor, they always encouraged me. It was just understood that I would take the entrance exam and was going to study medicine. Now I wouldn't get through the exam, but in those days it got me through to medical college.

'In 1958 I entered Lady Hardinge Medical College in Delhi. It was hard work and I won a couple of scholarships. I think life was very simple those days.

'My mother was a very hard worker. She was not educated.

I have a younger brother who was educated in one of the best institutions, the Doon School, and I was very aware of the fact that my father could ill-afford fees for both of us. It used to be a great pleasure to see his happiness when we did well. For example, when I stood first in Senior Cambridge, he wouldn't stop boasting about the scholarship. My parents really had a lot of respect for me. They were very simple, totally honest people. My mother was not formally educated, yet on her own she could understand English, she could read the English newspaper. She was really a respected citizen of Dehradun. Anybody in trouble always came to her. She was a very wise person.

'In medical college I really enjoyed all the studies. I also took part in plays and sports. I won't say I did brilliantly, but I did well in my examination. I got the Delhi University Medal for services. Some senior doctors told me, the field of medicine is very competitive. Of course, looking at the competition now, I don't think it was competitive at all. I decided I would go in for pediatrics. Then it so happened that there was a job in pathology advertised and the only reason I applied was because as house surgeons we used to get only one hundred and fifty rupees a month. Today house surgeons get four to five thousand rupees a month. And this job at the Medical Institute was for five hundred rupees. Also, I was fascinated with the Medical Institute. It so happened that I got the job. Till then I had no interest in pathology. I thought I'd take it and I said I'd work for six months and earn some money. Once I started pathology, I got very involved with it and decided to do my MD in pathology from there.

'My brother, after he did his schooling, went to Allahabad University for two years. My brother is an artist and he was the best painter the school had, an excellent painter. Then he went to Oxford. He decided not to come back, and it was a great, great disappointment for my father. Ever since then my parents have been sad. I suppose I have always been very soft as far as my brother is concerned, and now sometimes I feel maybe I shouldn't have, because looking back, he has been totally irresponsible towards my parents. I always defended him and consoled my parents.

'Now I've lost both my parents. My mother passed away this past December. It was a big loss to me. They used to live in Dehradun. My father died about twelve years ago. He was not well, so I brought him here for treatment. But he died very peacefully. He literally died praying. He was a very spiritual person and he realized that it was time for him to go.

'He was eighty-two. My mother was seventy-nine when she passed away. She suffered from breast cancer and also nearly had her eye operated. Her cancer surgery was at the time I was just a student. I brought her from Dehradun and looked after her. All these things must have left a deep impression on my mind. It was around that time that I met my husband.

'Ours is an inter-caste marriage, not inter-religious; they're Kshatriyas, we came from a very high-class Brahmin family. I knew there would be some opposition. When I told my parents, my mother said, "Couldn't you find a Brahmin?" She came to Delhi. I said, "Okay, meet him, but don't ask me to get married to anybody else." I knew it was blackmail. Very few parents would agree to that. But she did agree and later she adored him. At the same time, I had respect for his family.

'When we got married, my father-in-law was a major general in the army. He was also a very distinguished, very nice, god-fearing man. My mother-in-law died long ago, when her youngest child was born. My husband, seventeen years old at the time, brought up his younger brothers and sisters. After our marriage, my younger brother-in-law and his pregnant wife stayed with us. It was like a joint family. My brother-in-law wasn't working, my sister-in-law was just studying. We had an understanding and no questions were asked. My father-in-law used to do the monthly accounts and expenditures.

'Then, immediately, I was pregnant with my first son. During that time I was preparing for my MD thesis. After my MD examination I worked for just six months. My husband got a fellowship to go to England and I went with him. During that period my father-in-law expired suddenly of a massive heart attack. When we came back after a year and a half, we were running the house, and my brother-in-law and sister-in-law stayed with us. After sometime I told my mother to move in with us as there was no point in her staying alone in Dehradun. The children were growing up and I could not depend on an ayah any more. Then my mother shifted in. In winter she used to go to an ashram, and through her we got exposed to Ingatguru Shankaracharya of Joshimath—not the present one but the previous one, a really enlightened holy man.

'I consider him as my guru. When he comes to Delhi he stays with us. He is a very nice person. Previously I didn't go looking around for a guru. I was educated in a convent. In my Senior Cambridge one of my subjects was Scripture, and I topped in that. I was a favourite with the nuns. It was very, very Christian oriented, and I still remember all of us had to go to the chapel which I used to love. I used to love the organ music. I had nothing against going to the chapel but the year we joined the school we all objected. We said, we will only go to the chapel service once a month. It is just the principle of it. Why only Christian service? Half of the world is composed of Hindus, Muslims, Parsis, so why only Christians? So, for the first time services were given to Hindus, Muslims and Christians . . .

'. . . I won't say I have been spiritual, but I was interested in philosophy. I have never been bored with it. I always liked a little discourse, something from the Gita. If somebody said something different, it always interested me. I did go to the temple, shut my eyes and pray with humility. In Paris the first thing we did was go to Notre Dame and pray for a good half hour. The atmosphere was so sacred. I would do the same in a mosque because the atmosphere is just the same.

'I have a lovely relationship with my guru. He could talk on any subject, depending on the type of audience. He's an expert on Vedanta. Over the years, I've developed a great deal of respect for him. Ours is a non-Brahmin household—meat, eggs, everything is cooked. So, the first time he came and stayed, we of course could not have any meat, eggs, onions, and so on, in the house. In the beginning it was a little problematic. Then my husband got very interested, having become aware of the goodness in him. There were good vibes around. Positive vibrations are what is important.

'He only comes to Delhi when there's some work, but when he comes he stays with us. Then it gets a little chaotic in the house as many people come to see him. We never advertise, but people do come to know. The whole house is full of life. Even the children have great regard for him. This time he was here for fifteen days. He had as disciples some Britishers who had been coming to him over the years. Then there was this famous man who started the London School of Economics. This old man is eighty-six and he comes all the way on an appointment basis. He came this time with two interpreters. They had sessions for ten to fifteen days. Each question is translated into Hindi. Then he gives his answer, which is translated into English. Everything is taped.

'For people who have been scientifically trained, especially doctors, it's really not like pure science. But how can you not believe? Because you see death, you see so much suffering, there has to be some sense of spirituality. I mean, people just came to it naturally because there is so much of suffering. I don't think there's anybody who'd say "I don't believe in God". I don't know what God is, but I think it makes a lot of sense. I tell the children, one way of bettering yourself is to say a prayer every day. It doesn't matter what form, whether it is this or that, it is the intent that matters. Any intelligent person would know there is one God; there can't be two fighting in heaven. Prayer is a process by which you better yourself. If nothing else, just minutes of detachment from the world around us. Ultimately it leads to a little introspection and some peace of mind.

'At the medical institute I had a very demanding job. I was the only girl and there were six boys. I took this position that as a girl I wanted no concessions. We had a very tight schedule of teaching, research, post-mortem. It was really very hectic. Even when I was carrying my first son I was working full-time at the medical institute. My husband was also in a very gruelling job. When I had my first child, my son, it was a caesarian, and I almost bled to death. When I did come home I was extremely anaemic. I had to call my mother to help me, but then she went back and I had only one month's leave. It was very difficult. Sometimes I felt my husband could have helped, but it wasn't forthcoming. And no matter how busy you are, there are some things which a wife has to do. You know, if a particular shirt is not in the cupboard, then he's going to ask you, "Where is my shirt?" But if my blouse is not lying in the cupboard, I'll not go asking him, "Where is my blouse?" This is what I'm trying to say. Petty things, but a lot can be made out of it if you are on edge. In most people's lives major scenes don't happen.

'From a woman's point of view, the sacrifices in a married life have to be of a different variety from the sacrifices made by a man. I'm sure there are many things I could do which a dutiful wife can do, cooking at home, things like that. I remember we were not earning much when we married. I was getting five hundred rupees, my husband was getting six hundred rupees, that's all. So I said, "From now on I will shop for vegetables and groceries." My husband said, "Have you gone crazy? You hardly get any time. You want to waste your time buying the sabji? Forget about it. If you have spare time, relax and spend it with the children. I will do the shopping."

'It is strange but I do feel guilty now. All the time I had this feeling that I didn't do enough for the house. You know, the dusting, changing the curtains. Although the material was lying there, it would take me three months before I called the tailor for stitching the curtains. When he came I would not have the time to speak to him.

'With my children, I am absolutely, totally, intimately involved. I was also very intimately involved with their studies, down to doing their homework, participating in their school lives, even getting to know their friends. But my husband didn't know what the children were doing in school, not even which class they were in. All the decisions were taken by me—which tuition to be given, what not to be given, what forms to be got, etc. All that he knew was that they were preparing for their examinations. Of course, if they ever came to him for help, he was always there. Now that the children are grown up and lead their own lives, we're more like friends I suppose.

'I didn't get any sex education from my mother. It's a very

silly thing to say, but when I got my period I was in the Convent of Mary and Jesus school, and I thought I had got blood dysentery. I didn't even know what periods were. Then my mother explained it.

'When it came to my daughters, they were in a co-education school and we always talked very freely. When they got their period I explained everything. They came from some session where the teacher drew the male and female organs, and then I did that science lesson with them. It was all very natural. I always told them, "Look, the boys and girls are all your friends. Before a boy asks you out, just think in your mind, whether you really are going to enjoy yourself. If you think you're going to have such a whale of a time, go. If not, just stay in a group, stay with friends." And they all used to go for parties and outings. I trusted them. None of my three children ever went around with some guy.

'I did not have an arranged marriage for my children. Now I'm telling my younger daughter, stop thinking too much with your mind, think with your heart, and enjoy the relationship. If it doesn't come out all right, never mind. You're very mature. And I am not in the picture.

'I don't know how my sexuality unfolded. I can't say how strong a part of me this thing is. I was always in a girls' institution. The first time of my exposure was when I went to the medical institute. You see, a certain maturity is required. You can't allow things to go to your head. I think it's very important for a woman or for a girl. This way of thinking has helped my elder daughter. She was the most beautiful girl in her school. I always used to tell her, good looks for a woman can be a great disadvantage. You stop being an achiever and start doing all sorts of silly things. So it used to annoy me very much if somebody said, "I'm good-looking." I must say that I never really was curious about sex. I didn't feel the need. I had many friends, I was in the hostel, there were no checks on my movement. And then, I really got attracted to my husband and from that point of view I've been lucky.

'I have been very satisfied with our sexual life. There was no exposure at all, hardly any TV, hardly any films. I'm one of those who hardly went to movies and things like that. I used to be a great reader. Now times are different. Sexuality is something you feel—you want to be with a person, touched by that person, and to touch that person.

'Now this will not apply to the girls of today. You just have to see this wretched programme *Santa Barbara*. Most of the young people have seen it. It is just so vulgar. There's not a single positive human relationship in this programme. Imagine what effect this is going to have on young people.

'What effect is it going to have on the orthodox Brahmin family? I don't mind explicit things, but this is beyond explicit. There is no sacrosanct relationship, just hypocricy.

The children know everything. We see X-rated movies together. It's a joke. My daughter says "Mom, this is not meant for you or Father." They have a very different concept. They are very aware and yet in control . . .

'. . . Ordinary working women are under great pressure. They will end up being nervous wrecks, including maybe even my daughter. Looking back, sometimes, I do feel I must have missed out on some parts of their childhood. In the last few years I've been having these thoughts, that maybe I shouldn't have worked so hard. I should have spent some more time with them. I had done many things, but I now wonder what I missed out on. One regret I have is that I kept my interests totally submerged—even reading which used to be a great passion with me. I haven't read a good book for many years because I don't have the time. I barely get the time to read the newspapers and a couple of magazines, that's all. Even, being a doctor I managed to cope with the house, the children, with this, with that, a lot of relatives and commitments. I've had hundreds of patients and operations. It is totally exhausting. So exhausting that sometimes I don't know whether I'm coming or going.

'However, I get a great deal of satisfaction. There are patients who think I am next to God. They say that they're alive because of me. There's no time even to think, you just do it. It's your duty. I think that's why I do it.

'My children are very proud of the fact that I work. Of course, now it's, "don't work so much". That's a different matter, but they never once said "this has happened to us because you were not there"—not once.

'My patients are of different type, no pattern in particular. Many women generally complain a lot and have psychological problems. Many of their ailments stem from neglect at home, loneliness, sexual abuse and such things. I think that affects women of all ages, from the young bride to the elderly. Overall, the girl child is neglected. If there is not enough milk, I'm sure the girl child will not be given it.

'It disturbs me that young schoolgoing girls from well-to-do families waste so much time on their looks and hair-cuts and show so little interest intellectual pursuits. Therefore they just go astray. They come to Delhi, they come to the hostels here, young girls away from home and away from parental influence, which in many cases is probably not very strong. They just join these party circuits, and it's the end of any career. I feel very disturbed because I feel this is the time that a girl can make something of her life. These are the most formative years, and sometimes they end up in my clinic.

'However, some girls, as I know from among my elder daughter's friends, are really good girls. They have done their BA. Now the parents are waiting to get them married. But boys from the typical arranged set-up just don't appeal to them. And now the girls are twenty-four or twenty-five. They don't have a good job. You can already see a lot of frustrations. Then there is hardly any opportunity in Delhi for young girls and women to mix with boys. This young girl who's got an excellent job, and an MBA, said she hardly goes out. If they go out with young men, half of them just want one thing out of it. I think it's a very depressing thing. There's no reason why girls, and women, can't be mixing in healthy relationships with the opposite sex and maybe find compatible partners. They don't find compatible partners because there's no opportunity for mixing.

'Then, too, our *sanskaras* are very deep. I've seen it in my parents. Religion is ingrained in us as a philosophy. You can't throw it away. A friend of ours came to India for the first time—she belonged to one of Sardar families settled in the Philippines—and I was so surprised when this girl would go to the gurudwara. Otherwise, she was totally anglicized. She couldn't speak a word of Hindi, and is now in the States. Her husband is a Hindu. Even for their two little children, who are Americans and were born and brought up there, the first thing is the gurdwara and Vaishno Devi.

'Religion is a part of a civilization. It's not like every Sunday you go to church, it's a very day-to-day thing. And even if you are Christian here, it's different from Christianity abroad. It's very Indianised. Brahmin Christians get married to Brahmin Christians.

'I've had *janam patris* (birth charts) drawn for all my children when they were born. I feel the horoscope must be there, but I don't go around having it shown. I have had my palm read. There may be times when I do it out of curiosity, if I have an opportunity, to find out what's in store for me. I think there is a lot to horoscopes. My mother used to say, "Get your horoscope made from panditji." If there was something, the panditji would say, "Do this or that." For instance, once I went and bought a white stone for my husband. But I'm not going to be totally carried away by these kinds of things. I feel you've just got to make up your own mind about most things. On the other hand, a little bit of horoscope reading is very good. It's like psychiatry. It helps you in many, many stressful times.

'The passing away of my parents was a very spritual experience. My mother actually willed her death. She had become very frail. My brother had come home after nine years because of her, and the last four months she would keep telling him not to go back. And suddenly there was a decline in her condition. She wanted her last rites to be performed by him. For a Hindu, the last rites are performed by a son. She was seventy-nine and very weak. She probably reasoned with herself that if her son went, she would not be alive when he came back. He was booked for 6 January and on 10 December she passed away.

'She went into a spasm and when I asked her, she couldn't feel. She experienced an astral type of phenomenon. Next day we admitted her to the Medical Institute. The doctors said, "We examined her even with a CAT scan, nothing wrong." Always she was saying, "It is happening." Now I realize that this was an out-of-body experience.

'I'm very interested in life after death. I do believe in reincarnation, there's no question about it. Nothing can go into dust and finish. We're all molecules, we're all atoms that circulate. How can I not believe otherwise?

'All I can say is, of course the loss is there but it was a peaceful experience. She lived her life fully, and that's the best way to go. I think it was probably just the right time as she died exactly thirteen days before my brother was leaving for Europe, the way she would have liked, the Brahminical way.'

*

Professional women holding prestigious positions and well-paid jobs generally tend to feel competent and productive, and have high self-esteem. They may also derive interpersonal satisfaction from their family and / or job. Without the assistance of the spouse, extended family or domestic workers, they find it extremely difficult to manage their career and family simultaneously. Neglect of family members, demands at the workplace and feeling hard-pressed for time may inevitably frazzle these women and also have the dire consequences of creating a sense of guilt and fragmented self. However, implicit in their accounts are scattered clues as to how women perform the role of influentials. Although overwhelming demands are placed on them, they feel honoured and humbled to be in touch with the spiritual dimension in their lives.

The counsellor comments on the transformative event of her sister's accident that led to her vocation whereas the doctor aspired to enter the field of medicine all along. Both of them have had cross-cultural marriages and the husbands have supported their careers. Yet, mothers and grandmothers are primarily responsible for the socialization of children, and sex education is an integral part of this process even if the changing sexual mores and the behaviour of successive generations shocks them. The counsellor's parents were mildly religious but they inculcated a positive value system in their children's lives. She herself has turned out to be a deeply religious person and her 'inner strength' or shakti sustains her. The doctor's parents, on the other hand, were orthodox Brahmins while she seems to relish philosophy rather than religious rituals. She has also inherited the family guru. Introspection, detachment, prayer and the event of her mother's death have refuelled her spiritual quest. Thus, facing the awesome dimensions of life and death makes them discover the sacred spaces in their lives.

Living in a constant state of stress and disease has triggered due concern for the spiritual imperative in the lifelong journey toward wholeness, creativity, interdependence, transcendence, engagement and love. Besides economic and educational compulsions, the well-being of people plagued by infections and chronic diseases encourages women to contribute increasingly to modern medicine. The fate of women and earth, the eco-feminists maintain, can barely be disentangled as nature connects them deeply. The natural and/or socialized resources of their compassion and nurturance support and energize many hospitals, clinics, hospices and sanitoriums. Even family members are blessed by the curative aspects of their caring.

Today the desire to heal is being expressed in lifestyle changes in terms of exercise, nutrition, naturopathy and homeopathy. Although practitioners of mainstream medicine are at odds with the traditional healing systems, women tend to counter the allopathic onslaught and gravitate to alternatives such as Reiki, Pranic Healing, Tai-Chi-Chual, Holistic Health, Aroma Therapy and Reflexology as consumers and practitioners in the metropolis. Organizers of these workshops have mentioned to me that the majority of the participants attending their courses are women. Also, I have come across many women who are trying to introduce their husbands/fathers to these alternative therapies. As women attest, a new healing consciousness that balances the feminine and masculine aspects in their lives and integrates feelings, relationships and a search for self-knowledge in the healer-healee matrix is gathering spiritual momentum.

# Chapter 2

## *Change and Stability: The Designer and the Beautician*

In this age of discontinuity, women must cope with a vast array of inner and outer shifts and changes. The pursuit of new opportunities has been a mixed bag for many women. Employment outside the home, which they must take up to supplement the family income or because they are the support of the family, has not relieved women of responsibilities of children and housework. Dilemmas and unintended consequences of change arouse anger, anxiety, and an unfulfilled longing for self-validation. The spiritual task of reconciling the concern for change with a deeper need for stability is exemplified well in the accounts of the designer and the beautician.

### The Designer

I had met her at a dinner party during one of my fieldtrips to Mandawa in Rajasthan. Many years later, we happend to sit next to each other at a luncheon hosted by a mutual friend in Delhi. After our discussion about my current work, she spontaneously agreed to be my interviewee. She always dresses up in style and projects a fresh and confident look. Her forthrightness, expressiveness, and hospitality are striking in equal measure. She belongs to an upper-caste, upper-middle-class family from Bombay and is now living and running a successful business in Delhi. She relates:

'I look back today to where I began. I see I have evolved because of challenges, traumas, anguish, and joys that have been put in my life for one reason or another. An inherent strength deep down has been sustaining me. I've been fortunate to discover spiritual strength. There has also been a very strong, affectionate family background that I grew up with.

'I come from a joint family. I'm the ninth and last child of parents who also had nine or ten brothers and sisters. After Partition, when I was only three years old, our family migrated to Bombay. We were given a house in exchange for a house in Karachi, and suddenly we were like a hundred and ten people in the family because my father's brothers and sisters, who were not able to find a place, landed up in our house. So I really grew up with hundreds of cousins for a few years.

'I ended up like a tomboy rather than a girl. I mean, I never played with clothes, I'd be climbing trees, jumping and clawing like an animal. It was like a free-for-all. Many times it was like fifty people for a meal, and then we slept. It seemed as if every room had ten kids. It was almost like camping in a palace. And then my parents began to realize that it was doing no good for us kids. So we just left the house to the others and we bought an apartment. That was the first time I realized this was my family. I noticed my brothers, sisters, and my parents for the first time. I related to them on a one-to-one basis. Ineviably, a lot of restrictions came my way.

'I felt abandoned all the time. I would always get into mischief. I guess it was the need to be noticed. And not a day went by when I didn't get punished either in school or by my parents. I was always looking for ways to escape and just be by myself. I had a secluded spot. I was no more than ten or eleven years old. We would eat a lot of beach candy, and I would walk as far into the ocean as I could. There was a huge big rock which I would try to reach. As I grew up nobody could understand my feelings. I had a beautiful dream on the rock, and even though I had lots of friends and I was the gang leader and led everyone to mischief or fun or whatever, I never showed that rock to anybody. It was my pilgrimage spot and now frequently I go back there when I'm happy and pleased with myself.

'I hated all my brothers and sisters. There was nobody I loved in the family because I always felt, they don't love me, they don't understand, they know only how to restrict and lay down the rules. It was like a rebellion, a vicious circle. The more restrictions I had, the more I was bent on breaking them and the more trouble I was intent upon. I found I was very talented in sports. One of my brothers saw this and he managed to direct my attention to sports. Before I knew it, I became the number one high-jumper and I was participating in the Olympics in Maharashtra State. I was the youngest girl there, when I was not quite thirteen, and the record hasn't been broken.

'Then I suddenly channelized my energy. The biggest dream of my life became winning medals and certificates and things like that. The next two years I put all my energy into sports. My brother went off to Germany for further studies, and I felt I had lost the great support of this brother. He really cared and understood and he dreamed of my future. Once he was gone, I again felt friendless. My parents were already grandparents when I was born. I was a second generation kid who couldn't relate with her parents. I had an elder sister whom I felt closer to. She had kids who were my age. Her eldest kid was a boy who was my immediate best friend. I became the boisterous one of the two, and that was where the influence of being rough came, of being a fighter, of being a man, that sort of thing.

'I know that I loved my mother because she was one of those mothers who was Mataji to everybody. The whole world came to our door. She was a blessed lady and she gave a lot. My parents were very religious. They were Hindus when they got married and later converted to Sikhism. All my bothers wore turbans and beards. As we are Sindhi, our language and lifestyle at home is Sindhi, but our religion is Sikh. We were influenced a lot by the Punjab, and because of the family rites, we had to be home at six p.m. every evening, at sunset, to Rehras (evening prayer) and everyone in the family, twelve of us, had to say their verses for an hour. Only then were we allowed to have dinner.

Anyone who missed that was punished. They were very strict. That was one of the best things when I think back. Thank God, I had a great grounding in my faith.

'So, we were a very close united family; very supportive, but I always felt that I had to look up to them because I never understood their world. I was a new generation and secretly rebelled against everything that they stood for. Later, I took to reading Western magazines and I first discovered the pop music of the fifties on the radio. My father would only allow bhajans or classical music to be played and I had to listen secretly to pop music when the family was asleep. There were no transistors at that time. Actually when the house used to be asleep I used to quietly put my ear to the radio and listen, so that nobody else would be disturbed. I enjoyed that. They didn't know what was happening to their kid. She was getting influenced by the Western world. We all had our Western education in India. Then one by one family members went abroad and decided that they liked it there and didn't want to come back. My father felt there was no point in building up a business in India because there would be no one to take it over. So we sold it and migrated to London in the late fifties.

'I went there as a teenager and it was like a dream. I felt I would be thrilled because my thinking was Western-style. Anyhow, it turned out to be the biggest shock because now I had twice as many restrictions. They were so afraid for me. We were surrounded by televisions, everything was Western, and the girls were suddenly in danger. Three daughters were single; the two elder daughters were married and had settled down. Our brothers and parents were very watchful over the three girls, me in particular. I was not allowed a full education because they felt that I was too strong-headed. I was only allowed to take the primary courses, studying at home. I'd go secretly and sign up for architecture or interior decoration. By the time I attended class my brothers would find out and strike my name from the register. My rebellion was building up somewhere inside me. I wanted to get married and leave this cage. I hated England because there were so many restrictions and I suffered awful depression in winter. I would crave for and dream of India. I wanted to escape. I had little crushes here and there, and the fear that the family would disapprove. The boys were independent. Each one had his own family car. They were financially well-off.

'Occasionally I went to plays with the family. Girls would often want to be friends with me. But if ever a boyfriend of theirs came along and I happened to chat with him, that was forbidden. It was like double standards of the highest degree. There was no one on my side. It was me against everybody else. My parents did disapprove of my brother's gambling, but the boys were independent, and earning, and my parents couldn't control too much. I used to be allowed to go out with the youngest of my four brothers, who was three years older than me. By now I was twenty-one or twenty-two. We had our own friends. And more and more interesting people from India turned up. Things were opening up. We went to dance parties, but the question of dating was completely out of the question.

'Then we came to visit India to look for matches for the two sisters. The one immediately older than myself was told she was marrying a Sikh. She was very contented. She got married and settled down in India. I felt very stifled. My parents were rapidly getting older. They felt that because I was away, I was going to get married. It was scary in a way. Lots of men were chasing me in India, making me feel elated. You can't imagine how it bothered them, scared them. The first year I spent in India, at twenty-two or twenty-three, turned out to be the best year in my life. I made very, very good friends. Exciting proposals came from them.

'I really blossomed. I was a model and felt as if I was on top of the world. My parents didn't approve of even that. There was this big movie star that I was secretly in love with, but he didn't know it because I wasn't allowed to acknowledge that. My parents were getting nervous about him. He was madly in love and insisting on marrying me, and I was secretly in love. He was saying, "I don't care if your parents don't approve. I'll just kidnap you." I couldn't even say yes to him or cooperate with him. I just had to be dumb, demure, with a virgin mind, as I was brought up to be. But it was still the best thing. I wish that upon every girl. It was wonderful. He chased me with flowers all over the country. We were never allowed to meet. We would talk on the phone for hours in the night when the whole world was asleep. The romance bloomed in the abstract way.

'Meanwhile the usual proposals were coming from the Sindhis. I turned down so many fantastic proposals. I was cowed into saying yes to one because I didn't want to go back to London. We were married within a week of seeing each other.

'Later I was on my way to San Francisco where this huge disaster awaited me. My husband was already with somebody else. He had no time for me. He was coerced into marriage by his parents because he had another woman. They just got around my old parents. He wouldn't touch me. He was so angry he had been burdened with me that he treated me as a piece of excess baggage. For three months I was a virgin. He wouldn't touch me. I was just an unwanted person in his life. Imagine, I was on top of the world, I had everyone falling for me, with an incredible one-year romance. God, this was like the worst punishment. What a come-down! There was nothing to talk about. If I opened my mouth to ask him anything he would shut me up. I was just a brainless, stupid, tall, attractive girl who meant nothing to him. That's all I represented. He had a lover, a secret life going on. He didn't want me around.

'He totally undermined me in every single way. When his friends found out, they questioned him because I was so nice. I didn't speak to my parents about it. I was very angry by then. So I did go home three months later for three weeks, still a virgin, and my parents saw straightaway that I was miserable. He never called or cared, nothing, not a word. I broke down by the end of the second week. Then I expressed my unhappiness. So they called up his family and said it's over, and the family couldn't care less because it was his life. I lived in India, and he just never responded. He had a sister in Washington, to whom my family spoke, and she said, "Look it's their life. Let them decide." So it was decided that I would stay back, but within a week of being there I asked myself: Am I going to accept this failure? I was determined to go back to him, and the family was dead set against my going. But my mother saw, as a mother should. And it helped in a way. He thought he had lost me, and he began to take care a little. Our marriage was consummated, but he was still cruel. I got used to the cruelty. It was normal for me to be exhorted once a day at least, in front of people. It somehow made him feel superior, and able to accept me.

'Now I see that he had a sort of a complex, but at that time it was a shock. Friends helped. They saw all that was happening. They protected me. Finally, maybe I got used to it, I don't know. It didn't seem to be bothering me so much. In the meantime, another thing had happened. A man came into my life. He was the most celebrated man I ever knew. He was single. He had just broken up with his first wife, and he had gone on a world tour. It was his first trip to India. My husband had met him in California when we lived in San Francisco.

'My husband travelled a lot, and in one of his absences there was a big function. I was there with the wife of an Indian friend, and in an instant we were introduced. We shook hands and he didn't let go. I cannot tell what a wonderful experience it was. Meanwhile he was pulled away. After the function we went to a dinner. He sat in the distance where there was nobody just so that he could stare at me.

'I was scared. What is he thinking about? So, I turned my back and saw the couple who had brought me. Please take me home, I said. As we were leaving, he came up and invited me for a show, which I declined. It was obvious that he didn't want to lose us. Anyhow, on the way home my friend said, "Look, he will not remember who we are tomorrow." We reached home and she said, "Why don't we call him for a nightcap on his way home?" In fifteen minutes he was knocking at our door. It was magic from the moment we met. But I was still totally in love with my husband and was determined to win him. So, we became friends. My husband and I would go to LA, meet his family, eat with them. All the while he would give me indications and things, or call me alone at daytime. I would simply shut him off in a very nice way, keep talking about my husband. It went on for a few months. Our friends told my husband, "You know, you're going to lose your wife to him."

He said, "Oh, good for her. She needs to look around. I'm fed up with her attention." So he was encouraging.

'This star got no encouragement or response from me. He never thought that I would respond. When a year later we were about to be transferred and he was going off on a trip to Europe, he just called me up and said that he wanted to see me before I left. "Come, we'll have lunch together. Don't call your husband till the morning." He flew down. Then he got physical for the first time. He tried and I resisted. He was shocked because he was so used to glamorous, gorgeous women falling for him, and this rejection made him determined. Then he said, "I've known you for a whole year and your marriage doesn't exist. In the first month you succeeded in making me believe how happy you are, but your husband just sucks and you smile and put up with it. How can you?" Then he proposed to me. "You promise me you'll leave your husband and marry me one day."

'I called and told my family all this. They didn't know him, but they'd read all about him. They approved of anybody who loved me. Anyway, we moved to New York and months later we saw each other and we were falling in love now. My husband had become completely intolerant with me in New York. He had more pressures at work, and New York was too much for me. I couldn't adjust. Besides, he treated me more like an idiot because in a big city I was a small-town girl for him. Then I began to respond to this person and it was agreed that we would be together by the end of the year. After six months I left my husband and was back in London. By now we had been married for exactly two years and had no children. For the first time I was flourishing. My parents were so happy to see me like this. My brothers, everybody, was thrilled for me. My friend had been calling me from Los Angeles. He had another week of work, then he would come to London and officially get engaged to me. It was just about four weeks that I had been in London, and my husband had never bothered to call. My friend was flying in the next day to London. And that same day my husband suddenly calls me up from New York for the first time. I said to my husband, I want to separate and try without you, without these terrible fights we have been having. He said all the things I used to crave for—how much he loved me and cared, that he wanted to be given just one more chance, that he had been cruel. That day he was so expressive.

'Of course, I completely melted. And I was confused and heartbroken and didn't know what to do. Deep down I was confused and angry. I realized later my anger was with my parents. Anyhow, I just took a decision and went back to my husband. It was goodbye to my friend for ever. I got pregnant and had a daughter. And the marriage, for the first time, did work for a little while. I think it was the first happy time we had. Sharing and communication started between us which never existed before. He respected me for the first time. I was the mother of his child. He was crazy about his daughter. Within a year came another child, a daughter, and he blamed me entirely that we didn't have a son. I had failed him and this became a new chapter of misery. He just rejected the second daughter and said, "That daughter is yours and this one is mine, and we won't come in each other's way." He didn't love the children equally, although I suppose no parent can love equally. It became a whole new thing of torment. I just carried on with great shock and disappointment. Meanwhile I got a job, and it helped me come out of a life of vegetation.

'It gave me a great new beginning. I had to work initially with loud protests from my husband and then on the condition that he get all my salary. He was such a strange man. I was happy, feeling good. A whole world I didn't know about opened up. We began to communicate again. I was with the hotel, and he was with the airlines. I got a maid now to look after the kids, and I could be out and moving. Life looked up, but the insults never stopped. The more I grew the more he resented. Now I had to prove that I was actually stupid. I had to get an insult, otherwise it would be disaster.

'I don't know why I accepted it. I guess you become a creature of habit. He was teasing more and he hurt me more. Then, my friend entered my life. Suddenly one day, he called me at my office. He had made enquiries. I used to read about him in the papers and feel kind of sad. We started to see each other a little. And we realized how much happiness we could actually share; his marriage had failed but he could not make it public. He was a public figure. We just began to get hooked to each other and started having an affair. I think I really matured as a woman for the first time. And he also found total happiness. We both grew beautifully together. It lasted for ten years, as our marriages were failures, but we made a pact that we would never hurt the other's spouse. We were both such romantics and had so much love to give and get. I always felt that I had two husbands, and he had two wives. We were content and it was very pure.

'I will cherish my special feelings that I shared with him, for life. You can compartmentalize it. I felt that it is all part of the woman's strength where your body can relate physically to one and spiritually and emotionally to another. Definitely there was a hundred per cent distinction between the two. Eventually when I went on to a proper sexual relationship with my husband, it was very good. We were good sexually. Probably that was the only part of our marriage that worked. It was very infrequent. Most of the time we never talked to each other because we were fighting over small issues, mostly over our two daughters. It was a tragedy.

'The other one was a complex relationship with blissful joy. I never felt that physical orgasm is better, because I couldn't compare the two. They were different. One was strictly physical, and one was completely, totally spiritual. Sex can be the most spiritual experience, but it doesn't have to be. To experience such love makes a woman blossom, there's no doubt about it. I have been so fortunate to experience it for so many years. We met no more than ten times because we were not in the same city. There were times when I used to have amazing conversations with him. It was as good as having an orgasm.

'Had it not been for him, I would have been floundering. It was a total God-send. In marriage I thought one was meant to be shown pure ecstasy and joy, but at that time I felt that my marriage was the cruellest thing that had happened. So, I think I was compensated. Saturdays and Sundays we were home and couldn't talk to each other. Then, one day his wife saw us both in the street. Just as a taxi pulled up, she came out. She looked at us. She had never spoken to me ever and supposedly she didn't know who I was. Suddenly she knew who I was. I just walked away across the street as though someone was waiting for me at a curbside restaurant.

'Then I took off for India, and his wife disappeared from his life for about two weeks. He went completely crazy. I knew that she was hurting. She has no family at all, no father, mother, brothers, sisters or anyone. And she knew this was the way to get his sympathy emotionally. Slowly we switched our relationship into a strong friendship, a very beautiful friendship. By then my marriage was reaching a stage where it was becoming impossible. I was doing very well in my career, and my husband was stagnating. He was always on a limited salary, and he was not moving further because he had developed complexes so severe that he had no friends. In fact, he would never come out of it. I was growing, and making more money than him, and we were living in style because we used to spend a lot.

'He would put away his salary completely. He would live off mine. I had no control although I had managed to save a few thousand. He began to suspect that I was making money and stashing it away somewhere. There was no focus on me, only on my money, otherwise I was no use to him. His way of thinking had become like that. We had nothing left to talk about except: "I know, you must be earning. I bet you invested your money. I bet you've done that." I said, just go and find out what I've done and let me know. Our fights became worse, and I would dread coming home because it was the same question of money. It became so impossible that he got into physical fights with me. So I just picked the kids up and set off in the middle of the night and drove to my cousin's house which was just ten miles away. I called him in the morning and said, "It's over and I'm going to the court. You want to marry money, you don't want to marry a human being." I had bruises all over myself, and when you go to the family court and show this, they can give you custody, which is what I got straightaway.

'I had just about $10,000. I decided not to let him know because he'd take it, so I kept it a secret. I went to the court. My lawyer said, "He looks like a vicious man. I've dealt with these in the family courts before. He's going to do something to you. Hide your kids for some time." So I hid them for a few hours in a friend's house. My elder daughter knew. She was eleven years old at that time. She called him up and told him where she was. He quickly packed their bags, went there, picked them up, and took them out of my life to a boarding school in India. My sister's daughter happened to be at that school.

'I just crashed out totally. My life ended. My friends came around, supported me in every way, and helped me. And one of the brothers flew out to be there for me. That changed me. I realized a reason for living existed when my family came to my support and said, "Come on to London, everything will be fine." I said, "No, I'm not coming to London. I'm now going to live for myself. I'm going to fight my battles in this world without any guidance or support. I'm the one who's lost everything and I'll get it back. I'll stumble and find my way." In about ten or twelve days I found out that the children were in India. By then I was half mad. The first two years were very traumatic. He did everything possible to demolish me. He did everything you can imagine. He knew a lot of lawyers and filed all kinds of horrible cases against me. His parents lived here in Delhi—wicked, mean minds. We had no idea about Indian lifestyles and norms and whatnot. Everytime I arrived to see the kids in India, there would be some customs officer or police officer there to interrogate me. He would make false allegations—that she's a smuggler, or she's a racketeer, or whatever. The authorities became fed up as there was nothing to these cases. Then I said it was my ex-husband who had stolen the kids and was doing everything possible to stop me from coming. My $10,000 was depleted over the first year. I was penniless. The family came to the rescue, but I'd never wanted them to know that I needed the rescuing. I struggled to meet my own ends.

'That's how I started. I think it was the greatest test God put me to. I was new to India. I don't know how I faced all that. I carried the heaviest burden, all those tensions, illness. I had to fight for the children who would have no parent if I didn't keep my senses right. They had no future; the father was completely berserk. It was the sense of motherhood that kept me going. I did have to lie two or three times. I had to kidnap the children from school once. He took them out of school here and back to New York. There he put them in a horrible school in a very poor neighbourhood where he had moved and where they were entitled to free schooling. So from there I had to kidnap them and bring them back here. I had to do all kinds of things to protect them. It was like animals, dogs, protecting their puppies. Doing everything to protect them was what kept me going.

'He knew that I had cancer, that I needed surgery. I was operated upon in London about six years ago. I went through four to five years of anguish, day and night, with cancer. My hair was falling out. It was awful. I couldn't do any steady work. I was just lucky. Whatever I made, sold. When I could make twenty necklaces, a lawyer who wanted twenty necklaces bought them and paid in cash right away. This would see me all the way through till the next trip. The more turmoil there was, the more exciting it was to create. The ideas were new and fresh for India anyway. That was how it would sell. I was encouraged and confident that I had a future.

'Now my health is fine, though you never know once you've had cancer. You just have to be careful, which I have to be. There's always this nagging fear that it will spread for some reason. I feel I've placed my kids in a place where they're secure. If I have to go tomorrow I know I will have no regrets. I know they are okay. I've brought them to a level where they don't need a mother and father, actually.

'Now my daughters are twenty-three and twenty-two, and they help me in my business a bit. At first my business became their biggest enemy. I got so involved with the whole thing that for them it became a rival, the boyfriend I could have had. My workshop was in my house. Day and night I was with the traders. When the kids would come home for two months from school, I had very little time for them. I was committed and couldn't stop. So they resented my work. I didn't have time to be a role-model housewife. Today they are very happy and grateful. Now they adore, they love, they worship me. They are very close. They do know that they are in an enviable position. As a parent I relate to them much more than my parents related to me. So they are proud . . . . I just might want an arranged marriage for them unless I can put them in a position where they can be sure and decide. They have boyfriends, they have everything. I have given them too much, which I shouldn't have. But I didn't have time to be their mother and their father while being their provider. So they were spending a lot of time with their friends while I was travelling on business.

'I love to work. I love challenges. But I hate the working conditions. I end up being the one who has to deal with all sorts of people. Perfect in health I'm not, and if I could get a super secretary I would be the happiest person in the world. India is an amazingly challenging country and I've learned everything the hard way. I had to pay the price; and I feel that's the message that I have to pass on to Indian women. The reason why I thrive on challenges is because I saw my limitations as a woman. At the work place some of the villagers simply would not look at or talk to me because I was not worthy of their look. Some would talk to me, some not. Some villagers were emancipated enough to see the vision, which had drawn me there. Thank God. I have really educated them. I have modernized them. They look up to me, they can't believe what's hit them. The younger ones now in their teens or twemties are married and have kids already. They are wearing shirts and pants and sweaters. Their fathers are the ones who fuss and wear dhotis. They tell me, thank God, before we die we saw a dream which had seemed impossible. They are crude, every once in a while I have to put them in their places. I lose my voice because of that. They get out of hand with customers in the shop, the foreigners. The villagers' mind will take very long to actually change. Now I'm turned on by Bangalore because the women there are so sensitive, the people there are so sensitive. There is no sensitivity in north India at all. There the women are emancipated.

'During these traumatic years I used to have gurus. I went to Sai Baba in Pune, up to Bihar to Shivananda, you name it. I came away unmoved by them all and very calm. Then I went to Bangalore to see Sai Baba. I was so excited I was going to meet him the next day, and I was asking all kinds of questions. Someone told me to quit searching. You cannot go finding your guru, the guru will find you. And then when I had this operation, it was as if he knew.

'When I opened my first shop, two Americans looked in. I was fascinated by what they were picking up, so I went up and asked, where are you from? They said, "From New York. We want to buy the best you have because our guru is coming." They showed me a picture of a very beautiful young guru. She's a Bahumuktananda. And the way they were talking was appealing to me. They looked so highly evolved. They said, "Next month she'll be here." I said I'd like to come and attend her discourse. In the meanwhile, more and more Americans were arriving and my shop began to flourish. The guru arrived on my birthday, and my lifestyle changed as a result. It was an instant magical reaction. It was one notch above that meeting with my friend. I don't usually cry, but that day, for a straight three hours I didn't stop crying.

'She talked to a congregation of thousands. It was in 1987. We were so closely connected. Every day that she was here I would go flying to her like to a secret lover. I didn't want anyone to know because they might think I was crazy. Meditating, chanting—it was amazing. The best thing that came about was that I found security in the world. I didn't need to go looking for any guru, the guru was in me. I communicate with her once in a while, but I'm secure within my own life, very secure now. Touch wood. I feel very very fortunate.

'This has given me a lot of peace and strength. Once in a while I feel the need to quietly meditate on my own, and listen to taped music off and on. There's an ashram nearby. I don't go there now as much as I used to. I question myself why I am no longer drawn, and I don't know the answer. Urban life moved me into another world.

'I used to see some connection between my sexuality and spirituality. Before I met the guru I was free and single. I didn't belong to anybody. I had the odd boyfriend, and it was an important part of my life. Sex was an important part of one's life and emotion and all that.

'My guru aroused me sexually. She allowed people to feel that she was so powerful. The spiritual awakening opens up so many channels that it brings your body, mind, physical, and sexual emotions to a pitch. They are all linked. When listening to her talk, I got this incredible experience called shaktipower. This shaktipower completely illuminates you in every way. It's just a mind-blowing experience. It definitely wakens up all the chakras inside. It's like antennas opening up and seeing the vision in so many directions. I can't explain it. Suddenly you start reacting to the minds of people. Your life becomes much more enhanced, sharpened. Similarly, the first sexual relationship I had after this sent me flying through the roof. I was electrified totally. I think I scared the man away. I scared myself. He thought I'd had an epileptic fit or something. It scared me so much. My God! This has to remain precious and pure. It cannot be shared. Somehow I felt I shouldn't waste it. She was a living god to me at that time. I was thanking God for showing me this state. And then six years ago my interest in men and sex diminished. It definitely has diminished in the past two years. I have no friends or sex, and I don't care or even think about it. I feel this interest is locked inside me, that it's good for me, and if it is to come out again it has to be for somebody so worthy that I don't want to waste it.

'My mother's passing away was painful. She suffered a lot the last two months. She was such a divine, great woman, such a giver, and she had experienced a lot of pain in her life. One just couldn't do enough to show gratitude to her, she was such a great lady. So watching her pain the last two months was very difficult. She was surrounded again by the entire family. We all knew that she was going. This was way back in 1972. They both went on their own birth dates, my mother first, and my father, five months later.

'I always felt that my brothers towered over me. They affected me more than my two sisters. I resented it terribly. And deep down I think I must have made up my mind that I am going to show all the men in the world I'm greater than them. I think there's still that kind of competitiveness. They are very close. They love me, and I admire and respect my family. If I had to be born again I would like the same brothers and sisters. We were very close, but I still feel the need to prove to them that I am smarter than them. I am so proud of them, I look up to them. They have done well in life. They are good to their families, to their homes, to the environment. Everywhere they've made a good name for themselves. My friends tell me how proud I must be, or how much they enjoy meeting my family. But every time I get the opportunity I still love it when I can give a piece of good advice. Deep down I'm still competing. That is my inner script, my psychological script. I'm not restless or unhappy.

'I am a very fulfilled and satisfied person. I like to spread happiness. This is something I learnt from my friend. He enters the room and something in me lights up. I think I've inherited it from him and love to feel that I can give anything I have to the world. That is part of my spirituality. I always find that I relate one to one.

'Now I just want to experience each day. I love adventure. I know that I want to climb many heights, attain spiritual knowledge, and I want to try to connect the world together, East and West, not for the guru's messages but in terms of modern consciousness. And I don't know how I will do it, but I know there's a longing for it being manifested somewhere, through art, culture, music, minds. The West is so ripe and ready for our spirituality. I feel if ever there's a chance for India to be recognized for its greatness, this is the only area.

'I want my daughters to have individuality. The older one is a total individual. She's quite evolved, very creative. I'm in awe of her creativity. I still feel I failed in marriage. I lost that. If I had the chance, I would like to marry again and try to create a happy family unit. I'd love that relationship more than life as a mistress kind of thing although that can be another beautiful way. I still weep with joy when I see a perfect romance, two people in love, it's wonderful.'

**The Beautician**

I first encountered her about thirty years ago. She was known as the 'Sohni Kuri', or pretty girl, and was the centre of attraction amidst her friends. It was interesting to see how she had maintained her youthfulness, and how her life had developed.

After city-hopping in India, she is now based in Delhi—her city of origin. She belongs to an upper caste, lives in an upper-middle-class nuclear family, and has two children. She relates:

'I was basically a sensitive kind of person, but had a very self-assured veneer. So what happens with all sensitive people? They tend to get tossed around emotionally much more than people who are not sensitive. Things in the journey of your life change your course of direction. You don't even know why they've changed. Sometimes it will be better, sometimes it will be worse, but I do feel there is somebody on top who sort of makes moves that are better for you. At the time one may or may not understand.

'There are two aspects of my career. One is how to remain young, and the other is how to treat people who have problems remaining young. Treating the problem I think of as my social duty, giving back what society has given to me. All this is very crudely joined up to form a career. When I don't take money it's because they can't afford it or because they're older or family or whatever. The day when I'm financially able to do it, I will do more than I'm doing right now, because there are many persons who have come to me with such problems.

'Skin care is not only external, it is also internal, and treating people on that basis makes them more open and it works like a therapy. There are many persons who've told me it helps them become aware of what their problems are in the world. My career started because of my brother. He had bad skin problems. He couldn't be cured and he'd go into depression. So I thought to myself that there are people who need help. Why can't people be cured? I found out with the help of my grandfather, my father, and my own study.

'My grandfather had knowledge about the subject and my father had done an M.Sc. One of my subjects was biochemistry. I came out of a great state of depression as I realized that looks are a very important part of being successful. Everybody wants to be neatly, nicely groomed. So with this realization came the career.

'One can avoid situations that give you stress, but stress comes from all kinds of allied problems like hair-loss, wrinkles, discolouration. There are various treatments that one has evolved for various problems, such as keeping the skin young. Because we have been five years here and four years there, I had not made the business commercially viable. Now the children are grown up, and I don't have the guilt that I have neglected them. Hard work needs time and if you don't have time, then you can't be successful. Now this business is very viable. You meet lots of people through this form of career and it has a kind of a great quality, and doesn't mean just sitting in an office or an isolated kind of activity.

'I was very happy that I was born into a special family. It's not very often that one can say one's mother is highly educated. Even now I'm proud of the fact that she is able to tackle many a situation that women of her age can't. She drives a car, her mind is sharp. It's not been easy for her after my father passed away, but she has been able to come to terms with it. When the mother is educated and she allows her child to grow and is progressive, it is a fortunate situation. Whatever potential you might have in you as a youth, you are like a plant: if you nurture it, it can grow, but if you don't, it won't. That comes from progressive parents.

'The times are different now. My grandmother came from a generation when their father would say, do this. That was wrong. They didn't have the authority, the courage to question what the father said. Then came my mother's generation, and my mother's relationship with her mother was a very mixed kind of thing.

'Today I'm very protective about my mother. I almost feel I'm her mother. In fact, very often she feels that I'm the mother. With my daughter, it's different. She was born within a year of my marriage. I got married in my mid-twenties, and then there was a large gap between her and our second child. So she has been more of a companion, and today she is very mature for her age. She is more compassionate, she is more caring, she is able to relate to me and my contemporaries. Most people, if you tell them to spend some time with their parents, think it is a waste of time. But she wants to spend time with her parents. It is the generation which makes for an easy-going relationship. The way our son behaves with his father, my husband can never behave with his father.

'Earlier on, people wanted absolute authority. So even if they understood a child's position, they wouldn't allow themselves to be crossed in any manner. If they determined something to be right, it was right, whether it was right or not. Whereas today you can even discuss it with a child. I think it is this, what do you think? And then if a common consensus is given, well and good. I was very fond of my grandfather, he in turn was very fond of me. One can't imagine the stories he used to tell about my mother. For example, he told us that when she was in the seventh standard or something, he just took her to a boarding school and said, "You've got to stay here." It must have been terribly traumatic for her. I can't imagine any parent doing this today. It wasn't that he wasn't fond of her. I could see that he thought it was right. What happened is that previously it was an extended family, brothers of the father and all that. These days it has become more of a small family unit. So life has become very difficult compared to the earlier period since the demands on you are much more than before. Life then was simple, less complicated.

'Children today are also much more demanding. I would make a conscious effort to make them see that they must be satisfied with little. You can't have any amount. Once you get used to good wine, you can't get used to bad wine, right? It will lead to dissatisfaction. But if they are satisfied with little, then they are always satisfied. The peer pressure, moreover, is very great. I see a difference between our daughter and son. The peer pressure was more on my son than it was on my daughter. So, I was finding it a little more difficult with him.

'Fortunately I did not have too much tension. But a person like me can be tense with many a situation—servants in the house, for instance. It really depends on what the mood is. If the stability is there, then small things don't matter. If the stability is not there, small things will matter. There have been tensions when I have been sick, and of course, the period after my father died. I'm still affected by his death. Somehow you never feel parents can go away. You feel they'll always exist because they have been there since your childhood. You come back from school and you see them at home. You get married, and you see them there. So you feel they are a permanent fixture in your life, that they are there to handle the situation if you have a problem. Even if I feel protective about my mother, I still feel I can go to her if I have a problem. That is a tremendous feeling.

'My father wasn't a very pushy kind of man. He was a very nice, good man. It's a vacuum no one can fill, there's no doubt about that. Who can be your father? I know when my grandfather died he was ninety; even so my mother was affected by it. No way around that. It is an irreparable loss, a full stop. It's so final. After my father's death I think I got pretty stubborn, a little tougher. Previously I was willing to take a little nonsense from people, very often even among friends and among associates. I always say that if you can stitch khadi it won't matter, but if you stitch silk it will tear. I've gotten a little tougher, a little more worldlywise. I'm not sure about that, but I think I did . . .

' . . . I don't know what to really believe as far as reincarnation is concerned. One has read a lot of matter on that—from the Dalai Lama, and an association where they actually believe that they are getting data on reincarnation. One doesn't really know these things. It's like being in a valley and dreams are beating on the sides of the valley. Some people have very intuitive power and listen to it, and some people don't. There are some people who may try to remember that their concept of television and radio weren't there at all. I remember if somebody said, oh there are waves in the air, I would think, how does one really know? One doesn't really know because one has a limited view, limited intelligence, limited to what one is taught. One can't aspire to understand everything; it may be there, it may not be there.

'I am a religious person. I never sit back to think what the concept of spirituality is. I feel that I have been somebody who has been guiding, caring, almost a father-like figure. I wear a kada and have worn it since the beginning. I read the Sukhmani Sahib, I read the shlok every morning and night, I jap (count) the mala. If I were allowed to go to the mosque I'd probably do that too. So the children have been brought up in that kind of atmosphere. They go to the church, they go to the temple, any temple—south Indian, north Indian, west Indian, whatever—because I do feel very religious. It is wrong to isolate religion of various kinds. It's wrong for anybody, for instance a Muslim, to say that Allah is stronger than your God. He can't say that if you don't worship Allah, you can't go to heaven. Religion doesn't really mean that. It means every act should be a gift to God.

'People do good, and bad may happen to them, but eventually justice prevails. The question is whether I have inner strength. I am a very nervous, worrying kind of person who's very religious, who has a lot of faith, but I worry all the same. However, I don't want to have a guru. One has heard a lot of stories about persons who are gurus in name only. One is a little wary. I'm sure there must be lots of them who are holy people but there is a streak in me which, if I nurture, could lead me to become a sanyasin, to give up. So I wouldn't really tap it. This has been told to me by an astrologer. I don't know whether I really have this streak but that is what he told me. He said, "You keep yourself attached to family and worldly things if you have that streak in you."

'I feel the guru can be all kinds of things. In any case one only has family commitments. I do believe that we are a very closely knit family, a nuclear family. It's like a rectangle and each one is very important. Till now it has been going well. To me, the order of priority is children, mother, and then all the rest.

'Fortunately, I'm seeing not too many conflicts although there are some. I met my husband when I was sixteen. We got married six years later when I was twenty-two. I was very flexible. I was willing to change, to adapt. I was willing to let things go. If somebody said something I would pretend I hadn't heard it, which is something I wouldn't do now. My husband was very mature for his age. He was able to handle the situation. I played along, but the credit really goes to him. He is a strong man but a good man.

'In families, you have problems and problems. If only I could handle these kinds of problems. However, with a mature man who's also kind, things are easier. It hasn't been difficult, although when we got married, there was not much money. In the final analysis, it helps if people are cooperative and communicative—it's very important in a relationship. If it is a relationship where the person is not honest, you are groping in the dark. That is when you can stumble, get hurt. When a person is honest, everything is like daylight, everything is in the open.

'I always tell my children, do what you like but remember you should be able to come and tell me about it, and if you can't tell me about it, then it's automatically wrong. So don't do it, but if by any chance you have done wrong, then come and tell me about it. Our daughter can do what she likes; that is what I told her when she was sixteen. I let her go out, particularly in a place like Delhi, but it has to be an honest relationship. With friends, I value honesty more than anything else in a human being.

'Talking about sexuality and sex education, you've got to put my mother in her generation. You've got to compare her with other parents. And me, you've got to put me in my generation slot and compare me with my peers. Now my mother, compared to her peers, was very progressive as I told you. She did tell me that menstruation is not something to be frightened about. She had been frightened by her sister that this was some kind of disease. So she didn't want me to have that trauma. She said, "Don't be worried about it." But it's very difficult for the parents to talk about sex to their children. We have with our children a very open kind of relationship. My daughter was telling me, when in a group of friends in school, they asked how she knew it all, and she said that her mother told her, they were surprised.

'As far as my clients go, it's a full range of problems. One person came and said, I've come to say bye to you and thank you very much, but I'm going to commit suicide. There have been people like that, at one end, and at the other end people with minor problems. Skin and internal problems are related. So to work with a person you do not know is beneficial, for it's easier to unburden yourself to a stranger.

'The mother-in-law problem is a world-wide disease. When you care for a person honestly and you are willing to give them time, very often you achieve results even if you're not a psychiatrist. This is such a valuable thing. It's a great gift to people; it can be given with honest caring. There is certain kind of satisfaction that you get. Also, when the children grow up and they are leading their own lives, then you have to have satisfying work and not interfere in their lives.

'I think I have been using the word "fortunate" very often, but that is really the essence of life. So many things could have gone wrong at various times and didn't. I was fortunate in that—in my family background and then marrying into a family which was royal. So, literally no problems. We've stayed in the major cities of India, and one good thing is our having lived for a fair amount of time outside Delhi, exposed to different kinds of cultures, different types of people, different types of personalities, people in a different kind of environment. I'm a Delhi girl, but I think that over-abundance of one type of people, as in Delhi, is not good. We need to have an input of different types of cultures.

'Bombay is cosmopolitan. There is no cosmopolitan feeling in this city. The mind here gets narrowed down. Everybody in Delhi is wanting to have a fight. The man in the street is like a full glass. You just have to give him that extra drop, and he is willing to punch you. That's so unhealthy. The way they talk to you, the way they behave. You go to the market, the fellow says, "If you want to buy OK, otherwise don't touch." Haven't you come across people who talk like that in the most aggressive manner? In the other cities they are more polite.

'Walking on a street in Madras, Bombay, or Calcutta, at nine o'clock in the evening, you needn't worry. In Delhi you can't go to the Bengali Market, so close to my house, without an escort. There's a crudeness in the way they speak. It's a situation which really needs to be changed. You can imagine what's going to happen to a foreigner in a mini-skirt in Connaught Place at ten o'clock at night. I think that a Punjabi male, if he passes behind a woman without passing some kind of a remark, feels it's derogatory to his maleness. I hate to say that, I'm a Punjabi myself. Then they have this thing of saying "mother," "sister". The thing is, they are a hypocritical society. They will say, "Respect your mother and sister," but the girl on the street they don't want to respect at all. It's all a big facade. So the character of a person in Delhi hits you hardest when you have been exposed over a long period to any other city. Bombay is now going to be different, but you don't feel so much lack of respect for the female anywhere else in the country . . .

'. . . there are qualities in human beings, in each one, even your parents, your friends, which you admire. As I've often said, I admire my mother, her ability to have studied up to an MA in an era when women were not educated. Her ability to stand on her own, to have a sharp mind, to immediately handle situations, those are the qualities I admire in her. In my father I admire his gentleness, his total devotion to his children, which was beyond anything else. His warmth, his kindness, all that. He didn't have certain other qualities which my mother had. So each one has something to give, something that you admire, something that you don't admire. It is up to you to look at their good points and try to bring that into your life somehow.

'I worry not so much about marriage for my children as for their careers. Marriage is a question of destiny—when it happens, to whom it happens, how long it will last—which you can't control. So when you can't control it, you don't worry about it. A career is something you have to shape. It's your responsibility, and equally so for the son and daughter. When I thought I'd give this career to my daughter, I felt it was a sensible career for a girl to have. But at the back of my mind was a nagging doubt whether she would like to do it, whether it would be good for her in the long run, whether she will be a success? She's a perfectionist. I asked her, "Would you like to do it?" She said, "Mummy, this is your thing, I want to do my thing." For a couple of years I let it ride. Then I told her one day, at least learn it for yourself. You learn it, you have the ability to do it. If you want to make it a career, well and good. If you don't, it's up to you. She thought this made sense because she needed it. Now she's much more involved than I am. So there is a career for her.

'Very often, friends have told me that I could have been a Shahnaz Hussain, but she's there and I'm here. I think I'm happy with what I have, but sometimes there's a tinge of regret.'

*

Issues relating to the structural and psychological constraints imposed on men and women in creating an egalitarian relationship still remain unresolved in our country. These distinguished women largely speak for themselves, and it is quite possible that they may not agree with my categorizations. Nevertheless, they make a difference in life and society by questioning reality and continually trying to reshape it.

Personal and historical events caused interruptions in the lives of these aesthetic aspirants. Yet, they have been able to influence social trends and their pain has intensified the experience of a changed consciousness.

The designer exposes herself to the dangers of sudden and shocking experiences but feels fortunate to discover her spiritual strength or the 'Shakti power' in the process of exploring unknown territory. She lives on the experience of rebelling against the false social normativity and understands the perils and triumphs of her avant-garde role in society.

While the designer sought gurus for her spiritual development even though now she has extracted herself from this cultic retreat, the beautician seems to be wary of gurus. For her, family plays the role of a guru and helps her from feeling the unbearable tensions, rage or grief. However, both of them grapple with the ideas about communication, honesty and cooperation in relationships, self-worth, career and personal integrity, in the context of changes in women's roles. They try to adapt, conform or rebel.

It is not merely discontinuity in their everyday life or social mobility but a celebration of the dynamic and stable that is visible in the transitory and ephemeral present. Their respective profession transforms reality into images and breaks time into a series of perpetual presents. The beautician, for example, possesses an acute awareness of temporality and specializes in making people remain young and treats people who have problems remaining young.

These women do not always have an attitude of critical observation towards themselves, how they tell their stories, and how their language shapes oral texts and gives meaning to personal and historical events. Their unique style of speaking mirrors a multilayered texture in terms of their social class, self-perception, language and culture.

Externalization of interiority and the social virtues of communication are reflected in their lives. Nevertheless, with instantaneity of things, continual connection, communication and information network in their fields, they tend to lose private protection and the necessary distance for nurturing interiority.

While women retain and stabilize the positive aspects and discard that which harms, they refuse to conform entirely, either to tradition or to modernity. Situational wisdom determines their advancement in spirituality.

# Chapter 3

## *On Freedom and Creativity: The Writer, the Singer and the Librarian*

In order to understand an autobiographical trajectory adequately, it is necessary to acknowledge early background experiences and how they affect the subject's later decisions and attitudes. The troubles these women go through are reflective of social realities. Also, at a given time, the cognitional and philosophical orientation of the autobiographer forms the basis for interpreting certain significant events. The writer, singer and librarian illustrate the role of freedom in promoting or hindering their creative development and reveal the ways in which the creative act structures their relationship to reality, and inspires others.

### The Writer

For the past three decades, she has been in the news for her contributions to the cultural and literary fields in Delhi. Her bold articulate writing, while not her means of livelihood, has won her both critical acclaim and popularity. Many admire her dynamism and sensitivity.

She belongs to an upper-middle-class Sikh family and is in her late 50s. She now lives with her only daughter and son-in-law. We shared a good deal of ourselves in an emotional and spiritual exchange. She relates:

'Life is such an abstract thing. I have a whole ocean of experiences and non-experiences and wastages. A lot of it goes to waste. The ocean of my past is an area of darkness though it is alive and throbbing like emotion, not very much alive, yet pointing in the direction you want to throw your searchlight.

'I virtually did not have any childhood because my father was of the opinion that school spoils children, but for a little while I was in Sacred Heart School. It was not like today, where women feel they should get rid of their children by sending them away to nursery schools as soon as they are two-and-a-half. In those days, the right age for children to go to school was perhaps between four and five.

'My father said that a girl has to be educated in a proper way, and the proper way was to have a tutor at home. I only had one brother. He was younger and he was given all the freedom he wanted. He used to go to school and on excursions. He went to a school that was close to the house and was run by a very patriotic man. My father was at that time a 'pucca' Congressman, very patriotic, and some secret meetings were held at the back of his clinic. They used to have these meetings there because nobody would suspect a doctor.

'This patriotic man who ran the school did not believe in teaching children inside the four walls of the classroom. The classroom was in nature and real life. He used to take the children to a bakery and show them how a loaf of bread is baked. He also took them out to places where the birds chirped in the trees. I used to feel jealous because I was denied all this. My father thought that the only respectable way to educate a girl was at home. I do not know from where he got these ideas. Perhaps from my mother's background. My mamaji (uncle) who brought up my mother was a big zamindar and had a couple of villages, lots of property, in Gujranwala. A whole bazaar was named after him. Along with that he was a very religious man. My parents were very religious too, my mother more so. I was always fighting with my own emotional problems, resenting my father, but here in Delhi, when I started observing my father objectively, I felt admiration for him. Here he had this small clinic. In Lahore he had had a fabulous clinic. I do not know how he adjusted. He was around fifty at the time of Partition.

'I was not close to my parents because my mother was always very ill. Right from the age of eight I was working in the kitchen, helping the servants, and looking after her. I was mothering her and resenting it all the time. I used to feel so exhausted and then, over and above that, she would scold me if I did not give proper attention to my younger brother, because he was the favourite child. She used to treat me like a maid servant.

'I must have been jealous of my brother in my childhood. In our tradition there are all these foolish folk-songs in which girls idolize their brothers. I always thought I loved my brother, whereas, in fact, I do not know. If he is in trouble I will be very hurt, but I do not miss him. If he is happy without me, let him be happy. He is not threatened by my achievements and fame. He is really very famous. I am nothing in comparison to him, nothing at all. He is internationally famous. He has achieved so much in such a young life. Right now he has a ministerial post. What else can he aspire for? He is not a very money-minded person—that is a plus point with him. He has only aspired for excellence. Whether I have achieved as much, I do not know. I am creative in my very limited way.

'All my anger was against my parents since they treated us both differently. They treated me like a piece of shit and they treated him like a king. My grandfather, in some villages near Gujranwala, had orange orchards that produced blood-red maltas. If you cut them you will find a lot of reddish sparkling juice in them. My father, when he was free from the clinic, would supervise the extraction of juice because there were no mixies in those days. Everything had to be sparkling clean and even the knife had to be washed. He always gave the first glass to me, the second to my mother, the third to my brother, and the fourth for himself. I felt he treated me at least equally, but in his heart of hearts his whole concentration was on my brother's education. My father could not finish his medical degree as he lost his younger brother while he was in medical college. My father never gave that much love, but he thought probably I was good for him, in a superstitious way.

'The atmosphere in the house did not affect my development. If it had been possible, my father would have got me an English governess. That was his original idea. Later he changed his mind. The English governess would not be able to teach math, because these English do not know math. Finally, a teacher was employed. He would pick me up in his arms and take a round of the courtyard—I think the courtyard was about two furlongs—and teach me math. I never learnt math. He was so frustrated that one day he took off his turban and said that he would jump off our four-or-five-storey house. Eventually my father thought it was all a waste. He got me admitted to Sacred Heart School when I was around six. The children chanted all those silly little English rhymes. They used to talk among themselves in English as well. I used to feel very inferior, but the whole atmosphere was very peaceful. I was happy to be away from home. With tall eucalyptus trees surrounding that school, it was peaceful, with heavenly bliss on the faces of the nuns. That was the time when I thought that writing the name of Kaur with K was the wrong way of writing it because the nun who used to teach the silly Punjabi children the differentiation between pronouncing K and C, found it very hard to teach us. She said that K was masculine, it had to be spoken harshly. "See, my children, softer, puff it, puff it, make it softer. It is cat, not CAT. Say it softly, with grace, because C is feminine." Some seed must have dropped in my mind then, which later on made me change the spelling of Kaur.

'I was eight and a half and had been in that school for barely two years when a famous writer's father dropped in because his dear daughter had got married in Lahore. He had some time on his hand, and so he started teaching Punjabi. I did not know Punjabi, and all the hymns and prayers I knew, I had learnt by heart from my mother. She used to insist, "If you won't pray you will have to starve." He prepared me, a child of eight and a half, for the Buddhamani exam. In spite of my protests and crying, I was removed from the school. It was just a matter of six months. "Oh, you will go back to the school again," I was told but knew nobody would take me back. He taught me Heer Ranjah and so on, and I used to hate all this. The grammar in Gurbani was so difficult, it was hell. Eventually, he picked me up in his lap. I was crying. He took me to the examination hall, put me in a chair, and said, 'You write anything you feel like writing.' So that is how I became a Buddhamani at nine years and three months of age. The newspapers carried my photographs as the youngest child ever to appear for this exam. I think my father must have told the newspaper people as they were his patients. That became a burning question of discussion in the next senate meeting. A decision was made that nobody under twelve could appear for this exam. This was later raised to fifteen or sixteen. So, that became a kind of a record which can never be broken.

'After that I started reading some English books—Nelson Readers, grammar, this and that. I used to cry every day. Nobody to talk to, nowhere to go under the constant vigilance of my mother. I used to curse my teacher. He pitied me and took me to Khalsa School. It was safe and convenient, and attached to an all girls-college. Everything decent, with huge hedges on all sides, like the burqua which the muslims wore. Initially, I was sent in a covered tonga. One day, my classmate's father scolded my father. He said, "They are talking of getting independence for India and you can't give independence to these little children. I am going to buy a cycle for my daughter. You also buy one for your daughter." So, for one year perhaps, I went on a cycle with my friend. Those were the happiest days for me. That was the first step of liberation, but in the house the atmosphere remained the same—the looking after, and all the scolding. After Partition, everybody worried about my brother's studies, but nobody took my studies seriously. I went on a hunger strike and gradually managed to do my master's in economics. Later on, my father was proud of my qualifications.

'A girl child starts becoming aware of her femininity from day one. As soon as she becomes aware that she is being discriminated against, she knows that she is a female child.

Nobody told me about menstruation, it was a shock to me. A big shock. I was in Khalsa School and I was doing some cooking classes. Luckily, I was wearing a maroon-coloured salwar. My first awareness was that my salwar was soiled. I thought, maybe I had spoiled it in the cooking class, something spilled on it. When I went to the toilet, I was horrified. I thought I had injured myself, or that I was going to die because I used to hear that my Massi (aunt) had been poisoned by her husband and in the end she had vomited blood. It was blood, blood all over her, and she died. So, I thought maybe in the cooking class I had eaten something and I was also going to die. It was such a horrifying, shocking thing. I used to think of ways and means of how to commit suicide at that age. I was very lonely, very depressed, and felt very unwanted. I came and asked my mother about it. My mother beat her brow and said, "So early?" What does so early mean? Have I done anything wrong? So early? What does that mean? I must have been ten and a half then. And then she made me feel ashamed for the first time. She saw signs of my breasts growing. I thought it was something very bad—and the way she used to look with total hatred at my breasts. I thought it was again something wrong on my part, and this was some sort of celestial punishment.

'Then, she sat down at her sewing machine and took a piece of very hard, tough cotton fabric called "lattha". She just folded a large band and cut holes from both sides for the arms to fit in, and put two straps on the top of it and at the lowest edge. That was my first bra. I felt so suffocated, and it used to hurt and scratch my skin. Now I feel I know how Chinese girls must have felt when iron shoes were put on their feet. Can you believe that I used to wear that sort of bra throughout the last year of my school and my college days? Then, a friend introduced me to a regular bra, but I did not dare to buy one till my wedding day. I was seventeen when I got married.

'It is very strange that when a girl becomes an adolescent and becomes aware of her body, her mother and everyone around her wants to trim her in every way—trim her thoughts, trim her body, and, if they could, they would actually trim her life and stop her from growing. Her growing is always connected with a catastrophe in their minds. You must have heard the famous saying that girls grow up like venomous vine that spits venom or that bears grey, bitter leaves or fruits. This growing up is not a pleasant thing. When a son grows up, they say, "*Sardar vadraya* (He is blossoming)". His growing up is always considered to be a matter of pride. In almost every language you have this famous idiomatic expression that when the shoes of the father fit the feet of the son, that means the father should treat him as an equal and stop scolding him. But with the girl it is a different story. It is a catastrophe, maybe because of the impending terror of having to pay a dowry or the terror of having to send her away to another house. Perhaps, it is a mixture of all that.

'Everybody feels threatened by sexuality, especially because they think that a girl has to be a virgin when she reaches the bed of her husband. Even in Western societies, twenty or twenty-five years back, Italian, Spanish or even French films, for example, would show that after the marriage festivities of dancing, music, and eating, the bridegroom would take the bride away to the bridal chamber. He was supposed to show the bedsheet, a white bedsheet, with a red spot on it, to confirm that the bride was a virgin. Now, I think every parent is concerned with this sacred virginity and becomes scared once their daughter reaches puberty. I find this so amazing. What is so sacred about it? Even I used to feel that, but there comes a time in your life when everything becomes crystal clear. You rise up from the ashes of your own doubts and fears. Everything that has been handed down to you from your mother's mother's mother, all these traditions, look futile. In order to protect the girl in a male-dominated society, some atrocities are inflicted on the girl which go on wounding her psyche. Our self-image is not only thwarted, in a strange way it is crushed.

'You feel as if you are dirty, contaminated, and the whole image of sex or sexuality is taboo. You cannot talk about it. All that you know about sex is some whisper among your classmates, which is more dangerous. How do parents expect a girl to behave like a normal human being when she is thrown by her husband's bedside? How can she, when during her formative years a bitter pill has been pushed down her throat that sex is something dirty? So many marriages collapse because of this. The result is that the husband becomes impotent, or he thinks that this woman is no good. So, where does it leave the woman? Many times she is not mentally prepared to sleep with the husband, as sex is something to be avoided. So, when she has to succumb to the husband's desires, it is rape. You talk of gang rape and rape of unwilling women by goondas, but what about the rape by husbands, night after night, because of society?

'The woman is being used and that deflates her self-image further and that is what happened to me. I do not remember if I felt rejected emotionally. Perhaps, at times, because it was not a normal relationship. When I became pregnant, I did not know what was happening to me. I was nauseated. Nobody ever talked to me about anything. My husband never felt the need to talk to me even though he was a doctor. I was a thing to be used. After using me, he would go to sleep.

'I always thought that they would cut my tummy from the ribcage down to the navel, the way they cut open an orange, and they would take out the child and then they would stitch my tummy back like a gunny bag. I was so afraid, imagine cutting my body to take out this unwanted thing. It is also a myth when they show in films, in all our literature, women becoming blissfully happy when they feel they are going to be mothers, and the husband's face brightening up. Women are something unwanted. They have not known the pleasure of sex. If the child is conceived out of some sort of physical pleasure, if not spiritual, even then it will mean something. Otherwise, sex becomes something mechanical, an unwanted burden, a thing to be terrified ~~of~~.

'There is no way to calculate how many women feel great with their husbands. My grandmother used to tell me that even after she conceived she had not seen my grandfather's face because he would just sneak in at night and do his job quickly and get out before anybody in the house could know. In those days men were confined to the mardana and women to the zenana.

'Sex with my husband was always distasteful but later on there was somebody else. By then, though, I was a mother of two children. When I came into contact with this person, after I had left my husband, only then I felt it could be pleasurable. Pleasurable is not the word, it can be exalting. There comes a moment in time when everything stands still; you start rising up towards the stars. That experience of spirituality cannot be described. This happens only if you are with the man you love and you feel loved. Mutuality is essential. I do feel that in the moment of physical communication there can be a spiritual experience. You cannot negate your human impulses. I think our Sikh gurus also realized that and that is why it is said that marriage and children are essential if you want to attain higher spiritual experiences. Salvation comes according to your efforts. You do not need to go to the Himalayas or a secluded place or be a recluse or renounce your worldly relationships.

'Though we women have resented being mistreated by our mothers, fathers, brothers, and later on husbands, we tend at the same time to inflict, if not as rigidly, the same restrictions on our daughters. The fear of our mothers becomes part of our psyche. We think we have to bring up our daughters in the right way, and the right way is the same way in which our mothers brought us up. When my daughters entered the adolescent age, I had to separate from my husband. The fear became more intense. My mother, aunts, and the neighbours frightened me. They accumulate a sort of terror in you about the marriage, and the position of your daughters. My husband used to say that he would get them kidnapped and sell them in brothels, send them to Singapore and so on. He always used to threaten me in many ways. If the threats had not been there, perhaps I would have been more liberal, but not to the extent of breaking all the shackles, being truly liberated, which I became a couple of years later.

'I felt that my daughters were so simple and so foolish that everybody could take advantage of them. What will I do if they become pregnant? Therefore, I must marry them off early. All these things do not go with my personality, but then I was so terrified, frightened, and threatened. That is why I married off one of my daughters early when she was full of life. She was not afraid that she might get pregnant. When she died, that was the moment I changed. When I came back to reality seven or eight months later, then I realized that it was out of fear, which was no fault of mine, though I still blame myself for her death. She would not have died if I had not married her off so early. Then, all the thick chains which were around me for years, simply fell off. That was the time when I felt truly liberated.

'I had suffered enough. There was no dearth of suffering. But the loss of a child is a different sort of suffering, it shakes you up. I told my other daughter to marry only if she wanted to legitimize a child, but she never agreed because there was something in the marrow of her bones which always made her traditional. I gave her full freedom, and the result was that she married when she was thirty-four. So many times I had to fight with my father on this point. I told him, "You have done enough damage to me and I passed on that damage to one of my daughters. At least, let me save the other."

'I was also angry with everyone. Lots of anger, in fact. Even now, if somebody asks me, where are you going, that becomes like a hammer striking against my head. That is the sentence I have been resenting throughout my life. Even if my beloved daughter asks me out of love, out of concern, I still become angry.

'Now the only source of joy is my daughter's achievements in the field of art, or self-expression through my own writing. Otherwise, I am quite a disillusioned woman who has lost her faith.

'Once upon a time, I was quite ritualistically religious, woke up at four in the morning and prayed, but after losing my daughter I gave up everything. Now, after a long gap, I have started going to a Sunday congregation because my daughter is deeply interested in the spiritual path. Yet, I have not regained the faith. Maybe someone will have to help me . . .'

**The Singer**

I had been to some of her performances and was always amazed to see the transformation in her voice and face when she sang. As I stepped into her rented house early one day, she was immersed in her morning practice. Quietly, I sat down in a corner of her sacred chamber to listen as she rendered the lyrics exquisitely.

She comes from an upper-caste, middle-class background, is divorced and in her early forties. She lives alone in a posh colony of Delhi as her daughter attends a boarding-school. She relates:

'I think I would like to start with my work in the field of art. You know, I have another family. It's the Gharana. They are spoken of as family also.

'A lot of my growth, a lot of my understanding of the world and of myself as a person, and as a performer, came as a student of music. It's not that the biological family is not significant, but in this other family one should be able to receive training and learn with a great passion.

'I come from quite a large family of three brothers and two sisters. I am the eldest sister, which really makes me different. I am, of course, my mother in a way. She taught me so much. My enjoyment of literature, reading, and music is because she would read and listen to music with me. Whatever she read, I read. I respect her very much.

'I was eleven years old when she actually started working outside the house. She is a schoolteacher, but before that she used to write, and she always had a kind of commitment to her work. She is affectionate and loving, and at the same time, has a completely satisfied feeling about herself. I have no negative feeling towards her, but it's not necessary that I agree with her. I am grateful to her. She was important to me.

'Now that I am much older, lots of things have fallen into place. In the practical sense, I have difficulties because if you are not close to your parents, you don't feel very well. I am a very different kind of person. I am not much of a home daughter, I don't think any of us really is. Perhaps, because I am the eldest, I must have been very difficult. The main difficulty I would say is that of being committed to myself and my art. I am not really very much concerned with how much it affects someone else.

'If anyone had asked me as a child what I wanted to be, I would have said something like, I want to be a doctor and serve my country. But I have no patriotism. I have no sense of doing good for the community. Somewhere, perhaps, I am good, for I have a strong sense of beauty. Beautiful things are very important for me.

'Singing was wonderful for me. It was considered a part of a girl's education. I don't think anybody really expected that I would do it so seriously or make so many sacrifices for it.

'In terms of sacrifices, when I was quite young, I hardly went out. I would go to work and come back from work. I was totally stuck at work. I think I made some difficult choices. I got married in 1974. It was a very difficult marriage, not a nice one. I felt very, very traumatised and very unhappy about it. I found that at one stage, somehow, what was important for me was being denied. Finally I decided to put an end to my marriage. Although everything will be over soon, I don't expect hundred per cent happiness. I was married for twenty-five years. Separation is very difficult, it is not easy to accept. But it's OK. I also see that the hassles of legalities make your hatred very strong.

'It was all very hard. You cannot imagine the amount of practice that went into my singing and it was complicated by the fact that you had a new relationship. It's how much faith you put in, how much effort you put in, and how much you receive. It was the only thing that I enjoyed.

'The number of hours I put into my singing depends on many factors. For a long time I had a full-time job. If I was lucky, I managed an hour or two in the morning and maybe another in the evening. Now that I am not working, I have more time for practice. So I organize myself. At times, I get eight hours, other times, it's back to four. But I see that it's not less than two hours.

'I have a daughter. She is around fourteen. My relationship

with my daughter is a very ill-rewarding one for me. For thirteen out of fourteen years I was considered a non-parent, but the one year I actually was not a parent, I was traumatized. But looking after my daughter, as a friend, and watching her grow up has been a wonderful experience for me. I do not regret it at all. I do not think that women's identity comes with motherhood because there are many, many other ways. When she was born, she was given to me as my child and I think I learnt a lot from her and have grown a lot with her.

'As a single parent I had many difficulties. It is very challenging in a sense, because you are looking after another human being. Sometimes the mind tends to forget that this is a completely different human being. You can't impose anything over another being, you can't be overbearing. The child has her own life to live. She needs your support, but she has to grow and her life is her own. The duty of the parent is to help the child. My daughter is very communicative. We talk at par. I am fortunate that she is a very sensible kind of a child. She is able to understand when I explain something to her. But I suppose you have to respect your child as a human being and not as your child.

'In my natal family, I was the eldest daughter. When my sister was born, I had a difficult time with my mother. I remember that I didn't want to read. I was quite small, around four. Later, when I learnt to read, I never got my head out of it. I made a world of my own. It was a kind of way of finding a place for myself, which I felt I needed. But while growing up I was very fond of my sisters and I was very motherly towards them, specially my little sister who was much younger than me. They depended on me.

'The family talks a lot about my relationship with my sisters. Both my sisters are going through difficulties. One is in her earlier thirties, and one is in her late thirties. I think they are going through a kind of identity crisis over the work they are doing now and what it means to them. I find that they are not talking very much about it, and they are not able to address the questions clearly to themselves, or maybe they don't want to address them to me. I don't know really. Maybe because I am older, or have gone through these things myself, I feel I have a sixth sense. Maybe I am wrong about them. Maybe they need to look carefully at themselves, make their own commitments, articulate themselves, take their own decisions. But until they do that they will be in conflict. Anyway, they may deny it and say I am imagining it but this is what I feel. I certainly feel that various kinds of underlying tensions seem to be emerging.

'I feel I am OK. I know where I want to go. I know also that there is no end. I know that's what it is, that's where I want to go, that's what I want to do. It's kind of a paradoxical situation, that's where I want to be. I am quite happy with the world of music. It's not just sufficient for me to be able to sing, to practice as much as I can. I also want to write, to do the work I am doing, to watch my daughter grow. There are many, many unresolved problems. I just have a lot of faith that it will all be OK.

'They may not be resolved, or not, at least, in the way I imagine I would like to resolve them. What shall I say? I just feel this is the best possible moment. There is no other best moment. I am living for today. Tomorrow it will be something else. That's the way I live, and it gives me a lot of satisfaction. It is not as if I don't have moments, a moment when I panic and feel very depressed. Something can just put me off.

'Regarding my sexual development, I would like to shift that question slightly, and talk about the erotic, perhaps. When one says "sexual", there is a tendency to limit it to sexual relations. I think that as one grows up, one realizes that one's sexuality is much more than that. I think I would say that it's highly aesthetic. For me the understanding of my sexuality comes only though understanding it as an aesthetic and erotic need. When you look at Indian art, for instance in music and lyrics, you find that desire is not being expressed very directly. In describing a leaf you can have the most erotic kind of lyrics. When I think about that kind of feeling, I look at myself as an erotic being as an object of another's desire. Somehow, in myself, I don't know if I can explain. Sometimes when I am practicing early in the morning, the sun is rising, light is falling softly on the leaves and plants in the garden. I cannot tell you how enriching it is. I feel so comfortable, so relaxed, so good, so much one with these things that perhaps this is the emotion of happy sexuality.

'For many women of my generation menstruation is a very difficult experience. I am not very sure when I started menstruating. My mother must have thought that she was being very matter of fact and practical and sensible by saying only that it happens to everyone, it's OK, now you can have babies. But it was not a very happy explanation for me. I still feel it was terrible. I was confused and unhappy. I really hated this peculiar bleeding every month. I felt that my mother must be wrong. I was sure nobody else in the class was menstruating. It was such a shameful and horrible thing. Now I feel very sad because I did not know. I don't mean to romanticize menstruation—it is such a nuisance. You sometimes don't feel so good on those days. At the same time, I feel it is something that makes me very special. I mean that is what is making me different from a man. I am glad I am a woman. One of my friends often pointed out that it somehow links us closely with nature. I also feel happy that my body reflects the period of the moon, the growth of parts.

'My daughter hated it. It is perhaps time for children to change. We have to talk to them. It's not only between me and her but also something between her and her friends. We do the best we can. I am sure my mother did the best she could for me. I feel comfort and joy in that all these things bring you to spirituality. I don't think that it is something which can be talked about in, say, an hour.

'Spirituality has always been very important for me. A question I asked myself as a child was that of spiritual importance. I was interested in God and music and particularly in the image of Krishna. In many ways it is a kind of humanism, very beautiful. But now it's very difficult. I don't see it as a personalized God or a being outside myself. I feel, somehow, it is a search within myself, and there are many ways in which I am searching. Just working gives me a kind of knowledge of myself. I do have a guru. One is fortunate to have met him and talked to him. I used to read a lot of books I felt drawn to. It was a kind of mystery that used to intrigue me. I was attracted to the monastic tradition. Music and spirituality are located somewhere in the body. It's as much about the desire of the body as about the desire of the heart and the soul. They are all together, not separated.

'The predominant way in which we receive religion is that somehow it purifies your body. It took time for me to understand precisely the coexistence within me of the deeply erotic tradition of music and the highly monastic tradition of religion. I find it interesting. It means that I have to adjust to that situation, find my understanding through it. I am sure everyone has to do that. Everyone has to come to terms with God, body, and soul.

'I met my guru for the first time when I went to a small group to listen to a talk. I sat so close to him. The greatness of the moment was in me. My life changed. It was very sudden. At that time I was going through a very difficult life. My daughter was very young, and my sister was ill. I had difficulties with my parents. I was struggling with my music. I had a full-time job and as a student, I was never free of financial worries and emotional difficulties. I was very much alone. But at the same time, I had also begun to understand my strength. My guru said that maybe this is my life; I have to struggle. I can do it. I have the strength to do everything together—be a mother, an ordinary office worker, a singer.

'It was some time ago. But somehow I think my confidence in myself came from that moment. It's not that His Holiness will come and set everything right, but just that obviously there is something different and special in me. I am feeling deeply connected to him now. It is sufficient for me. I don't have to go to him. He has been a mirror to me. He has shown me something, my great good fortune, and that is sufficient.

'For many years after our first meeting things were very difficult. From time to time I had opportunities to meet him. I had once gone with four or five people to meet him. It was a turbulent time for me. He gave all of us a silver coin. I very often look at it. On one side there is a lotus, on the other some inscriptions. When I look at it, I say it's just a coin, a temporary thing. But it means many, many things to me. I no longer have fear and despair to the extent I did then. Of course it's not as if I have no fear. I have fear, but today I know that I can face it. Sometimes when I have had a difficult situation to face, the coin has fallen out on that side where the inscription is. It's always as if I am being told something. I don't mean that I can't be injured, or that somebody can't be rude to me, but I feel as a human being I cannot be destroyed. Now I recognize that I do not need anybody's approval. I don't need anybody to tell me what to do. If I enjoy what I am doing, that's sufficient. I realize I am not a fool, not an idiot.

'Coming back to my other family, perhaps the only difficulty I faced was soon after I got divorced. It was also a coincidence that I went to study singing with a couple of people who I can't be nasty about. Perhaps it has also got to do a lot with the fact that I was well brought up. I don't think people respond, face to face, very badly to me. But I have a very difficult relationship with my teacher, which is very much like a mother and daughter relationship. I am very fond of her. I don't think it was accidental that we met each other. I have explored a lot of things about myself in this relationship, and it has been hard to come to this stage where I can appreciate her as a teacher.

'The death of one of my teachers affected me deeply. He was like a father to me. He was very, very fond of me. I felt very much cared for and loved. It took me a long time to get over his death. I didn't want to work. It was terrible. For a couple of years I could not stop crying. I think it was also because I had very recently been separated from my husband. I still miss my teacher very much. I think whatever base in music I have, he gave it to me. I feel very much indebted to him.'

**The Librarian**

Occasionally I would run into her at social functions in Delhi. Her warm and vivacious nature had won her many friends, some of whom told me about her love of freedom and sense of abandon. My wish to explore her world was granted, and soon I found myself having sittings with her at her residence, usually on Sundays. I also visited her workplace. She was completely at ease in both premises. She is in her late 40s and belongs to an upper-middle-class Brahmin family of West Bengal. She lives with her husband and son in a newly built flat in South Delhi. She relates:

'I was very lucky to be born in a wonderful part of the world, Darjeeling, up in the mountains. I went to a very good school run by the Loretto nuns and teachers. I can see in flashback a lot of them—their faces, how wonderful they were to me, how much they encouraged me. I also have to give a lot of credit to my mother. My mother is still a strong woman. In fact, she's staying with me now for a few months. She was responsible in a lot of ways for me. She was born in a village, or a small town, I guess, and she married into a very well-to-do family in Bengal. My father was born in a village in East Bengal to a zamindar family, and the family were practically little kings in the principality. But she didn't come from a rich family at all. Her father was a doctor in a small village in East Bengal, and she came to Darjeeling.

'She went back, after my brother was born, to some kind of private tutorials with the nuns—Irish women—and was impressed by them. Therefore, she sent me to that school whereas my brother and sister never went there. She went to this school to learn English. The reason she wanted to read and write English was that she was very opposed to the British government. My father belonged to the Congress party and had gone to jail a number of times with Gandhiji. My mother came from a terrorist background—my grandfather had often given shelter to terrorists in his cellars in Chittagong. My father was a peaceful guy. He never raised his voice and never complained about life. My mother was just the opposite, fighting all the time.

'She was responsible for sending me to school. She would sit with me and make me apply mustard oil in my eyes so that it would wake me up, but she never slept. She sat with me, eating her paan, reading her books or praying, or grumbling about the servants, whatever it was. She stood beside me through school, and she did that for my brother and my sister.

Her aim was that we should wear the graduate gowns. It was remarkable. In little ways I was resentful, but not angry or alienated. I knew what she was doing was to better me.

'She was the person to open our door to others. We had strangers living in our house in Darjeeling because it was a tourist spot. To Indians or anyone who didn't have a hotel reservation, she would say, "Okay, come and stay with us." I do it today myself, but a lot of people don't understand how I do it. A lot of things, I have inherited from her.

'Then, after I finished my college, she wanted me to study for the IAS exam. I never wanted to sit for the IAS exam because I hated the idea of studying further. So then she gave up. I got a job in Calcutta and she came straight to me. When she saw I was settled, I could handle the city, she let me go into a hostel and she moved back to my father. Then there were lots of marriage proposals for me because of various reasons. "Okay, but if you don't want it, fine," she would say. She allowed me to meet them all, but I didn't marry till the age of thirty-six.

'After I was married for a few years, I had a slipped disc, and I had an operation. She came and stayed with me, and she was the one who forced me out of bed. She was scared that I wouldn't walk. I would keep on crying and crying. But every few hours she would say, "I'm feeling bored and my husband and I've left my grandchildren. Why don't you get up? I don't want to eat alone." She made me walk again. So, in all these ways she has supported me many, many times.

'There were times when I had problems with the job—a very good job—that I'm in. I was about to resign, and she was so great. She came back to Delhi and she said, "Okay, if you want to resign and are unhappy, resign, and you can sell my gold bangles and you can earn your living with the money. You can sell them and then look around for jobs." I was having problems with my husband because I married so late. In his own way, he was a very nice person. I'm a man, in a sense, a man and a woman at the same time, as I believe in Ardhanareshwar. He's a total man. So I was having problems.

'She rang me up from Calcutta saying, "Leave him and come back to Calcutta, I'll get you married again." There was also the time which when I was emotionally involved with a guy from the States. She said to me, "Why don't you go and live with him and see if you like it?" Which mother would say that, tell me, in India or anywhere? "Don't get married. Do it and see if you like it." I was very fortunate to have a mother like her.

'I would definitely say I was closer to my mother emotionally, but I respected my father very, very much for his values. My mother is like me. She frightens the pants off the taxi driver if he is cheating. "Let's go to the police station and I'll beat you up." I've done things like that too, both in Calcutta and Delhi.

'I went abroad to England for a holiday and got a job there in the School for Oriental and African Studies. I stayed back but I didn't like it. It was a problem settling outside India, and so I came to Delhi in about 1970 for a job and to be supportive to my family. My sister lost her husband and my father's whole right side became paralysed and he could hardly talk. That set off a panic button in me. My parents were so good to me in every respect. I really wanted to do something for them.

'I am a graduate in Indian history—MA in history, and history honours. I've done a library science course. Since I came to Delhi I got the wanderlust, travelling and wanting to move. I used to travel before but in small areas like Orissa, Bihar, and all that.

'I have a child who is eleven years old, and I was very disappointed that it was a boy. I love my son because he's an extension of us, but I really sobbed in my nursing home because it was a boy. I wanted a girl. He is going to a good school in Delhi and is going to grade VII now. I have a very interesting relationship with him. It's not a mother-and-son relationship, and at times people say that I don't do it right. We're equals. We have a kidding relationship and so we are better friends. At times I say I should have been a mother to him more, taken control of his behaviour and been domineering.

'Even my son does not dominate me. I don't think anyone can dominate me. I have a very interesting psychology of the mind. I feel nobody can control you mentally. When I think of punishing him physically, his mind is free. Like just now I'm talking to you but maybe I'm thinking of something else. Nobody can really control you. Freedom is the most important thing. My son's name means freedom, and that is how I brought him up.

'Regarding my femininity, I never have seen myself as a female object. A lot of men and a lot of women have thought of me as a female object, in the States and in India. You can understand what I mean. However, I've always thought of myself as a human being. I need strongly to do everything for myself. I dress for my pleasure. I wear a lot of ornaments and jewellery. If I had gone out to a party just now I would have put on my kajal beautifully and chosen the colour of my sari because of what the mirror is reflecting back to me, and not what society thinks. I've never been molested or assaulted in my life although I've moved around alone all the time. Even though I'm so old, I can say even now I am attractive. And twenty years ago I must have been really something. But I don't allow anything of that to come into my life. I'm not interested, never will be. I can't play these games. I think that way I've had a lot of healthy relationships. I've had a lot of very good friends, both men and women, because friendship for me is very, very important. I like to be alone. Everybody needs space. I need more space than anybody else, most probably, but I like people.

'My spirituality is again not bounded by any schools. My mother believes in a certain school, my sister too, I have friends who have faith in one school or the other. How they pray, how they do rituals, is a lot like Hindu practice. I've tried all those gurus and schools. I have not had a relationship with any guru, but I have carried one impression for a long time. I respected her a lot. And in a way she has taught me a lot. Anandameyi Ma. I can tell you of one encounter with her.

'I was working in the school and I had a big fight, and my husband didn't understand what the fight was about. He couldn't figure it out. He thought I was making a big issue out of it. The big issue was something about salary and student relationships with me and others. I heard that Ma was in Haridwar, and the way I found out was like a miracle. I was at a music concert in Modern School. A woman sat beside me and said, "Can you read Bengali?" And I don't even look Bengali. I said, "A little bit." Bengali is very beautiful to look at, so I said, "I'll try." But the conversation led to Ma, and she said, "She'll be in Haridwar town tomorrow or the day after," and went out. I asked my husband and my husband was wonderful. He is a Christian, and he knows I am capable of calling a cab and going. So he said okay. My son, he was about two years old, my husband, and my sister who was here, all went. Ma was not talking those days. She used to go into "mauna" (silence). So I wrote a note saying, I want you to help with my decision. She has millions of followers. So that she could remember me, I carried my son on my lap purposely to show that I'm a family person. I'm also an escapist, mentally. I escape all the time. And she said, "Everything is passing, even your family is passing." And that really changed my thinking. It really helped me and helps me even today.

'My family has always been interested in things spiritual. My father's first cousin is a man called Nikhilananda. He has written a lot of books on the Upanishads. He is Vivekananda's disciple, started the Ramakrishna Mission in the United States. And he died in Chicago at a ripe old age. I tried to read his books, but they were tough for me to understand. My father and mother go to a guru called Golaguru. These sages who've lived in the mountains are not like those who live in five-star hotels, jet-setters, these are serious types of gurus. There are gurus and gurus. And these are the people I've heard about.

'I like to do things my way. If you see my house, you'll see it follows a pattern, not because I'm trying to show off but I do things my way. If you could see all the sundry things we eat—I don't cook, it's a mishmash. Spirituality for me is also mishmash. However, definitely there's somebody up there, whether it's a he or a she. I'd like to believe it's a she; the person has to be caring.

'I also believe there has to be a reason for everything. I believe it very strongly. It pains me to see and hear about AIDS. But I'd rather die of AIDS than the virus of religion, like in Bosnia or South Africa or the United States or even Delhi. It's horrible to say that, but it pains me to see people doing this to people. I am not unique in that thinking.

'I don't meditate everyday, but I have some space and my spirituality. I do believe in reincarnation totally. My personal experience is that it makes sense. My sister has just come to Delhi. She was working with Indian Airlines and she retired. She is now fifty-nine. If you see her for even two days you'll feel like taking care of her. She's so nice, she's such a wonderful person, but she's suffered her whole life. Her husband died when she was thirty-two. She took care of our father for seventeen years. He was paralysed, that means he needed help with the potty and everything. She worked with Indian Airlines to make money. She took care of the whole house and had two kids that she brought up. And now she's taking care of my mother. There has to be a reason for all the injustices in the world.

'I don't know about other Indian girls, but when I got my period—when I was twelve or thirteen—I was really worried. I thought I had some disease or something. I was really worried and I started crying. I changed my panties. I was very tomboyish in my teens. Most of my friends were boys of my age—jumping from big trees to the grass, we did things like that. I used to play also with catapults, trying to kill birds, or throw stones and things like that. I played with dolls but not to that extent. My neighboorhood friends were all little boys. Anyway, I thought maybe I had hurt myself. I was really concerned and worried, and later on when I realized it was not going away, I had to tell my mother. My mother called my sister and she came and said, "It happens to all girls and you had to get it too." I was wondering, why should I get it. Now it sounds so amusing, but then I was really upset. I thought that it wouldn't come back, but it did, and slowly became a pattern. It wasn't told to me that you're going to be an adult, that it's necessary if you want to have a child or a sexual relationship when you're married. All that was definitely not explained to me.

'I became aware of it through school because I had Health Science in those days, Senior Cambridge, and there used to be chapters on the subject. That's how it happened. Then the whole process of how the child is born came to me late, when I was working. I must have been twenty-two. It came as late as that. How a child is born, the actual fact that it doesn't come from the belly button—that's what a lot of girls think. It's not obvious that it comes from somewhere else.

'I've been told that in different parts of India, when a girl gets her period they have a party for her, new saris and things like that, but in my part of India, which is urban, that's not there. However, it was a part of growing up. I didn't like it, something I remember now. Same thing now with bras. I was not comfortable. I had no desire to wear them because it's such a cumbersome activity. Even now I think it's stupid. I don't enjoy wearing one. My mother, come to think of it, used to buy bras and all those things, but never enjoyed wearing it as such. I was very uncomfortable when I realized that my breasts were developing, as they say. I didn't like it because I liked dressing in pants and T-shirts, also dresses. Comfort was a priority.

'I had a sort of masculine attitude towards life. Like I never thought of boyfriends and girlfriends. I always wanted to work. From my childhood days I wanted to earn my money and not depend on anyone. That was a very big thing, that I had to be financially independent. I think this idea was put into me very subconsciously by my mother, but then it grew inside me because she was always interested in educating me.

'In my case, I have my own bank account. I deal with my own money. If I need some money, I borrow from my husband and give it back. Sometimes I forget, of course, but I definitely have mine, and he has his. I married at the age of thirty-six and had my first child at thirty-eight. I worked for so long. To think that somebody has to buy me ice-cream or a sari or a book that I want, I can't accept it. Even if you give me a gift—after a couple of months, I'll give you one, maybe bigger than what I have. It's a hang-up I got. I can never take favours from people that are far beyond my means. That puts me down. I don't want to owe anything to anybody.

'It's my freedom, more than liberation. I think there is a difference between liberation and freedom. We could look up the dictionary or thesaurus and see what exactly it means.

Freedom means no binding. I think in liberation you are enslaved, and you have to get out of it. I don't know; I'm just thinking aloud. I prefer the word "freedom" to the word "liberation". I bought a T-shirt in the States with a picture of birds and it says, "Let me be me". That is the most important thing for me. Let me be what I am.

'At times I know who I am and at times I don't. There are times when I'm totally mixed up inside, and times when I'm totally at peace with myself. Today if you ask me, I would say I'm made up of a lot of experiences in life. I've had a beautiful relationship with my very good friends with whom we travelled a lot in India. We'd read poems. A beautiful Russian poem, "Lies you do not tell children", has a meaning which I really liked. For me, the present is very important. I don't know of the future, it's is so uncertain. Whether it is nature or intelligence controlling the future, we don't know. That's a question mark. But you know the present. I can live for the present. I can't control tomorrow because I don't know what will happen tomorrow.

'I think we live emotionally in the past. I can think back about my friends in Darjeeling. There were also adults who affected me—especially the Irish nuns. One friend I still have, a Chinese friend in Benaras now, has gone her way, and I've gone my way. She got married at a very young age, I think she was seventeen and we were in standards seven or eight when she got married. I really sobbed. It was a love marriage for her, but she was going away from Darjeeling. That was my first parting, and since then I've had many partings. Working in an organization, you come to know people and then they leave. It was very painful but at the same time I picked myself up and carried on from one relationship to another. When I become involved, I go all the way. I don't keep anything for myself. A lot of people don't want to give their time. I've been very fortunate with a lot of beautiful relationships which might have lasted only for a few years, but it was worth it.

'I think the Irish nuns affected me religiously. It was their discipline, the love for learning, the love for education, the dedication to work. They dedicated themselves to their work as teachers and that has come down to me as a career person. I look back and think how beautiful their teaching was. Such dedication is lacking in my son, and I know what is happening in education. It's really a pity, very, very sad, and I wish the Irish nuns were here today for our children. But what was not beautiful, I would say, is that I was brought up in a cocoon. Not only me but a lot of my friends were brought up in a cocoon by the Irish nuns, where black was black and white was white as far as Catholics were concerned.

'As to whether being a Hindu makes me go through a conflict with Christianity, I would say yes and no. Because my mother and father were very supportive, I used to go to church. Though I don't have a good voice, I was in the choir. So I used to go to the midnight service and sing, and used to attend mass. I really wanted to become a Catholic nun. You saw these nuns with a rosary going around quietly; there was some kind of a peace. For all you know there was turmoil inside, but at least the outside image was something peaceful and beautiful. But do you know what? My mother's friends in Darjeeling would say, "She's going to church, she's going to be a Christian, what are you doing?" And my mother used to say, "She's not doing anything wrong. She is going to the house of God." It might sound strange today. But then it sounded beautiful. And there was no turmoil.

'And then I came to Calcutta. I was staying in a hostel run by Spanish nuns and I found that they were horrible. I think they didn't have any values. That really disappointed me. Then a very close member of the family, my sister's husband, died when he was about thirty-five. My belief in God or Christ vanished. I did not become an atheist but neither did I have any feelings for Yeshu when I started working and came to Delhi, staying on my own. I feel that what the nuns had taught about God was different. That you pray to God and come back like Cinderella, that the fairy godmother would settle the issue with a wand. That's where Hinduism came to help me. There is a pain, there is a scheme, there is a cause and effect, there is a reason for things. I came to terms with myself and that's where

Anandameyi Ma figured in my life. I could finally speak about my husband and my relationship with him.

'I experienced great difficulty as a single woman because the attitude of men towards women in Delhi was very different from the attitude of men in Calcutta where I started my career. But somehow or the other my mother had given me a role model. It's really crazy how you role-model people. She had never told me, "Do this". But I've seen her in action controlling crowds when they had little riots in Darjeeling. I have seen her fighting with the police, fighting with shopkeepers or taxi drivers. So these techniques I had imbibed, I guess. If I had a fight with a scooter driver I would pick up my chappals and beat him up. I've done that. I was never scared. You know the thing I was scared of was that I would be molested or raped; it has never happened.

What I used to do was protect myself. I wouldn't go out at night to Chandni Chowk and say, hey, I'm here. I used to go to music concerts very often, and I would keep the taxi waiting. So the same taximan would take me back. This technique I had learnt from my mother, of becoming very close friends with the taxi driver. I would tell him about my family, how many children I have. In England, where I was working, once coming back very late at night, a young man started running after me. I had an umbrella and I hit him in his you-know-what. I was close to my house, luckily. In New York, once I was in the Port Authority bus station standing in line to buy a bus ticket. There was a younger man—he was not a big-built man—trying to pinch me from the back. So I stepped out and said loudly, "Why don't you take somebody of your kind! Why are you pinching me?" People around me were embarrassed, and he just moved away. Then there is another instance involving a Brazilian girlfriend of mine. We had gone to see a play and were coming back by the tube in New York. I had told her, let's not go in the tube, let's go by taxi. Between the two of us we had enough money. She said, "No, come on, let's go in the tube." We took the metro and a man coming in said, "Oh, how beautiful you are." I looked up at him and then continued to stare. The only thing that must have occured to him was, Jesus, she doesn't understand a word of English, and he left. I look at men as young little things, like my son is. I don't feel any hatred for them.

'Coming back to my husband, I've been married to him for thirteen years now. I met him through my work, and I had no intention of marrying him or marrying anyone, for that matter. I was not interested in marriage. I was not romantically inclined towards him. We became friends gradually. However, he will tell you, "As soon as she saw me she wanted to marry me."

'My husband himself slowly influenced me to get involved with this relationship of marriage. I would say that when I got married I imagined it to be very romantic. Though I had degrees and my art books, we were all brought up on Mills and Boon in a way. I may not have read that many Mills and Boon, but we all have read that women fantasize. I woke up from the Catholics, saying that God is not like a fairy godmother that comes in with a wand and touches cancer and makes it go away. God doesn't do that. He might give the strength to face it. Slowly I realized, God, I had made a bit of a mistake. I wanted to run away from my husband because I thought marriage was awful.

'I wanted him to be all the people I admire. After seeing Clarke Gable, I wanted all the attributes in him. Everyone expects that, not only me. I wanted to take more than give. I thought my role was being challenged and curtailed. My husband is very intelligent, and he figured out what sort of a woman I was. He definitely wanted to curtail my physical movement because I would be out at any hour of the night. You could ring me at ten o'clock and say, "Hey, let's go for a drive, are you free?" I'd say, "Yes, let's go." I've done that, and you can't do that if you are married. So, it was stopped. It was very, very tough for me. Slowly, I learned to compromise totally, though there are days when I resent it. I'm happy with him. But for all you know, after three days I'll say I can't stand him, I'm leaving him. We've had our ups and downs for sure, but I reaped the benefits. My relationship with him, I'll say, is not too bad.

'I do not know how he views this relationship. I have never channelled the questions to him. I think his good point is his fantastic power, and he has a tremendous amount of patience. These are two qualities which I really admire in him. It's a nice balance because I do not have patience. I come first in my life. It might sound very self-centred on my side, egocentric, but I give only up to a point. I definitely come first in my life. I enjoy the "I" moment, it's a very big thing in my life. It's like I would cook dinner and tell you to come, but if you're taking your time and I'm hungry, I'll start eating.

'It is difficult for me to say something about my sexuality. I can't, but if you ask me questions then I can. I have to think about it. The first sexual relationship I had was not with my husband. I wouldn't say it was unpleasant, because I loved him. I'm glad I didn't marry him, but I had a pleasant time. It was a surprise, and it was beautiful. I was really upset later on, when it happened with somebody else. I didn't want to have another relationship with anyone else, because I was so emotionally connected with the previous person. Due to certain reasons, my first relationship didn't mature into a permanent one, and that was very, very painful for me. It didn't affect my marriage in any way. I had a very casual attitude toward life. I don't think anything is permanent. Anything can happen. If my husband leaves me tomorrow and goes away with another, it's fine. That's the attitude I have—it may be an attitude to protect myself.

'The other thing that affects me is travelling, sitting in a train. I love train travel, I love the journey, a journey into myself, into the world, into the womb, into nothingness, into all sorts of things. I love the Indian railway, it's my railway. It's because you create your space in spite of having people around you. The first time I went to Benaras, I went to the Viswanath temple and said, "How sick! How can people pray in this mess? How can you concentrate?" Then I realized it was beautiful in a way there. I sat there and sorted it out for myself. I'm not saying it was the right attitude, but I sorted myself out, for myself, in spite of the cow shit, the noise, and the pushing and everything.

'My husband and I travel a lot, and I think that is the time when we really come together, because he loves driving. So we travelled from here to Ladakh, Lahul, Spiti, and Kinnaur. I've gone to Ajanta and Ellora. I've gone down south two to three times by road, and I just love it. I've seen the length and breadth of the country.

'My mother and sister are my real-life role models. My father was paralysed in 1969. I saw him getting paralysed, called a phsyiotherapist who saw to it that he could walk, came to Calcutta. Then I got a telephone call that my brother-in-law had had a stroke. I went there, and my brother-in-law died within ten to fifteen days. My father asked how my brother-in-law was. I didn't have the guts to tell him that he had gone. My sister came and told him, and consoled him. She was crying and consoling him at the same time by saying, "Don't worry, I'm here for you."

'You're talking of a role model? There are millions of women in India, the strong women that you're thinking of, and everyone has a story to tell. I came back to Calcutta and got my sister a house, because I knew she could not stay in that house where my brother-in-law had died. She took up a job, and she and my mother looked after Father for eighteen years.

'It was very, very difficult. I wanted him to die, I was praying for him to die. But my sister, especially, thought I was crazy to think of it. She was very angry. She said, "You don't even have to send money, I'm looking after him." The reason for wanting to put an end to it was because he was suffering so much. He had been a body builder, a horseback rider, and here he was with bedsores. It was terrible. I would sit in the other room, and my sister did everything for him. She refused to have a nurse, though we had the money to pay. She wanted to take care of him. That's her. Nobody is going to write about such women.

'I have read a lot of books on Krishnamurthiji. I've been to him. I would say he's horrible, he wasn't marked for me, he was marked for others. I felt that they wanted you to control others through his message. If you had read his books and had then met him, you could see that he contradicted himself. It shows if you read his books. I'm such a small person to talk about him, but I felt that. I don't want anything to do any more with anyone who has power as a guru. It doesn't impress me unless I see them. When I went to Kedarnath and Badrinath, I would go to

Gangotri and see the sadhus. I would go and sit with them. Some of them were really serious people. I would appreciate them from a distance, but I didn't want to become their chela.

'I've always wanted to know what there is in life, life after death, from reading Aurobindo, Vivekananda, and others. I have questioned many tantrics, and I feel spirituality is something highly subjective, differing from person to person. My concept is that you have some inner kind of tranquillity and peace, and you come to terms with your turmoil. I would distinguish it from religion, because religions are really rituals.

'I used to believe in rituals once upon a time, but I don't any more. I just want to say that I'm married into a Christian family. My in-laws are very, very nice. I have two sisters-in-law. They are all very fond of me, though I'm capable of anything, I'll say anything. Once my mother-in-law came to stay for three or four months with me. I would drop her at the church and pick her up. Once my mother-in-law said, "Oh, because you're like my third daughter, I can rely on you. I can confide in you much more than I do to my daughters. I really pray that one day you become Christian." "Mother, maybe in my next life," I said. They know I'm capable of saying things like that because I like to shock people. That's an impish thing in me.

'My in-laws are very ritualistic in their religion.There are some people who need it, whether it's Hindu rituals or Christian rituals. I was in Kashmir once. I stayed in a houseboat owned by a very famous houseboat owner. I had met the old man recently. The old lady and I became friends. She couldn't speak a word other than Kashmiri. The old man taught me how to read the namaz, and I did it. Then he asked me (my husband was with me), "Do you want to go to the mosque this afternoon?" I said, yes. So he said, "You don't wear a dupatta?" I said, no. So his wife gave me a dupatta, which I still have. Then we went to the mosque. Again I went there as a ritual. I definitely believe there's someone up there, but I've not figured him or her out. I would say it was nareshwar, it was the mother, but you see all the pain. I feel I am a mother, a woman who gives, because the whole concept of a woman is that of a giver. That is what I'm comfortable with.

'I certainly had sibling rivalry with my brother. My brother, who lives in Calcutta but comes now and then to Delhi, has a dominating nature. The rivalry started to develop when we were both in England at the same time. He's a loser. It was pretty bad. Anyhow, he got married here. I hardly see him because each time we see each other we have a fight, an argument, or something. I am an escapist. I didn't like any kind of argument for too long a time. At the same time I miss my brother. Whenever I see a married woman's relationship with her brother, I wish it was mine. I have a friend. She has three brothers who are like the three musketeers. They are so close, they really protect her. She is looked after. My brother doesn't protect me in any sense. I don't have any relationship with him, and I miss that.

'As you can see, I haven't dyed my hair. I want to look more grey, actually. I wish I had the energy to sit in a hair-dressing salon and dye it.

'I want to have a house up in the hills where I could go for walks and muse, but I don't see it happening. That's a dream I have . . . I want to die of a massive heart attack. The movie that really affected me was *All That Jazz.* You don't know how many times I've seen it, nine to ten times. I'd love to buy the video.

'I've calmed down a lot with age—a lot of people tell me that. My temper has come down. I'm more tolerant. I accept things. I'm happy. Moments of weakness or pain, I do have those. I become very callous when I have pain. I go totally into myself, become spiritual about it in an escapist way. I won't go into it in anger unless I'm very upset. If I'm upset I go to a beauty parlour for an aesthetic job or buy a sari, but when something affects me emotionally, I become very, very spiritual about it, become totally withdrawn, and think about it.

'I have a fear of prolonged illness like my father had, something where I'm not going to improve. I don't know who'll look after my son then, because my sister is much older than me. Technically she should die before me. Otherwise, I do not have the fear of death. And I don't brood over my problems. That is my magic for myself.'

*

Clearly, creative activity, be it art, literature or music, combines the inner and outer voyage of self-discovery. Yet, any quantum of external freedom per se will not encourage creativity or produce an inner state of tranquillity and enlightenment. Through their artistic expression, these women touch their inner essence, communicate uniquely, represent the spirit of the age, and pave their own paths in life. The power of the creative act itself sanctifies their spiritual strivings. Human beings are heir to infinite suffering, confusion and chaos in Samsara. Creativity helps one to transmute one's pain into ecstasy. But the question remains: do individuals create in order to attain enlightenment, and further, what motivates the enlightened individuals to create?

Genuine talent makes its way without requiring special encouragement as seen in the case of the writer. She, in fact, thrives on emotional conflicts and opposition. Her sensitivity to her environment and insights into human nature raise diverse issues, especially discrimination against girls—the trimming of their body, speech and mind—and marital rape. She still harbours a lot of anger and resentment against her immediate family. However, salvation can be reached through one's own efforts, and in her case the ultimate shock of her daughter's death truly liberated her. Basically, it is her outstanding persistence that drives her to write, work and help others.

For the singer, it is the aesthetic dimension of the erotic that impels her to search within. Extremely devoted to her practice, she has the faith to resolve her problems. The spiritual task at hand is to reconcile the erotic tradition of music and the monastic discipline of religion. Her very first encounter with her guru changed her life as she realized the greatness of the moment within herself. Her other family has groomed her in the field of music, making her quest for perfection an endlessly delightful process.

The sort of education and family environment that encourage spontaneous and independent thought among children, emerges in the account of the librarian. Her creativity lies in the fact that she is free to try out in a flexible fashion all manner of relationships, as is apparent in her marriage, her wanderlust and her mishmash spirituality. Love for learning, education and dedication to work is her path for spiritual practice. Her intense awareness of impermanence is a gift from the gurus, even though she is sceptical about them.

At times, however, these talented individuals are viewed with suspicion as they do not conform to the conventional.

Our socio-cultural environment can thus facilitate freedom of symbolic expression in order to foster creativity and draw out whatever is most inward in the minds of men and women. Once we have learnt to contact ourselves, then, we can perhaps experience that lightness of being which comes from discovering our in her selves.

# Chapter 4

# *Initiation and Kinship: The Housewife and the American*

The nuclear family is the dominant social unit in urban centres, but it is not the exclusive or exhaustive form. Kinship and friendship ties remain important and incline the individual out of himself/herself to search beyond his/her narcissism and finitude. The issue here is to recognize women's sacrality and the logic of their particular articulation. The process of initiating the phenomenon of caring and communication in their family, extended kinship network or community, is reflected in the accounts of the housewife and the American.

**The Housewife**

My association with her lasted for a few years. We had worked together on the executive committee of a charitable organization in Delhi. The politeness and social skills she used while conducting herself at the meetings had always impressed me. I was a little surprised when she permitted me to interview her because she had always maintained a certain distance and a sense of privacy.

She welcomed me to her large house in a posh colony in New Delhi. Her husband joined us for tea, but later left us to ourselves. I could not help but admire the collection of books and paintings in her sitting-room. We slowly warmed up and proceeded with our work.

She is in her late fifties and belongs to an educated, upper-caste and upper-middle-class joint family. She narrated:

'I was born into a family of five children. My father came from a zamindari family, but he opted for a career and joined the Indian Administrative Service. So, my childhood was spent as the daughter of a service person. I have two elder sisters. I think that was important, though I had parents who never made me feel that being a third daughter was in any way unfortunate. However, I was very conscious of the fact that my father's zamindari properties would definitely not come to us unless there was a son. But again, my parents never put any emphasis on it.

'Those who really influenced my nature, my character, were my two sisters. My eldest sister was brilliant. She ultimately became a doctor and got degrees from colleges in America and England. She was also a very dominating person. By the time I was born, my father was well into his career. My mother and he had to entertain and go out a lot, so my eldest sister was very protective and kind towards me. But being brilliant, she was extremely short-tempered when it came to the fact that I was not a quick learner, and I think that affected me.

'I think I was frightened. It was nothing serious, but I think it made me a bit of a slow starter. My second sister was of a much more pleasant nature—a very happy-go-lucky person, very pretty and also very clever.

'So I had two very dominating sisters who made it quite clear that they were superior. I think in one way I was fortunate. I never rebelled, I just quietly did my own thing for which I'm very grateful. I had an exceptionally beautiful mother, elegant and very charming. My relationship was very good with both my mother and my father. My father sometimes used to feel a little disappointed in me, and he used to tell me that your sisters have achieved so much and you must try to do your best also. He was a very God-fearing, gentle, wise man. Rather than put me down, I think he motivated me.

'My mother had been married at the age of six. But she was

very fortunate. My father's family brought her up and gave her education up to Senior Cambridge and took her abroad for finishing school.

'She wanted all her children to be highly educated because she only went up to Senior Cambridge. She would say: "Whatever happens, my five children are all going to be highly educated for sure, whether they use it or not is not important." I think that was an important thing. Then, because of my father's career, I was very fortunate that at the age of six I went to England. I stayed there till I was twelve, through the war years. Having parents who believe in the old values, having gone through six years of bombing in London, I think it inculcated in me a sense of discipline, a sense of values. You see a lot of suffering and you learn many things as a child during the war—never to waste food, to be very careful . . .

'When, we came back to India, I did my Senior Cambridge in Delhi from a convent. As you know, a convent upbringing teaches you the Bible, and, in a way, it is extremely good, because it exposes you to religion.

'My father was always scholarly. He took great pride in learning. He used to read the Gita, the Quran, the Holy Bible. He was very proud that when he retired he spent his days writing comparative notes on what he had learnt from the three religious books. We were always encouraged to possess and read the Gita and the Bible.

'My mother was also very religious in her own simple way of doing puja. My father was not religious, he was scholarly—always looking into the truth of things and life rather than saying a prayer to Krishna, which my mother did. All these things had an effect on me and my whole world. My father read Gandhiji's *My Experiments with Truth* and we always had an ongoing dialogue with him about it. When we lived in foreign countries, foreigners would ask us at college to say a few words about the Gita. My father would give us ideas and we'd put together a lecture. Another thing my father told us was, "If you want to buy any books or travel, I'll always help you." He didn't like a privileged life. I have never been to a beauty parlour, we never had excessive clothes. He was moderate in life. Books cost a lot of money in western countries then. When we were abroad he helped us travel, which was also a lovely thing. Just as I was entering college, he got a posting in America. So he sent me to the best college, which was his way of doing things. I stayed there for four years and graduated. Anything to do with my education, he encouraged me.

'I did a BA honours in economics. I feel an American education for me was a very great stimulant. I didn't realize it then but now I realize what a first-class university with wonderful minds and wonderful people did for me. I just felt I had flowered and blossomed. I loved those four years. I did well and took part in activities and all of a sudden I realized, My gosh! I'm not such a slow learner as I thought myself to be. It was a wonderful experience and I always look back at those years as very, very important ones. I made some lasting friendships. I have friends whom I knew when I was six years old, and they seek me out. I still keep up with many friends from America. I'm very fortunate that I made very good friends in life.

'When I came back to India, I worked a little bit at the Cottage Industries in their research section for handicrafts. Then I helped an American who was here with the Ford Foundation. He organized the first group of Indian painters in Delhi, and because I was working closely with him I took a lot of responsibility for what we call Aid Painters. It was the first time in Delhi that these painters had exhibited together. Those were happy associations.

'And then I got married in 1958. It wasn't an arranged marriage. I met my husband in Calcutta. It was a chance meeting. I had gone there for a few days. My cousins took me to a party and we met. It was inter-caste, inter-state, inter everything. But our parents had heard of each other, and once they got to know each other, there was no problem.

'We share a lot of common interests. It's been a life of doing a lot of things together—reading, collecting art and playing golf. We have two children—two boys—and we moved to Delhi about twenty-five years ago and have lived here ever since. Then my husband decided to leave service and start his own factory at Calcutta. As I had some grounding in economics, I decided to help, which I have done for twenty years. It was great running a factory. People were a little surprised to have a woman in the factory. But I got wonderful feedback from bank managers and customers. Then in 1985 I found that the atmosphere in India was changing, the values were changing, and I didn't want to be involved.

'Before 1985 I'd decided that my family, my husband, my children came first. A career never entered my mind because my parents had clearly told me while educating me, "If, God forbid, one day you have to earn a living, you have to be able to earn. But if you don't have to, then you should be an excellent wife and mother, always supporting your family." That was how we were brought up. And therefore I didn't entertain or even try for something. Though sometimes I felt that if I had a career of my own, I'd have something different. At least, if the whole family knows the mother is going to be the central figure, I think it does help. I certainly felt that it was a very anchoring force. A mother is a very important person. If she gives the impression that the family comes first, then it gives a great deal of security to the family. Since I never had to earn to supplement the family budget, I had a secure existence.

'Now I don't know. Things are changing. My observation and experience is that girls' parents are not only telling them that we educate you to make sure you stand on your feet, but we want you to be a person. If you feel like having a career you should indulge yourself in that direction or whatever. That is very important, that's what I feel is the difference between my generation and the next. The girls are definitely very talented and they should be encouraged. But I think it's going to bring a lot of strains and stresses. When one comes back from work, one's tired. But if you don't have a cook, a bearer, and somebody to keep your home, it must be very tough, very tough indeed.

'See, we were very fortunate. Servants were around when we were growing up. I had an ayah for both my children. It's a privilege. She was like a mother to my children. That breed of servants has gone. So the girls have a much harder time. I feel that women have different emphases now. I don't know what's better, I can't say.

'I also feel that my sons and other people's sons all have to change, also. If their wives want to go out and be persons in their own right, I think they should encourage their wives. In my family they don't make their wives earn for income. They do whatever they like to develop and organize their skills. Both my daughters-in-law are employed.

'We have a joint family, and we all live together. Recently, we were fortunate to be able to get the eldest son and his wife a set of rooms with a little kitchenette. So now we are physically in the same premises but they have their own home. My other daughter-in-law and son are with us. We told them to do whatever they could to have a place of their own. She is happy with me. When there's a good relationship between people, then everything can be sorted out. It is all done without any tension or strain. If there is a good relationship, a problem is usually ironed out.

'I married into a much more conservative (with capital letters) family than my own. They were very Anglicised and had lived abroad most of their lives but were basically very Indian. My mother-in-law couldn't speak English and can hardly speak Hindi, but we had a beautiful relationship. They were so kind. They treated me like their daughter, and so I looked upon them as my parents. My husband bridged the gap and always explained if I didn't understand certain actions and reactions. I think the son has to take a lot of responsibility in a joint family.

'My first exposure to spirituality was when I was eight years old. My father had a Swiss governess for the two sons that were born very late in life. She was a deeply religious person, and she had a great influence on my second sister who was just a little older than me. She would read us stories from the Bible and she got us to love the Bible. We went to convent school, and the Bible was again endorsed in my education.

'My parents and in-laws all lived to a very old age. My father was almost ninety when he died; my mother was eighty-seven. All of them had a wonderful life. But my brother died when his career was just about to take off. He was just fifty-one. To understand why it happened to him, I went to the Ramakrishna Mission Gita classes which were held when I was running the factory. I took one hour off every day to attend the course. That was in the late 1960s or early 1970s. I didn't do very much until two years ago when a wonderful swami had come to teach us. And I've really enjoyed that. It was the first time I had a very well-educated, English-speaking swami for a teacher. I am enjoying it.

'My husband has always been interested in philosophies of religion. Our association with Buddhism started in 1979. I do not have a guru; they say when you are ripe, then the guru appears. However, many influences have come into our lives. They've come because we've looked for them. I have great respect for Lama Zopa Rimpoche. I decided that now I must work without looking for profit, and so I joined the SOS children's movement and have done a little. I love to do studies on the mothers and the children, on different aspects of the organization, and then present them to the board. It's a wonderful organization, very well run.

'As you grow older you become a little lazy. I took a decision that in my old age I would spend my time beneficially. I learnt French because I thought it was the only relaxation which challenged your mind and kept you thinking. I made lovely friends and have had good relationships. I find that has been one of my finest qualities, that I've been able to retain my friendships. And recently, I joined a book club which meets once a month. It gives me the discipline to read and think and do a little research. I've joined the university-level course of Indian Arts Heritage at the India Museum. I'm really enjoying it. I put in a little study and reading to make the course worthwhile and meaningful. I also travel a little. I think these are my little old-age insurance policies to keep active. I am doing all the things that, while I was working or bringing up my family and children, I didn't have time to do.

'Coming back to spirituality and my study of the Gita with Swamiji, there are two things which are very important. The first thing is that Hinduism, the Gita and the Vedanta, is not a religion. It is a journey into knowing yourself, and the most important thing is that you must take responsibility for everything you do. If something goes wrong you must ask yourself what you did wrong and not try to change the other person. This is something that Swamiji has beautifully brought out in the shlokas of the Gita—what Krishna was trying to say about such things as doing your duty. In Buddhism I've often sought compassion; you see, it's not easy to be compassionate. And that's one thing I think Buddha really wanted you to have. The Vedanta is a little bit self-centred, but you need both to lead your life.

'Regarding my sexual development, well, we never talked about it at school. My parents never told me anything either. It is something you acquire from a good friend. In my case I had a sister who was a doctor and had a very good relationship with me. She told me the basics. My sisters and I took things in our stride. We never paid much attention to menstruation. If we were not well, we just took rest. And that was that. And sexually, I think a loving relationship exists in a love marriage when there's respect on both sides. In our generation, things are done and communicated without too much talking.

'Having children was a joy. Deciding how many we wanted, and when, bringing them up . . . Luckily we both had the same sense of duty. So, there's no conflict. Sex is something which is private, to be respected, and not talked about everywhere. And it wasn't given so much emphasis. I'm not so sure if giving it so much emphasis is helping. If you talk about it, you talk to the person concerned. Today, it's much more open and I find it a little vulgar. I'm talking about the general trend.

'In some ways, I think, marriage is better if two people have lived together before, and really got to know each other. In some cases that would have been a better thing than marriage, but it's not good as a general rule. I know of a girl who lived with a man for eight years. Her mother in South Africa had some operation and so she had to go there. In her absence, he got involved with another woman. And one day he walked out of their relationship. That was devastating for her. So you see, you have to be emotionally and economically independent these days.

'I'm a very heavy sleeper. Once I go to bed, I sleep. But I have had one recurring dream which I am going to share with you. I had this fear as a child that I was never going to pass an exam. My sisters were toppers, especially the eldest. Even after marriage I used to dream that I was due to take an exam, but that I was unable to open a book. I kept procrastinating and telling myself, you must get on and study or you will fail. It's the only dream I've had, though I haven't had it for a long time now.

'My daily life keeps me nicely busy. I get up at about seven. The water shortage in Delhi is a new aspect of my life, and I go to the bathrooms and kitchen and put on the taps while I'm making my morning tea. Then I put the dog out and have my cup of tea. I like to read the newspaper. And then my husband and I have to go to work. We still have plenty to discuss. I still look after my own financial work and some of the factory work which I haven't totally freed myself from. I am always rushing in the morning. When I come back for lunch, I like to lie down for half an hour. We like watching select programmes on TV. We listen to the news twice a day. In the afternoon I often read. Then we go off to work at four o'clock and come back at 6.30 and have a very relaxing evening. We spend the evening with the family. We all have dinner together. Then I go straight to bed at nine.

'Two women have been models for me. When I was very young, a very dear friend of mine, Lady Rama Rao, was the flag bearer of our family—a brilliant, beautiful, double MA. She had been a very good friend of my father. From childhood I grew up with Lady Rama Rao as my model. She spoke beautiful English, she lectured, was a brilliant woman, and very loving. Even if she had ten meetings and I came to her and said, "Can you help me?" she would work out her time and give me her undivided attention. I admired her greatly. The second model was Tara Ali Baig. I had the privilege of working five years with her before she died. I used to admire Tara's enormous energy and brilliant mind. Tara could enjoy a party; she would go at five in the morning to the village and be totally at home. She was very elegant and charming in everything she did. Both these women were very feminine. So, they were my models.'

**The American**

She joined our meditation group four years ago and has been attending it occasionally. I found her inclination toward spirituality and devotion to her family relationships rather remarkable. She belongs to an upper-caste upper-middle-class South Indian family from Bangalore. She is an American citizen and now lives in Delhi with her husband and son. After having lived in the United States for over a decade, it has not been easy for her to cope with the everyday problems and concerns of domestic life here.

Her home had a semi-western, semi-traditional ambience. A blown-up picture of their family guru stood prominently in the TV room, where I sat with her talking, listening, and sipping a soft drink. She related:

'I was born in Bangalore. I grew up in a house with two sisters and two brothers. I was the fourth one. My father was very spiritual, a very outgoing person.

'It was like a joint family. We had nine uncles—my father's brothers and my mother's brothers, my mother's mother and my father's mother. We had all kinds of people in the house. In all, we were about twenty-five to thirty people there.

'It was a learning experience, living in a joint family, because when you come out into the world you really have to live in any circumstances given to you. We three sisters were really protected by my father. But still it was nice growing up with everybody, and now you know who's who and you have a big family to go back to.

'We brothers and sisters had a very good relationship. There was no rivalry or anything. My older sister and I grew up with my grandmother and grandfather, and we came to live with my parents when I was seven years old. So my older sister and I were very close. When she got married, it was like losing somebody special whom I could talk to. My mother could give her attention to all of us, and we also had Grandmother around the house. So we had attention from her as well. Actually, my mother's aunt was the one who brought us all up.

'I had an arranged marriage. I was eighteen years old when I got married. I had just finished my B.Sc. My father was so eager to get me married. My older sister married soon after she graduated. He thought that girls should be married young. He had probably his sister's case in mind, who didn't get married till after he had his own clinic and started working. So he felt that his girls should get married before they started working or having their own career. He asked me before he really made his decision and I had no problem in getting married. I married into the same caste. They lived in the same town too. The only thing was that my husband had come from America. He was there for two years before coming back to get married. He was a professional. So was my father; he was a dentist. My mother was educated upto SSLC, and she used to work in my father's clinic to assist him.

'I really matured after I got married, because I was out of the house and on my own. I was with my in-laws for nearly three months, waiting for my visa papers in order to go to the States. That was some experience. It was a different family altogether, a family where there were no girls. They did not know about a girl's feelings or anything. I just wanted to get out of that house and go and live with my husband. We fought sometimes. My relationship with my mother-in-law was a difficult one.

'Basically, the in-laws were very difficult because they had certain expectations from the marriage of their older son. They didn't come out and say in the beginning how the wedding was to be done and what they wanted. They expected certain things, whereas my husband didn't want anything from my parents. He just wanted a simple wedding. He overruled them during the wedding, and my mother-in-law was very disappointed. So, she wanted to take the whole thing out on me. She was very dissatisfied, and she kept talking about my parents and how bad they were. Every day I kept hearing this. I was very close to my father and I couldn't bear it. It was very difficult to understand them.

'I had a very good relationship with my brother who was still studying then. I used to keep writing to him and asking him what I should do. Like everybody else, my brother used to say, "Just keep quiet. You just don't talk to them, don't say anything. You are going away anyway." But it didn't stop. My whole family thought it would stop, but my in-laws had a very big influence on my husband. My mother-in-law used to keep writing letters even after I went to live in America with my husband. Whenever I got a letter, I used to think, my goodness, there goes the peace in the house. We used to have fights. He never understood me, or I never understood him. I used to pray to God that even if nobody else understands, at least my husband should understand one day. I had patience, I never talked back, I never did anything. It really worked. It was like he understood what was going on, and now he tries to stay neutral. It's difficult for him also, I feel, to support his wife or his mother. But he tries. My mother-in-law has now changed a lot. She thinks I'm the best daughter-in-law she could have had, and she's happy now. She doesn't talk about what happened in the past.

'She's changed for the better. She does expect certain things—like she wants to come here now. She thinks I should give up everything, and just be with her, maybe for a month or so. It becomes difficult for me because I have a circle of friends, a number of things I'm doing, and she expects that I should give up everything and spend time with her. That causes a little bit of tension, but then later on I say, OK, she'll be here only for a month, just take it as it comes. You don't have to see your friends for that time.

'The tension will never go away, because she's a person who expects a lot. They have three brothers in the family, and my husband is the oldest son and he is the only one who is married. I'm the only daughter-in-law in the house. She tries to claim everything from me or my husband, which causes a lot of tension. She's about seventy-two years old. She doesn't feel her age, and she thinks she can do everything. She tries to interfere with my son. He doesn't listen, and she feels, oh my, he's grown up, and that she doesn't have anyone to dote on. She doesn't have anything to do—that's become a big problem.

'My son is sixteen years old. Kids nowadays, especially teenagers, want to be on their own. We don't even force him to come and sit with us. If he wants to do a certain thing, he'll do it. We tell him, it's his life. He has to learn to live with his mistakes. We just guide him, but she thinks we're not doing the right thing. I keep telling him that it's just for a few weeks and she's going away. And that she's also trying to bear with us. Nothing we can do about it.

'I read a lot of spiritual books and I listen to a lot of bhajans and other things which keep my mind at peace. Spirituality, I think, was inside me all the time, because we grew up in a household where my father used to do pujas every day. The whole family believes in Sai Baba. We used to go to see him. We used to spend some time there and listen to his discourses. And even the family I got married into, they were staunch believers.

'My husband was a believer, but still he didn't want to do too much about it. When we were in the States, we used to go for bhajans and everything, but we never had too much time. Four years ago when we came back to India, I started reading books. I really got into it when I felt I didn't have anything to do. Then the whole thing, what my father was telling us, whatever I'd heard from the beginning, made sense to me. And I thought, this is where I should be spending time.

'Every morning my father used to do puja by six o'clock. He wanted us to be out of bed, have a shower or bath, and come for the arti. And we never did that, any of us, because we used to be sleeping. He had to finish his arti, and then wake us up. Every day he would tell us, "This is not right. You shouldn't do this. You should get up before this." We had about twenty-five people in the house, and in the old days, we used to lie in bed and wait for the one and only bathroom to get vacant. The thing I missed when I went away the first time were the mantras, the chanting. It was then I realized that if I have to hear those things, I have to learn to do it. I can't just listen to it and keep quiet. That's when I said I should learn certain things, do things, the way I thought my parents were doing them. We do celebrate all the Hindu festivals. Even in America we used to do pujas. My husband used to think festivals meant just praying to God; that's where it ended for him. For me, it doesn't end there. We do the pujas and pray to God, but we also celebrate festivals. Like the evening of a festival, there would a big dinner, and we would have some people over. I grew up in such a big family that if we had a festival, we had all the nieces and cousins, and everybody there in one house. So I thought that is how it should be done. But my husband's house is different. They like to have just their family, not the whole neighbourhood.

'I grew up with the idea that the guru is my God, he is the only person whom I can trust. My parents said, when you are really in deep trouble, nobody else can do anything. He is the only person who can. And now, when I look back on certain things in my life, I see that he was the only one who saved me.

'I could tell you the story of my son. My son was born when all the doctors told me I could never have a kid because I had some medical problem. I was really disappointed. Those days, my mother used to read the *Guru Charitra*, and I got the book from my sister. I didn't have anything in mind when I started reading. I just prayed to God that whatever happened was fine. For seven days I used to get up at four o'clock in the morning and read the book. That year I conceived. All the doctors were surprised how it had happened. Later on they said there was something wrong in the testing they did and I could have any number of kids I wanted, but I really didn't want any more kids.

'What I wanted was to work. We both decided that we just wanted one kid. He was three and a half years old when we moved into a new house. Just about then, he fell ill. It started with a high fever. I took him to the doctor, and treated him for an ear infection. The fever didn't come down. On the fourth day my son was getting very weak. I called my husband and told him I was taking him to the doctor, the temperature was not coming down. The doctor said, "Something is wrong here." We had to do a spinal tap, and he was admitted into hospital immediately. By the time my husband came, it was four o'clock in the afternoon. They started doing the testing. The spinal tap was supposed to be very delicate. They kept telling us, "Sign these papers," because if they missed and punctured the spine with the needle, the child might become invalid. They told us that they had to do this just to find out why he had so much fever. The fever was like 105°, 106°. They couldn't control it.

'They did the spinal tap and we both said, OK, God is there. They didn't come up with anything. They kept testing in the hospital—all sorts of blood tests, all kinds of nuclear medicine tests. And in America, if the test doesn't show what it has to be treated for, they don't treat you further. So all they did was to try and bring down the fever until they were sure what to give. To control his fever, every two hours they gave him Tylenol, and this affected his kidney and liver and he started holding water in his body. The baby looked puffy and nobody knew what was happening. And later on, after the fourth day, they couldn't even give him Tylenol or asprin to control the fever. They had to put the child in a cold thermal blanket just to bring the temperature down. I used to also put him in the cold water tub. That was horrible.

'By this time we both had been in the hospital for six days. We hadn't informed anyone where we were. My brother kept calling at home and couldn't get hold of us. He came to see what was happening and found out from the neighbour that we were in the hospital. Then he came to the hospital.

'Then they started giving my son blood and put him in intensive care. That's when we called my parents, told them what was happening, and asked them to go to Sai Baba and find out what to do. So my father went and asked him. He said, "Nothing is going to happen to him, he is going to be all right." Then he sent vibhuti (sacred ash) to us through some friend of his who was going to America and said that he would be all right.

'When he told us that, our son's temperature started dropping. The doctors didn't know how the temperature came down because he hadn't been treated for anything. After the temperature started dropping, one of the doctors said, "We'll just give him five types of antibiotics to see what happens." So they started with the antibiotics and asked us to sign a paper saying that these antibiotics were to be given in very high dosage and may affect the kid's growth, they might make him mentally retarded. Otherwise they were going to do exploratory surgery to find out what was happening. My husband wouldn't sign the paper and said, "You can give him the antibiotics, but I won't sign to release him for exploratory surgery." They wanted to open him up from top to bottom and see what was happening. We both said we would not sign. The doctors were about to take us to court. We didn't sign and by then our friend had come from India. He brought us vibhuti prasad. The temperature dropped like anything—they didn't know how—and in one day, it came down to normal. They took him out of intensive care and said, "You'll have to wait and see what's happening." But the temperature was normal for two days and we said that we were going home. We knew nothing was going to happen to him. All this happened during three weeks in May-June. We came to India in December that year. We visited Bangalore and saw Sai Baba. He spoke to us and said there was nothing wrong.

'He didn't say what had happened. He said, "There is nothing to worry, he just had fever, that's all, nothing is going to happen to him any more. He's all right now." He gave me a locket for him which he wears around his neck all the time. From that day on, we all felt like he was given a second birth, a second chance. For nearly six months the doctors kept calling us, saying they wanted to test him for certain things. We didn't allow them to do it. They had sent the blood-test results to California and to Atlanta. Both places said things like "fever from unknown origin". Nobody could figure it out and pinpoint what had happened. These are the things which make you believe in God. It is only God who can help. He is the only one who can give guidance.

'I got into a meditation group in Delhi, which really interested me most. I was introduced to it by a friend. I really like the group. I don't take it as a religion when I go there. It's a nice experience to be there. You're doing something constructive. I look forward to it, whenever I can do it. You have to do meditation to control your mind. You have to control your mind in everything.

'I never considered myself a professional, even though I worked for fifteen years as a programmer. Not that I had to work. I felt, when I stayed in the States, it was what everybody did, and what I should be doing, but I never felt really satisfied. I really like to be at home and take care of the home, of the needs of my kid and my husband. I feel really satisfied with the role of a mother, a possessive one at that. My son can do whatever he wants, but I feel until he is grown up and on his own, he should be taught certain things in life, even though he may not like it. We also tell him that he should read certain books and learn about the culture of India.

'We had been in the States for nearly fifteen years and my husband especially wanted to bring up our son in India, saying that he should know his background. In the States, if the mind is not strong, you fall apart very quickly because you've nothing to back you up. I feel that Americans don't believe in God, so they feel they must do everything. I think that is taking too much on oneself. You must have somebody else to bank upon, because if something goes wrong in your life, you shouldn't feel you're alone. Even if you feel depressed, you shouldn't have to feel that you must have a drink or something else to get out of it.

'My son also believes in God. Before he goes to sleep, he has a shower and then he goes to the puja room for two or three minutes and prays for whatever little things he wants. That's enough as a routine for him, and he can pick up whatever he wants later.

'I studied about sexuality when I was growing up. We were taught in school what to expect, being girls, and also, my mother told us certain things in her own way. So menstruation never came as a shock. I knew what to expect with my husband because I had home economics as a subject—child development, child birth, which really interested me. So it never came to me as a shock. My husband says that I was scared and it's true, I was really scared on the first day. I wanted to tell him that I didn't want to get pregnant until I came to the States, because I had to wait for three or four months for the visa. He himself brought it up, and there was no problem. I never thought of sex as something scary. I was just scared to talk to him because I didn't know how to begin. I enjoyed it and we talked about it, and now we have been married for nineteen years.

'When it's an arranged marriage, you don't know the other person, so you can't just talk to him, a stranger. I could talk to my brothers, my cousins, and everybody, but it was not the same thing. He's your husband, he is going to be your husband for the rest of your life, so you want to start on the right foot. He's a stranger anyway, to begin with. You just can't say whatever comes into your head. It took three-four years for me to establish a rapport with him.

'In any case, life goes on. You have your reservations and he has his reservations. Since we were both in a strange country we couldn't just go back to talk to our parents or anybody else. We were forced to talk to each other. My husband is a person who just can't keep anything to himself. I can keep everything to myself, not say anything to anyone, but he can't do that. He has to get it off his chest. If he doesn't like something, he has to say it.

'We both grew up in very different environments. I grew up in a very outspoken family even though I didn't talk much. I thought that was how the whole world was going to be. But in my mother-in-law's house they are very sensitive people and my husband was very sensitive when we got married. For instance, one day, early in our marriage, I made something and placed it on the table. He came home and said, "Can I take it?" I said, 'You should go and ask the astrologer if you can eat or not.' He really took it seriously and never touched it. And then I told him it was a joke. I always joked. The whole day he didn't touch it and kept quiet, and it took him a long while to get over that. He has come a long way. He has changed. He knows me now.

'If you ask him, he'll say I dominate him. It depends on the situation, on what the subject is going to be. We do ask each other before we do anything. We're not trying to hide from each other. Anything we do, we talk about it. It took him and my in-laws time to understand me, because I grew up with boys in the family. But to my in-laws it was like, don't talk to men. One day my husband's cousin came to the house and I opened the door. That I was sitting and talking to him shocked my father-in-law. "Why are you sitting and talking to him? It's none of your business, go inside. I'll sit and talk to him." That was a shock to me. What did I do wrong? I just sat there, and talked to the cousin till my husband came home. I didn't understand. I thought, they're trying to get back at me for something. When I really understood, I said, they're not used to certain things in the house. I just can't go into somebody's house and change everything around. If I can't change, how can they change? I'll lead my life and see how things go.

'When I went to America, my husband was the only one amongst his friends who was married. We often had eight bachelors for dinner. Friends would come and say, we're going to eat here today. For the first six months I said OK. One of them practically lived in our house. He would come on Friday and never went home till Sunday night.

'I was used to the family system. Instead of cooking for two, I always make food in large quantities. I can never cook only a little and say this is only for today and it has to be finished. There's always going to be leftovers which I give away. At least now, I give it away to people here. But there we had to eat it. I used to feel in the beginning that I was missing something by living in a nuclear family. But later on I felt this was nice, this was one way of getting to know your husband, and another way to learn how to manage yourself. If I had lived in a joint family all this time, my in-laws would have managed everything and I would never have learnt anything.

'I started taking responsibility for everything. Today if the milk doesn't come, I'm responsible. If the lights don't work in the house, I'm responsible. So I know how to handle things. But now I was ready to go back to a joint family because my son was growing up alone, he should know his cousins, he should know his family. We're not going to be with him for ever and ever, and he should have somebody else to turn to, even just to talk. I felt I should have had another kid, so that at least my son would have had somebody to talk to. I used to feel that a lot, but now I don't. Now I feel he knows how to handle things. He's very outgoing, knows how to adjust to people. Even though we couldn't make it every time, we used to send him home to India every year. Now he does know the family, and he was very close to my father, who died last year.

'He misses my father. He wouldn't tell us, but he was lonely. My husband talked to him and said, "This is what you're unhappy about." My father gave me everything he had and whatever my son wanted, he used to cater to him. He used to come all the way to my in-laws' house just to pick him up. He took him to restaurants, he took him shopping, and he was fully engaged with him.

'It's very hard to accept my father's death. Still, sometimes I see the scene when they took out the body. This happened eight months back. I don't sit and cry or anything, but sometimes the memory of it comes back. My whole life, I think, has changed. He was there for us all the time. He was very close to my husband also. My husband misses him a lot. In my in-laws' house he couldn't have a drink or anything, so they both used to tell us a lie to go out every afternoon and have a drink. My father used to come every day—it's almost eleven kilometres from our house—just to pick him up or pick up my son. My husband became very close to my father in those last four years. God knows what they talked about. My father was a person who couldn't ever open up and talk to anybody. But he could talk to my husband, and some of the things he used to tell my husband would even be concealed from me. I miss him a lot. This time I really missed him the most at the airport. Whatever time we took the flight out of Bangalore he used to show up, take us to the airport, and stay with us till the flight took off. When we went through the security check he used to be sitting there, and he would wait till the flight took off. That's when I missed him.

'When we got the news from the hospital from my brother that he had died, I had to go and tell my mother. That was very difficult. Sometimes I wonder where he is. We do believe in rebirth. I've accepted that he is no more, but he lives in my mind. I am thankful to God that he gave us the opportunity to be here so I can spend more time with him. I spent four years with him here, and I saw him more often than any of my brothers and sisters.

'I don't dream about him, but I always dream about the body—the scene where they're taking him out of the house. Otherwise I haven't dreamt about him. I had to get over this because we had to help my mother. It was not right for me or my sister to sit and cry. We wanted to make her feel that Dad's OK, that she's not going to be left out now. She knew, we knew, that life was going to change, but the first fifteen days were really difficult. Now my mother has adjusted. My life, I know, will never be the same.'

*

Under conditions of migration, change and stress, family support affects economic and personal relationships. The physical location and the socio-cultural context affect the life-style of these women. For the housewife in India, even living in a nuclear family, kinship ties are the most significant, whereas for the American, family, a product of continuous interaction, symbolizes a sense of commitment in an ever-changing world in which relations among individuals are constantly challenged, tested and transformed.

Being housewives is not the sole identity or activity for these women. The housewife syndrome—associated with physical and psychological exhaustion, thankless work, boredom and loneliness—does not seem to afflict them as the housewife helps her husband with his business and reaches out to the community through her social work while the American has been employed as a computer programmer.

The role of women as receivers, absorbers, assimilators and accomodaters in the family does not render them passive. Instead, the woman initiates the process of caring and communication. The nurturant task in the family is demanding and takes vast amounts of energy and enthusiasm. Thus, women symbolize an ever-flowing energy—passive and dynamic, peaceful, wrathful and destructive—depending on the family situations and their inner state of being. In each relationship, women acquire a new face—a mask intended to produce a certain effect. At a transcendental level, this helps to arrive at an understanding of the nature of illusion, paradox and transformation. Aesthetic qualities and dramatic dimension of masking in relationships—having religious and mythological origins—seems to represent a point of transition and bestows power to their mask.

The housewife's journey into knowing herself by taking responsibility for everything she does enables her to iron out her family problems and her spiritual quest, she feels, has been a humbling experience. For the American, establishing a deep conjugal communication—something you have to work for in an arranged marriage—helps her to face the changing circumstances and the intergenerational conflict in the family. Setting up a nuclear household developed her sense of individuality and responsibility, but still she depends on her family guru who saved her son's life, and who is a source of strength during times of crisis.

Women's intuitive understanding and skilful communication thus facilitate profound awareness, and initiate cooperation or conflict, but for what, and with whom, and at what price, will ultimately depend on their intention.

# Chapter 5

# *Cause and Activism: The Freedom Fighter and the Teacher*

Even if the readers have not been able to go through the women's stories with unremitting earnestness, hopefully, they have been able to develop an unbroken chain of argument for the validity of this exercise. The trained eye of the sociologist perceives the social constraints that deny the interviewees social space to either reveal or conceal. Women variously situated in the social and cultural structure tend to practice and promote the autobiographical narrative in distinct ways. For the participants, the conversational mode is a joint involvement that creates a world inhabited by many significant others. It is Goffman's unio mystica, a socialized trance. In studying the lives of the freedom fighter and the teacher, it becomes clear that social cause and struggle stimulated their spirit and structured their rebellion, social ferment and activism.

**The Freedom Fighter**

Her revolutionary spirit was still intact at the age of sixty, even though disenchantment had crept into her life. I had known her for twenty years and often admired her struggle to support and uplift her family. However, widowhood had suddenly brought meaninglessness into her life. She hails from a middle-class

Punjabi background and has three married children. Our meeting took place on a wintry day, in the cosy kitchen of her home, where she now lives alone. Slowly she unfolded her story:

'The first very important episode in my life was when I was sent away from my parents, almost 1,200 miles away. My father was strict. He had middle-class notions that children learn better when they are away from their parents. I was very emotionally attached to my mother and could not bear the separation. Before I was even sent to the hostel, I started having bad dreams. Sleepless nights, bed wetting, and all sorts of problems affected me. I was six years old then.

'Although my elder sister was with me and my aunt's two daughters were also in the hostel and were happy, I could not adjust. It had a very bad effect on me. For four and a half years, I could not see my parents at all. They were so far away. In summer holidays, in winter holidays, we had to go to our village to our uncle and aunt where I would hear them saying, "This is a burden on us" and things like that. I became very insecure; I was frightened of everything. When I came to Siliguri they finally came to see me.

'My father tried to persuade me to stay there for another three to four years but I cried and created such hell on the Ludhiana platform that my mother said to my father, "I will give education to my daughter at home. I do not want to kill my child in this process". That's how I was taken home by my mother. But my elder sister and the two other sisters remained in the hostel, had their education, and did whatever our parents wanted them to do.

'I started recovering once I was back with the family in Punjab. There was no sort of fear or suppression from my father. I started singing, laughing. Suddenly, when I was twelve years old, my father announced that he had engaged me to such and such a person. I was in shock. It really shook me that they had suddenly decided to engage me to somebody and throw me out. My father was in Calcutta and my mother was here in Moga. She wanted me to have higher education. She was pro-education whereas my father was not. Middle standard was enough for him. This was a peculiar era, and people from well-known families were going through a conflict of ideas. In 1944, my father suddenly decided that from Moga we should go elsewhere. This was to a new colony with new ideas, started by a progressive man. So we went there and throughout that first year, until right after my marriage, I had a problem of continuous fever. I also had malaria several times. I was the only one in the family who had this problem. Nobody else suffered like that. From 1935-45, all those years, there was no quinine available in the country. Consequently, I missed one-third of the school days. But then I could study ten hours, sixteen hours, eighteen hours a day, with concentration. When my father announced my engagement, I said that I will not let this happen to me. The boy came to see me. I was sixteen. I felt horrible. I wanted to put him off so that he would not have a good opinion about me. He went to his mother and said that she is very beautiful but she cannot cook.

'I studied a lot—poetry, books, novels, etc. My mother was very kind to me. I was given all the good things. There was always something to be done—mending, sewing, stitching. So that's how knitting and craft were taught to me. My sister took charge of the kitchen and domestic things.

'The plan of my father was that the whole family should come back to Calcutta. We were bundled up in the train and we went there. I passed my exams with very good results in spite of my illness.

'The discipline of my father was so crushing for me in the house that I told my mother I wanted to go to Punjab and stay in a hostel. She said: "What for? Learn some music here. I will arrange for you to learn music and the sitar, and anyway, you are going to marry at the age of sixteen." When the result of my matriculation came I was only fifteen years old. I started fasting then. I used to go to my friend's house nearby, and her family spoke to my mother. So she pressurized my father to let me go: "Let her do what she wants to do." Then my father decided to send me to Shanti Niketan. But I didn't think I would feel safe staying in Shanti Niketan, fearing the wedding party would come and take me away, so I insisted that I study only in Punjab.

I was sent to Lahore. But there was a great deal of political unrest there. I came to Ludhiana and my brother looked after me for some time. In this respect my brother was quite an enlightened person. He was the president and secretary of the Youth Federation of the Congress Party. I started working with him. We collected pamphlets to be distributed to the people. He used to tell people that I was at medical college and if I was caught red-handed in these activities, it might affect my career.

'I used to go out in the winter with two hundred pamphlets, telling the people about the British Raj and why we must fight. After some time, for some reason, my mother—either she was fed up with my father or she was worried about me and my brother being too far away from her—decided to come to Ludhiana so all the children could stay together. I had the opportunity to come and see her once in a week. Now I participated in a lot of mass meetings, holding the flag and shouting slogans, and attended conferences also. I was chosen on account of my good voice to lead a group of singers on the stage, for the all India Congress Conference. There were 30,000 to 40,000 people. Later I was beaten by my mother. She felt she had been trying to support and help us, but because of our activities she would get a scolding from our father.

'She was unable to cope with the situation and the thought that she didn't have control over the family. So, from then on friction started. But she still wanted me to carry on with my studies and I promised I would not marry until I had my degree. Finally, I had a love marriage. He was my teacher, and when I first met him, he thought I was sixteen years old, though I hadn't yet turned fourteen then. He came to know that we were from Ludhiana. He met my mother and started coming to our house, but still I didn't know anything. The thought that my parents wanted to marry me off was pressurising me inside. Once or twice I decided to end my life. One day I had gone out with my mother. I wanted to plunge into the river. At that time, on that particular day, I thought to myself, life is such a precious thing. It should not be destroyed. From then, gradually on my part, I started communicating with him, talking to him, getting help in math and English. I wanted my BA degree, but when I heard that my father was coming in 1947, I sought the blessing of a senior teacher and decided to get married secretly. Our parents did not know.

'I was sixteen years old when I got married on the seventh of July. We kept quiet about it. Our age difference is seventeen years. Because of the disturbed political situation, he didn't want me to come along and stay with him in the village. And then there were the 1947 riots. We were safer in the city. He was in the village. He had to hide himself since all the time he was saying, Hindus and Muslims are the same, don't do this. One day all the Muslims in his village were herded together early in the morning before breakfast. About six hundred or seven hundred were taken out of their houses to an open space in the village and they were butchered with the sword. Only one child and one or two adults were saved. When this happened, the very next day he left the village.

'My father happened to come in October. I had decided to stay with my husband. I wrote a letter to my mother, a beautiful letter, apologizing. I wrote not to look for me and not to report to the police as I was going to my house. She accepted it. She knew in her heart that my husband was a good man. However, when Father realized that the situation had gone that far, he was willing to throw a party and accept me in the family. This was a surprise.

'My husband lost his father at the age of four. He had stayed in the Congress Party, and paid frequent visits to the jail. Everyone spoke very highly about him. Luckily my mother-in-law gave me a lot of support. She brought up all my three children. She said, "I am not a literate person. If I sit down, I am not going to read a newspaper. This is job I can do. You do your job." After the breast feed she would take the child away. She would sleep with the children, sit next to them, bathe them—all the duties of a mother. And I took my full-time job. First I was an untrained teacher. I worked in a school in the village where there is no electricity, hand pump, no one to cook, etc. Then I taught in the middle school. Later on I became a lecturer in Ludhiana. While there, I saw an advertisement for teacher's training. I applied. Nobody spoke for me, I had no reference. I was given the job and that's how I went to London. I was praised and appreciated by the teacher and principal. Everyone said, "She is very good". My sisters, elder sister as well as younger, became very jealous and that jealousy lasted a long time. It's still there.

'This jealousy came up because of the fact that I managed to get my way. I married the man I wanted to marry. I didn't listen to anybody. There was another factor: My elder sister had an affair with someone, but she had to marry someone else. My younger sister was engaged to somebody, but she was married off to someone else. I was the only one who did whatever I wanted and was successful. That made them jealous. So we never really came closer. My younger sister was influenced by my elder sister, who poisoned her against me. She fabricated stories, partly true, and told my children that I had sexual relations before marriage and I was already pregnant before the wedding in the village.

'They didn't know that I had the blessings of my teacher. There was no question of any relationship before marriage. He was very strict, very idealistic, and he knew the danger. But my sister stayed in my house and told these stories. I left the house at the age of sixteen when she was six years old. How could she tell these stories to my children? That means she heard them from my elder sister.

'Regarding my sexual life, I would say that on the whole my husband was a very considerate man. But he was very demanding, with a very strong sexuality. I was more concerned about pursuing my career but he never forced himself on me. That is the beauty of it. By God's grace, there was no tension in the family. It is strange but I had heard those old stories: don't let anybody kiss you, or touch you, or else you will get pregnant. I was so scared of the slightest touch. I realized only after my marriage that there was no harm in it. Although I loved him very much, I didn't let him come near me. I was very strict.

'Before marriage, menstruation was difficult. I had heavy periods and often used to faint. I was taken to a specialist, who said I was going to have this problem solved after my first child was born. My first child came when I was sixteen years and ten months old. We were very happy. The girl was a healthy child. But I think my husband's demands on me were greater than my demands on him. I wanted us to go out together, to kiss and to cuddle. My relationship with him was more on the poetic level. I would like, instead of going to bed, to go up and see the moon, the stars, and moonlight—observing and feeling nature. I would dash out of the house and go for a walk. Now he has gone and I miss him very much. Sometimes I feel, maybe I was cruel to him by denying him.

'Our marriage was based on true love. It was beautiful. I was young and beautiful, and though he was not that handsome, he was good-looking in his time. But I never had this feeling of him and him alone, above all else. I am a mixture of many things. I don't know where it comes from. I related with other men as well. But that part of me remains unfulfilled. If I was keen to go out with someone, I could not go, and I was frustrated. I threw a tantrum and complained. Why can't we go and sit somewhere where there were other men, where we can have some intellectual talk of political problems? My husband tried to help me in this matter. But people thought maybe I had relations with those men. They misunderstood me. Now I wish I had. Damn this society, since they had already accused me.

'My husband made a mess of his life. He couldn't concentrate on one issue. He was always branching off into many issues at the same time. He had a nervous breakdown three times. But all this was overcome by our deep love for each other.

'Motherhood was mixed up with my own romantic life. When I wanted to do something, I would just leave the children and go. Maybe I could leave them because I knew my mother-in-law was there and could look after them better than me. And I never left them for the night. If I wanted to go anywhere, it was just for the day. I would spend time on their education. There was a time when the younger one didn't want to have further education. It was because of my persuasion that she carried on, and it was the same with my son. He didn't want to study. Then, eventually, he decided to get a degree. If they hadn't been in my house they would have never got this education. There were so many distractions—restaurants, cinema, theatre. Now my son says that education was a waste of time and money.

'All my children have had love marriages. There have been lots of problems because of inter-caste, inter-religion, and inter-national marriages. I always put the point of humanity above everything. I am also a religious person. I think of Krishna, I think of man and mankind. Many times I think about the possibility of an afterlife. Many times, I think of my soul. In very, very dark moments of my life, such thoughts have helped me come out of that darkness. After my mother-in-law died I was deeply grieved. She used to come in my dreams. My mother never did. But my mother-in-law used to appear in my dreams and console me. I have a feeling that she was always there. Now I don't see her, and I feel that perhaps something has been transformed.

'It's funny, but I dreamt about my husband only twice, although every night I called him to meet me in my dreams. One night I dreamt that I was in a lift going up. As the lift door opened I saw him standing there. Vague but not clear. Then I said to him in my dream, "How come you are here?" He said, "Look there," and there was a beautiful place and I woke up. And second was when I had overslept and it was time to go to school. I first heard a voice saying, "Get up, you are late for school." Just two occasions, and I've never seen him after that. That means wherever he is, he is happy.

'After his death, I was completely shattered. You know, Indian men are horrible. They think women are there to serve them, whereas my husband served me. He was very kind to me. He had his own ways. You could not stop him from drinking. He would not take my advice. I pleaded and begged. But I know it was his need. He would have been dead long ago if he had not kept on drinking. So I started drinking with him. Years went by. I used to sit with him in the night till ten o'clock, two o'clock. I used to sit up and wait for him so that we could eat together. He brought the best German, French and Italian drinks for me. I used to have a little bit. If I continued work quite late till, say, eleven o'clock and I got tired, then I would have a drink. The drinking is another issue which has been taken up by all three children. And I keep telling them my life is my husband's life, whether society approves of it or not.

'In other words, I think they could not tolerate a strong relationship between me and their father. Our daughter started saying, "They don't care about me. They will just drink and sleep together!" They thought we didn't care. On the contrary, we cared very much. My children are not as straight as I have been in my life. I had very clear views from my childhood. My husband was a different person. He felt that woman should be treated the same as man because he had seen this in village life. My daughters were treated at par. So they feel they are like sons, but they think that under pressure I will give everything to the son, which is not true. Consequently, my older daughter does not come to my house now. She doesn't ring up as much as she used to, and brother and sister are not on talking terms.

'Now I live on my own. If my mother was in the same position, I would have done a thousand things for her. Since my husband's death, my health has been deteriorating gradually. I have lost all my children. Because they are being impressed by these people from other communities. All my children are suffering. Maybe I am wrong in thinking that if we had chosen at least one of my children's spouses from the strictly Punjabi community, at least one of them would have been more considerate. But none of them is considerate. Well, they have their own lives. There is no time slot for me.

'You get a lot of consolation singing. When I am very sad and on my own, I just start singing. Good poetry brings me near to God. My husband's death has changed me a great deal. I have longer periods of depression—feeling that life is not worth living, that it's meaningless. Why am I living? What should I do? All these questions keep coming up over and over again. You are not born according to your sweet will, and you don't die when you feel like dying. Maybe I will do something, but what, I don't know. I am very confused. There used to be an aim in my life. For instance, I thought that we would make an ashram for these freedom fighters so that we have a chance to come together, stay there, and have lots of discussions. And we will not charge anybody. That was my dream but all that is gone after his death. Now I don't go out with men. I just go where there is a gathering. I don't go with anybody to sing or for sightseeing.

'Nobody comes to my house now. I don't even invite anybody. I am very unhappy about my son, for he is always the first one to cast aspersions on me. Maybe if the children had been more of the Eastern type, more caring, then I would have come out of this depression quicker. I am more depressed because of the behaviour of the children, which came about right after his death. If they had shown this side of their character, this feeling about me, while he was alive, I would never have cared much. But after his death I needed consolation, support, emotional closeness. Instead of that I got these horrible, nasty accusations—that I never cared, or I neglected them; that I had love affairs with many men. It has hurt me very much. I think the basic undercurrent was that they wanted the property!

'My knowledge ultimately saved me. This feeling that I know much more than other ladies, than common people, gives me more strength. I know my daughter-in-law knows law and has degrees. For me degrees mean nothing unless you try to understand or at least try to question your existence. What is your position in the universe? Are we insignificant or not? We are insignificant if we can tell people how many stars there are, but we are significant if we can change the course of history. In the national movement I felt that we were changing the course of history. If I am helping some helpless people then I am significant. If I take care of a child whose mother has left him suddenly before Christmas, and whose father cannot take care of him, then I feel I am significant. Maybe I got it from my husband. It is very fulfilling and gives me more strength to go on doing whatever I can do.

'Somehow, I was not happy with life. There is a basic unhappiness within me. Even when I was very happy there was a touch of sadness in me, and that sadness always pushed me to know more, to learn more, to do something more.

'I never expected that I would have to struggle so much in

my life. Somehow, I wanted to create a life of deep understanding around me without any conflict. This is just a dream. So many things you want, but you can't have . . .

'I never had a guru. I do not believe in them in the way other people do. If I know people who have more knowledge than me, I should sit in their presence and learn something from them, but not blindly follow them and say, this is my guru. I feel that a setting sun can sometimes give you something, and that can be your guru. One day I went out and saw a glowing sunset. There was this wide canal, and at the banks of the canal there were wandering cows and a shepherd playing the flute and I felt a joy I cannot describe, something ethereal, powerful. I don't know if you can call that God. I felt that this thin shepherd playing the flute had helped me get to that stage of ecstasy. Without him there, it would not have been. I did not have a religious guru to go to and worship because I had this history of being sick and in bed for long hours. All I could do was read. As I mentioned, at the age of thirteen I had read all the novels of Munshi Premchand, and the English translations of Tagore. I underlined in red those words I did not understand—my English was very poor at that age—and looked them up in the dictionary. Poets were my gurus.

*Khud ko kar buland itna*
*ki har takdir se pehle*
*khuda bande se yeh puche*
*ki bata teri razza kya hai.*
(Make yourself so great
that before determining your destiny
God must ask you,
tell me, what is your desire?)'

**The Teacher**

I had heard about her teaching skills and popularity from her former students. A few years ago, she retired from a reputed public school in Delhi. She writes books for children and takes part in community welfare activities. After receiving her consent, and doing the initial spade work, I went to her residence, located east of the Yamuna.

She lives with her doctor husband in a newly constructed house. Both her children (a son and a daughter) are married and have their respective households. Her husband has a private practice and operates from home. She belongs to an educated, middle-class Sikh family with a progressive outlook. While we were sipping tea, her husband made sure that we were comfortable and then instructed the house workers not to barge into the bedroom where we were sitting. Initially, she was self-conscious and hesitant to articulate her experiences. Gradually, she overcame her shyness and related:

'I was born in a small village and was later taken to a hill station, now in Pakistan. Ours is a big family, lots of brothers and sisters, and cousins. We are seven sisters and six brothers. My mother gave birth to about fourteen children and I am the thirteenth—and eleventh daughter—in the family. We had three brothers. The one younger to me died. The whole environment was rich and alive with people and their feelings.

'As far as I can remember, during my childhood I was so much within myself that I didn't really care much for anybody. There were rivalries with my sister who was just a little older than me, but it didn't bother me to a great extent. I was not deprived of anything because my father gave me a lot of strength and a lot of love. My father was an engineer. When I was born he got a promotion. So, maybe there was this private, special vibration from him when I was born that gave me strength. When I was born he told my mother not to allow anyone to come and condole with her on my birth, because I was a very special child. Later I came to know that it must have been some kind of projection, a positive feeling he had for me.

'Then, we were transferred to Rawalpindi, where we had a big house with lots of plants and flowers. Because we lived in a big house, there was more of nature around us, and people too. It looked to me as if everybody was minding his own business in the family and not interfering in anybody else's affairs.

'Nobody even told me when my menstruation began, how

to manage it. I just learnt about it through the natural process of my feelings. I didn't go to anyone, not even my mother, or my sister. I didn't even discuss it with my friends. I just managed it on my own. If one process did not work, I tried the other. I tried using a band-aid or sometimes I tied my own clothes and threw them away. Sometimes I kept newspapers on my bed so that I didn't spoil my bed sheet, and then threw those papers away. My mother must have discovered it, but she didn't tell me anything about it. I became quite introverted. I started keeping things to myself and never thought of sharing them with others. I think it was some sort of complex. Later on, I used whatever material was available. It was just through observation I discovered the periodicity of menstruation. I used to have a lot of pain during my periods, and my mother used to give me some medicine.

'My education was never a strain. I was never goaded. Later, our parents wanted to leave us with our brother. He had been transferred to Gurgaon, where the medium of instruction at school was English. One of my sisters, and I, were left with our elder brother for some time. I didn't resent it much. In the holidays when we came to stay with our parents, we told them we didn't want to go back. We said we would rather learn Hindi and stay with them. Going back to our brother, who was rather angry and cruel, was a bit disheartening. We were very afraid of him as he was very authoritative.

'At the same time, my bhabi (sister-in-law) was very nice and gentle. So there was this balance in the emotional attachment. When we were in Gurgaon, we got interested in dramatics and that was an enlightening development for both of us. We used to have a Ramlila in one corner of our house. We both used to play Rama and Sita. That was how we grew up, learning about honesty, about obeying parents and the ethics of life.

'Then, we also had servants. We used to get quite friendly while watching them work. All their children were also around. We would be sitting under a tree, or climbing trees, enjoying ourselves, and teasing our servants. It was great fun, and our father used to take a lot of interest in outdoor activities. He used to take us cycling for long distances. In the morning we used to go for walks and then go into the garden.

'My mother influenced me the most. I have inherited from her the love of children, and kindness. Whenever we went to the village there were a lot of people who used to come and work for us. I never found her getting angry with anybody—always well-wishing, always giving them something in terms of money and affection. She treated everyone equally, with no discrimination at all. That was the kind of environment in which we were brought up.

'The only toys I remember, which I really played with, were dolls. We made dolls, fixed them, and got them married. The dolls would have kids. My bhabi had one delivery at home and I had peeped in and seen how a child was born. I have a very hazy image as I was just ten years old. It wasn't a shock. It was fun watching.

'I didn't go to one regular school. For two years, I studied in Delhi. There, we were fascinated by one particular teacher. She was smart. We wanted to go to her house, meet her, talk to her. So we hired a tonga and went to her house. She belonged to a very high-class family. She had all her photographs pasted in an album, right from her childhood. It was a very nice experience, very romantic. Thinking about your past with pictures was a great thing. I thought that when I had children I would do the same, which I did manage.

'After that, for my education I went to Shanti Niketan. In between there was a sort of unpleasant experience with my brother-in-law because we were always discouraged by him. "You are not fit for studies," he would say. He discouraged us from ever reaching our goals. My father was very keen that I should go in for medicine, but I had a second class in the tenth, a second class in the twelfth, and those labels debar you from going this side or that side. So I went to Shanti Niketan—a place where one goes for arts and humanities. Somehow or the other, I got the science classes and picked physics, chemistry and biology. I was quite happy with those subjects. I was the only girl in a large group of boys and we were all made to sit together. I remember I could not follow the chemistry teacher at all, how he magically changed one odour to the other, doing experiments. I was shy to go and ask him, and I was also shy of talking to the boys.

'When I came back home during that time, the Second World War was on. The Japanese had come up to Singapore. Our parents wanted us to go back all the same. I met people of so many states, the environment was so romantic. The Bengalis were around. I even met Tagore. But then he died that very year. He left a deep impact on me. He would organize programmes of music and dance. I couldn't sing, but that is how I got interested in music later on. Sometimes the seed is sown at some place and later it begins to sprout.

'I became close to a woman who was older than me. She was a source of support because she knew my sisters, and she knew that I was a little overpowered by them. I had a very loving, very affectionate kind of feeling for her. We were friends for a long time. Then she got married. I kept up correspondence with her, but now that is almost over. Her daughter was also very affectionate. There was another friend of mine who was very tall, trim, and dark-complexioned. As they say, opposites attract each other, and we became friends.

'After Shanti Niketan we came to Lahore. Then I shifted completely to humanities. I took geography. It became my pet subject. I used to go to school which was four and half miles from our village. My father had hired a tonga for me to go to school. He wanted me, even at that time, to stay in the hostel. But hostel food didn't suit me, I used to get sick. So he thought it was better for me to stay at home. I was wondering how he could trust that tongawala to take and bring us back. At times, I used to be alone and then we started sharing with others. But on the whole there was a lot of trust, which is very much lacking today. Even with that kind of trust, at times we did have a bad conductor and unpleasant experiences, but we found that these people were brought up with many restrictions on sex. An uncle or a servant taking a child to his room and trying to satisfy himself in his own way was not surprising.

'Then, it happened with my uncle, a very loving uncle. We used to go and stay with him. He used to take care of us. He had a habit of playing with our bodies. His friends sometimes would come to play with us and we would be told to go and have a bath. He would just try to hug our naked bodies. Within yourself there are spontaneous vibes which arouse and protect you from really going completely with it unless and until someone forces you. The child has that sense of a forbidden thing. A child knows when to withdraw.

'There was a great amount of homosexuality between friends. Sleeping together and playing together teaches you. At times, boys are even shy of you in certain things. You take the initiative, and they will protect themselves. I had this experience. When I was six, two of us friends were discovering sex, about the difference between a boy and a girl. That is, you know, the age when you are more attracted to your own sex. It is afterwards, at the age of twelve or thirteen, that you are attracted to the other sex.

'My eldest brother-in-law was really a dangerous man in our lives. Our sister, the third older sister to me, had been a victim of his sexual appetite. By the time he came to us, we were quite aware of it. He would try to brush past against us and somehow make his male organ touch our body. My sister knew about it and others came to know of it to. Even my father. As a result, we took precautions, so he stopped coming to stay with us.

'My parents were quite liberal. My father became liberal after coming in contact with Punjabi books and literature. My mother also learnt to read, though she was uneducated. We two sisters educated our mother and taught her how to read Gurmukhi. Later on, she developed so much interest in reading novels, that we would find her sitting in a corner and enjoying a book. Then we taught her to knit.

'My parents were religious people initially, but they were never fanatic. My father joined the movement of 'Akalis' before independence. He was a sympathizer, not an active member in this movement of wearing swadeshi and not wearing videshi.

'My grandfather was also a teacher. Maybe I inherited that interest from him. I also developed interest in music, and playing the sitar, and the music sessions we had were quite interesting. Our music teacher was very romantic, andwith him, music was an intense experience—his style of teaching was so moving. I took a BA in sitar and also played twice in public. Unfortunately I didn't have what they call a musical ear. After Partition we had to leave Lahore and come to Ludhiana, where I had another teacher.

'When I got married, it was very important for me to get a job because my husband was a whole-timer. After marriage I did my MA. Then I had my son. I went to my sister's and delivered my baby there. This was a very big support. My delivery was by forceps under general anaesthesia. When my son was six months old I did my B.Ed. and came back to Delhi. I was offered a job in Karnal. I took up this job and left it as soon as I got a teaching job in Delhi.

'Teaching has been a fulfilling experience. When I joined the school I didn't know that I would be liked by so many people, because in my childhood no one had admired me. I always felt suppressed by my elder sister. She was more agile, better looking, more mature.

'Once my brother had a choice to take one of us to Kashmir for a holiday. Of course my elder sister was picked, and I was left behind with my parents. That was the time my father suffered a terrible pain in the eye. Every two hours he needed medicine and I had to be with him. If I had gone to Kashmir, I would have missed being with my father. God has often created situations in my life more for my benefit. Maybe my sister enjoyed herself a great deal in Kashmir but I didn't feel bad. Rather, I felt closer to my parents at that time because the three of us were in the house together.

'I did have a lot of admirers in school and even my dresses were admired—the matching clothes I wore. I became very fashion conscious, and started wearing *chinon, chittons*, etc. In 1953 our chemistry teacher took a photograph of me and my friend. I still have it. In that photograph I looked like Geeta Bali, the actress. That gave me quite a bit of self-confidence.

'I had done my B.Ed in Hindi and my English was very poor in the beginning. I didn't know the grammar very well. I didn't know what to do with the verb. So I improved my grasp of English, especially as the medium of instruction here was

English. In fact, language has to be taught to children right from the beginning. One's total intelligence and intellectual comprehension depends upon language.

'I had a good relationship with my students. I very rarely got angry. The first lesson I learnt in the first year of my joining the school was never to take the student to the principal for a complaint, because I did it once and I found I had made a fool of myself. I wanted to be helpful to students in their learning process.

'All by myself I organized a project for my children on the Himalayas, and had a huge exhibition in a big school hall. I was interested in advancing my education and used to attend seminars and workshops. From America, a social studies teacher had come and organized a workshop in the Central Institute of Education. I enjoyed it and learned a lot. I also used to celebrate UN day with the help of students. I was in charge of the exhibitions in the school, the youth hostel group, taking the students during holidays to various places like Kathmandu, Kulu Manali, and even Europe.

'Children at different stages behave in their own peculiar ways and they really can make you angry. To get angry at them all the time is not the right thing. Usually the students cheat. We found that the education system is such that cheating is a logical consequence of it. Once a little child asked, "Why can't I open the book to see the answer? Normally, when you do not know, you can find the answer at the back of the book." I found a lot of logic in the answer. It's not only children who misbehave, it's we who misbehave because we don't understand them. Mischievous misconduct and anger arise only when you don't understand them.

'We have to find that meaning for them, because we have been on this planet before the children. We are projecting our fears on to our next generation more than the positive things, or the happiness that is around. That is why there is so much confusion and violence. Also, it's the older generation who has to see that your child has a higher status than yours. This awareness came to me at a much later stage. You can call it a new dimension. I feel that education should be for creating oneness in humanity. That is the real education.

'I didn't follow this system of raising my children, because I didn't know all this then. At times I feel bad, because in the case of your second child you are more relaxed. With your first child you are more tense, and all your ethical principles are forced on the first child. So, I wanted my son to be as obedient as Lord Ramachandra. I would be as good a mother as Gokki's mother was. I looked on him as my product, as my extension. I remember I took my son's wedding as my project. I felt I had to do it the way I wanted. I didn't even ask anybody what his aspirations were, what he wanted. Of course, he chose the girl for himself, that much liberty I gave him. With a totally good heart I accepted it. But when the time came I didn't take any suggestion from him or try to know his desires. I refused to take money he offered me to spend on his wedding. That was the greatest mistake of my life. And he is quite angry because his desires were not fulfilled.

'I was quite a dominating mother. When he was a child I used to think that I had to pick up his shoes, get him ready, teach him, and all kinds of things. In a way he resented it. He started saying, "I am so grown up, why do you still do all this for me?" He showed a kind of helplessness and resentment as a child. Later on I became aware of this and read a book to him, *I'm OK, You're OK.* I changed my attitude towards him and my approach. I am very progressive.

'My approach towards my daughter was more liberal because the situations were different and every child has its own impact on the environment. In her case the environmental conditions were also different. She caught a slightly better side of me than my son could get. Even the father's relationship with the daughter is more relaxed than with the son. He was quite harsh and would often get angry. Another thing which my son must have felt was that I used to read bedtime stories to my daughter, sitting near her bed, but he used to be lying in his bed all alone. I didn't realize. He must have felt abandoned. That is why he is away in America. That is why, probably, he is an angry person. Also, he is not having a very good relationship with his wife.

'My husband has been cooperative. There have been no difficulties in getting support for my work, my going out, or my participating in various seminars. I didn't even ask him for permission to go; he used to tell me to go. The only thing we quarrelled about was our approach towards our children and their activities. The rest of the things were sort of OK. But, unlike him, I was not very exuberant about having sex. There were times when he would not talk to me for three to four days. That's the time I felt that if something had to happen, it should happen quickly, so that we could end the tension. When he would prolong it, I used to become so angry that instead of saying anything to him, I would just become a little violent and break plates which I had in my hand or bang the frying pan. However, he would just sit like a stone as if nothing was bothering him. He used to be so very indifferent. Then it used to get resolved gradually because you know the family bond is surely there. Another factor which bonded us together was our common interest in watching movies, drama, going out together for sightseeing, taking children with us, etc.

'I did have problems with my in-laws. They were very loving but they didn't have any way of showing love. When I got married I had a feeling that I was not welcome there. There was a lot of distance, and resentment. Initially I had to struggle against that resentment. His father was very supportive, but he was quite an indifferent man. Then, all of a sudden—I don't know what happened to me—I got my son's hair shorn off. I didn't even ask my husband. I was cruel to my son in getting his hair cut without even talking to the boy. I should have talked to him and prepared him for that. My husband was in the army, and during the holidays, when I took my son there, my husband was totally shocked. He didn't say anything immediately, but later he said, "Until and unless you let the hair of your child grow you are not permitted to come home."

'You know, for five years we did not go to my in-laws' house. In between I had a daughter also. But I have no negative feelings towards them. And an awareness came to my mind that my son should not be barred from having his grandparents' love. One day this thought came to me and I stopped cutting his hair. We went to his father's home for some gathering. The best and the most mature part of the meeting was that not a single mention was made about what had happened in the past. And we made a new beginning. There was a transformation within me, which made me feel that in women the strength lies within themselves. Maturity comes with experience, with education, and with awareness.

'You know, retirement didn't mean anything to me, except that the salary stoped coming every month. So I felt liberated from being an earning member of the family. I joined various groups, I started writing some poems in Hindi.

'In terms of spirituality, I have never been ritualistically religious or a believer in rituals. Initially, in our family, every evening we used to say our prayers before meals. My mother, grandmother, and later my mother-in-law, used to wake us up at four in the morning and take us to the temple. In gurudwaras we got interested in hymns and understood their religious significance. My parents encouraged us in this feeling. Since retirement, religious practice is not coming back to me in that form, but I feel that all truth has a spiritual base. Respect for human beings and respect for children, especially for children, has become my spiritual dimension. Education, working for the oneness of humanity, is the base of spirituality. And you cannot get it by preaching, you get it by practice. You have to practice it with your own children right from the beginning.

'I relate to my grandchildren in a better way now. I find my grandchild doing such things as sitting on his toy, tossing it up and down. I don't stop him because what matters to me is his enjoyment, and not that the toy is getting spoilt, dirty, or squeezed. Enjoyment is the top priority in the early part of childhood. If the child is full of happiness he will be a satisfied adult. However, when I watch my daughter, I can see that she is more frustrated because her situation is totally different now. She has been brought up in a single family unit. Now, after marriage, she is in a joint family. Although she is coping, she comes and complains to me. I listen to her. We also have to prepare our children to face failure, and not just success.

'I have not thought of death or dying. I do want to achieve more than what I am achieving now. But what I feel is that every day brings more satisfaction in some way or the other.'

*

Structural cleavages that divide society into potentially organized groups with opposing interests played its part in creating an idealistic frame of mind for these women. Poets and political leaders inspired the freedom fighter and the teacher to be proactive and not merely reactive during catastrophic times. Designated periods of historical time signify the conditions of their action and point to their political goals, means, norms, and efforts. Filiation with the freedom and class struggle produced an impulse to study society in a scientific way. Orthodox Marxism has been spurned, yet a humanistic variety of Marxist philosophy still influences their life. Instead of clinging to the myth of revolution, their struggle today is to resist power which prevails everywhere and cannot be transcended. So, their struggle is endless. Although depression and regret set in sometimes, utopian longing has eventually changed into a reformist approach.

'This is also reflected in their personal life. For instance, the freedom fighter fasted to resist her parents' authority, and to have her own way, and even had a secret marriage. Whereas, the teacher, in order to defy her in-laws, sheared her son's hair—a sacrilegious act for the Sikhs. Both of them seem to have a difficult relationship with their children, particularly their angry and possessive sons. Her children's indifference wounds the freedom fighter but ultimately her knowledge and love for nature saves her.

'Besides inheriting her interest in teaching from her grandfather, the teacher's meeting with Tagore influenced her life project. Growth is a never ending process and she has started writing poetry in old age while the freedom fighter finds singing very therapeutic, especially after her husband's death. Apparently, retirement has not affected these women adversely as they have satisfactory health and economic security. Both of them are vigourous and competent members of society. While still remaining active in certain fields and disengaged in others, they are successful agers and demonstrate that age is a poor predictor of a person's physical, social or intellectual competence. Also, the pervasive feeling of spiritual weariness cannot be detected in their accounts. Thus, a life of spirit, devoted to the cause of social transformation, makes women take up activism. In an effort to eradicate or minimize social suffering, they voluntarily embrace personal suffering—a condition revelatory of knowledge, wisdom and compassion.

# Chapter 6

# *Self-Reflections*

My subjects' experiences and understanding provide phenomenologically grounded insight into urban women's spirituality, sociality and sexuality. Such insight is also self-reflective, conscious of its historical embeddedness, interests, and method. For this study to be relevant to social realities, it has to lend itself to a humanizing practice and must remain at the level of probabilities. In this chapter, I undertake a personal pilgrimage—a journey into the sacred inner places. One's family is a site—a temple or a shrine—and family relationships are its objects of refuge. Thus, the researcher and reader are required to have personal empathy in order to enter the subject's consciousness and arrive at some sort of sociological truth.

**Family Relationships**

During 1994, the year of the family, the United Nations stressed the need to preserve this most basic human institution. In India, there was a major thrust on the regulation of the family through fertility planning. Ethical responses to reproductive technologies were called for. Such technologies have brought about changes in kinship patterns (such as different social and biological parents); non-sexual reproduction; extension of the lifespan of women and reproduction at a later stage;

amniocentesis, leading to enormous investment in male children, and genetic counselling. The role of the family has contracted in modern societies in the face of state welfare programmes. However, with increasing privatization, there has been a retreat of welfare activities, as a result of which the family has been over-burdened with issues of health and education.

Academicians have given much attention to the structure, function, composition, and the future of the family[1], but interpersonal relationships from a woman's perspective, by and large, have not been studied in depth. In individuals, and the family, it is through the successive stages of dependence, independence and interdependence that the highest potential of the human process is achieved. Each stage has intrinsic worth and yet is swallowed into the creative tension and harmony of interdependence.

As shown in an earlier study,[2] the family keeps women in a double-bind—it oppresses them but also provides them support and protection. The family context is a reference point through which women must work out the means and mode of their survival and personal progress. They profess a family ideology even though there is clearly a gap between the promise and the reality of their family lives. Nevertheless, women who have questioned this institution are still conceiving alternative family forms, while, at the same time, they are applying legal, medical, and therapeutic means in an effort to restore the family.

Although the family is a ground for nurturing intimate relationships, many of the tensions and conflicts associated with family life derive from outside social phenomena, such as unemployment, divorce, dowry, the woman's employment, sexual violence, etc. So, in a period of rapid change, it is impossible to ignore the strains and stresses in family relationships and some of the most corrosive influences on the family are the changing values and priorities, consumerism, the gender hierarchy, occupational constraints, and ineffective laws[3].

Not that sheer boredom or a blissful and prosperous family life cannot motivate women to have spiritual goals, but it is often the suffering and turbulence in family relationships, especially the illness or death of a loved one, that trigger discord and dissatisfaction in women and form the cooperative conditions for their spiritual quest. At the same time, it can probably be said that women tend to follow the graduated path of family relationships as a necessary and natural condition for their spiritual development. In no way am I attempting to undermine the socialization process that makes women opt for a religions alternative to family life. Yet, it seems that mixed cultural messages can, and often do, lead to a conflict between the cult of filial piety and women being or becoming the vehicles of spirituality or sexuality.

Generally speaking, social and psychological ambivalences in family relationships produce loneliness. On the one hand, my subjects clearly express and experience the hostility in family relationships: the complicated course of their emotional development; jealousy; causes of parental hatred; sibling rivalry, repression, and sexual inhibition. On the other hand, they talk about love and admiration; gratitude; attachment to parents; having parent substitutes; self-determination and autonomy.

Conflicting interests of parents and children; exaggerated love concealing hate in relationships; vicarious fulfillment through children's pleasures and successes; love or hatred of the parent of the child's own sex; parent-child hostility in old age; envy of children's superiority; presence or absence of strong or weak parents; a prolonged parental jurisdiction; and inevitability of estrangement indicate that until women transcend their fixed repertoire of responses, they simply hurt others and transmit their tensions outwards. Women can hence give an adequate expression to the life-flow by aspiring for self transformation in order to break down the fixed conceptual and emotional reality and work on a more wholesome and positive self-image.

Apparently, for urban women, development of their spirituality is analogous to self-realization, and the happiness of others. The family becomes the site of their spiritual struggle, and family relationships its central concern. In particular, development and acceptance of one's feminine potential through encounters with the mother/mother-in-law, sister/sister-in-law, daughter/daughter-in-law or the 'other' woman poses a real challenge to one's sense of self.

The discourse on the much-valued mother-son relationship has been continuing for generations in India. Only recently have feminists highlighted the discrimination against the girl child in various fields and generated a debate about their growing-up experiences. My research, however, shows that raising sons and daughters is richer and far more complex than has been previously described. The son obviously receives more demonstrative attention from the mother, but the connections and contradictions with the daughter are closer and deeper, and have to be worked out and resolved. Scholars have suggested that the mother-daughter relationship intensifies in a nuclear family[4] as age at marriage increases in urban areas owing to the daughter's educational and professional pursuits.

All women are daughters, but they do not necessarily become mothers. The issue of motherhood must be confronted because the potentiality of motherhood—if not at a physical then at the mental or spiritual level—is always present. Moreover, biological motherhood does not necessarily entail emotional motherhood. Today the contemporary art scene in India is replete with images of the mother-daughter bond, and women writers, for instance Krishna Sobti[5] and Mrinal Pandey[6], have been dealing with this theme.

Change is taking place rapidly in the urban areas, and mothers and daughters of all ages are living through a time of transition. Historically speaking, women have been portrayed as daughters, wives, and mothers of men. Constructing the relationship between mothers and daughters, and describing the patterns of development, could have beneficial resonances for many women. Today in the West, women also feel that the mother-daughter revolution unlocks the door to the possibility of a very different world and that this powerful germ of a new revolution could transform the lives of men and women for the better.[7] To enter into this inquiry I have reflected upon my own experience with my mother who passed away a few years ago.

It was in August—the month when India gained independence—that my mother delivered me on the top floor of a yellow mansion overlooking Qutab Minar. I often heard my aunts and my mother talk about my birth and childhood. 'You did not even take half an hour to be born. I was dressing up your sister for school and right then you announced your coming. Before your father could even bring the mid-wife, you had already arrived. You came out with great speed and ease and it was not painful at all.

'All along, while I was carrying you, I felt very ecstatic. I was working for the Peace Movement after the Second World War and travelling to different places for a signature campaign.'

It seems I met thousands of people while I was still in the womb. After my birth, my mother was awarded the World Peace Prize (for collecting one lakh and twenty-seven thousand signatures in one year) and in 1953 she went to Europe to receive it. Some eminent Indian ideologues travelled with her. Later they would tease me about my mother leaving me with my grandmother and paternal aunt when I was just three months old. These two surrogate mothers of mine were widows, and very religious. My mother returned when I was six months old. In those three months of her absence, it seems I got addicted to drinking a lot of milk and accustomed to multiple mothers. Mother was utterly dissatisfied with the way I had been looked after. She resumed charge of me and literally liberated me physically by giving me a good massage and changing my attire so that I could breathe comfortably. From then onwards, she reared me in an almost Western way, for example, sending me to a good English-medium school and giving me increasing autonomy as I grew older. As a result, I developed a good deal of independence.

I was the second daughter. To what extent I may have disappointed my parents by not being a boy (at a conscious or an unconscious level), I do not know. Certainly, they never gave me that feeling. However, I can say that either I was reared as a son would have been, or, maybe, I just demanded or commanded the respect, privileges, and freedom that a son enjoys in Indian society.

In contrast to the mothers of many of my friends, my mother took pains to train and groom me and would even beat me when I would disobey her or could not perform to her expectations. I would challenge her authority in a quiet way. It seems that my active nature and sense of self-righteousness offended her. Consequently, we had a challenging and intense relationship.

I knew my mother as a stern person for the first twenty years of my life, and as a friend for the next twenty years. Nonetheless, she was extremely hard-working, protective, and warm. Her devotion to work and to the upliftment of people, especially women, left a deep mark on me. At times, I was hyper-critical of my mother. We would regularly discuss our differences and occasionally have tiffs. Yet, we maintained a reasonably good comfort level with each other. When we discovered she had cancer, I realized the spiritual journey that lay ahead for both of us. Death became an object of meditation, not only for the two of us but for the rest of the family as well.

It all started while I was abroad in the summer of 1990. A couple of times I dreamt that Mother was sick and was being hospitalized. In the dream, she said to me that she did not want to die. I assured her that I would return soon and everything would be fine.

Within a month of my return, we were shocked to learn that she had breast cancer and that the cancer had spread elsewhere in her body. Doctors gave her six months at the most. Initially I had difficulty discussing the disease frankly with her, but gradually I disclosed even the minutest details of her condition. It was best for her to know about the stage of her disease so that she could muster up the strength to fight it and to contend with the interminable pain. Immediately, she was put on medication and given radiotherapy. There was some temporary relief of pain. She was averse to chemotherapy, but after many sessions with various doctors, she agreed to go in for it. This would improve not only the chances of her survival beyond six months but also the quality of her life.

Relatives and friends poured in regularly to see her, and with some she had meaningful conversations. My elder sister, based in the United States, visited us thrice during the twenty months of Mom's illness. She was a great moral support. My younger sister took care of her daily needs. There was a marked improvement in Mom's relationship with others, especially my father. I could see that the thought of ultimate separation frightened them. An undercurrent of sadness affected most of our interactions, no matter how hard we tried to behave normally. There were moments of helplessness and despair, anger and denial, with occasional emotional eruptions. It was all a part of the mourning process for us.

Mother's illness gave her the opportunity to be introduced to the spiritual realm. She received blessings from my spiritual master. A brief encounter with him tapped a new dimension in her and triggered a process of inner healing. She felt absolutely blissful and fortunate to be soothed by him.

Fifty years ago, she had dropped the religious chord in her life to concentrate on improving the material conditions of the world. Deep down she was quite idealistic. In her childhood and adolescence, religious ritual enabled her to evade and transcend the stepmotherly treatment she received in her natal family and also to find a desirable husband. Once she told me that her life story was similar to that of Cinderella's. Confronting her own mortality had now forced her to become philosophical and to ponder ultimate reality.

She remained active throughout her illness except for the last four months when she was bedridden. With great fortitude she maintained a brave front and always had a pleasing countenance that amazed everybody. The doctors even remarked, 'We have not seen a patient like her. She is always cheerful and smiling.' Her body accepted two cycles of chemotherapy rather well, despite such side-effects as weakness, nausea, and hair loss. But the first dose of the third cycle was too strong for her and she collapsed. This made her give up the treatment, and she opted for ayurvedic medicine. Along with it she did her breathing exercises and recited her mantras silently. Now she did not want to be disturbed by visitors. She preferred to be alone or with immediate family members. In her room one sensed a sublime silence.

The nature of her dreams had also changed—from the

mundane affairs of everyday life to deep psychic explorations. Finally the doctors gave up and she had to mark time till she renounced her body. It seemed to me that the doctors were becoming indifferent, that they had lost interest in their patient, and I resented it. Was their experiment now over, and had they generated enough data for their research? However, much later it dawned on me that the doctors probably were reacting quite naturally. Maybe it was difficult for them to face their perceived failure or limitations.

Seeing Mother's bodily self suffer and decline on a daily basis was trying for all of us. I tried to talk to her about the dying process, to prepare her to face it without fear. Her condition epitomized the evanescence and impermanence of worldly existence. Meditation and support from spiritual-minded friends enabled me to face the deep distress that Mother's irremediable illness had caused in me, and to be a source of strength for her. She was well aware of this and chose me as her confidante during the last phase of her life. She wanted to exercise her unassailable right to euthanasia, but I convinced her that even if she had the freedom to carry it out, living through her suffering would dissolve her negative karma in this very incarnation. Also, imagining herself assuming the suffering on behalf of all those dying from cancer would actually transform her dying process into a positive experience. This was usually the advice spiritual teachers gave to her. Many well-wishers offered prayers for her peaceful end as well.

She was in great pain. We had to put her on morphine for the last three weeks. Her voice had become feeble and she was losing weight. She aged visibly in those three weeks and had a shrunken look. Nonetheless, her face started radiating peace and light as the end approached. She appeared to accept her condition, and she was calm and composed even though she became like an infant who required round-the-clock care and attention. At times, morphine would have a hallucinatory effect and she would have visions of Buddha, Jesus, and Guru Nanak, all dressed in white. At other times the household chores would obsess her, and she would think of either cooking or washing clothes, and would worry about my father's health. She wanted to hide all her suffering from him.

All sorts of sounds disturbed her and she desired absolute quiet. It was as if the doorbell or the telephone woud break her concentration and pull her down from a higher state of consciousness. She did not claim to achieve knowledge of the highest reality, but expressed a rough idea about some subtle essence of a higher state of being. Such a state of consciousness made her feel wholesome and healed. Human beings, she felt, were too engaged with and attached to earthly matters (which now seemed to be illusions to her) to glimpse even slightly that pure state of consciousness. And if she ever got another chance to return in the human form, she desired to do more good for people.

She was in coma for the last five days of her life. Nevertheless she could still hear us and, at times, responded by changing her breathing pattern or causing her eyes to moisten.

Early in the morning on the last day of her life, I dreamt that she was being given a gorgeous farewell and was being transported by an aeroplane. I felt I had to say my last words to her right away. So, quietly, I thanked her for being a great woman and a great mother, and told her that we all loved her and that she need not worry about anything. It seems that she was waiting to hear these words. She departed that evening, looking beautifully peaceful. Though I was very sad to see her go, I was grateful for the spiritual transformation she had undergone. I was satisfied that I had done my best to prepare her to meet her end in a quiet and conscious manner. People who viewed her body said she looked more beautiful than ever before.

The voyage across the ocean of Samsara came in my mother's sixty-fifth year and brought to a close the business between me and her. The tensions between us had dissolved during this last phase, and we had come to terms with each other totally. Her death revealed to me the role we had played in each other's life.

A week after Mother's passing, her ninety-year-old stepmother, who gave her a rough time in her childhood, also died. We discovered later that my grandmother got to know telepathically about my mother's death and asked for forgiveness over and over again. Perhaps, something between the two of them was being resolved. To me, it seemed that she wanted to follow my mother to the next world. Strange are the ways in which nature connects mothers and daughters in their spiritual transformation in this worldly and cyclic existence.

By the sheer act of being born, all human beings are destined to go through life's suffering. Instances that depict man's efforts to direct his own destiny often pit his freedom against both fate and fortune. Nonetheless, certitude is not attainable in human relations. Death, the great unmasker, is definite; only its time is indefinite. Yet, in our consciousness, death is never a possibility for ourselves and has always been distasteful to man. Thus, it is consideration of mortality that helps one to face the pain and fear that the death of a loved one brings, putting an end to false emotions and base desires. To ensure that one's death will be a source of strength to those who survive is what my mother taught me—and that this can only be so when one has lived a genuinely good life. In many cases, the course of one's life changes drastically after a near-death experience or the death of a dear family member. Death invariably reveals and makes one think about the spiritual path, if not force one to follow it. (See the life stories of the scientist, the writer, the counsellor, the American, and the singer.)

My mother did not perceive me merely as an extension of herself, that is, in terms of a wife or mother. She desired and dared to raise me differently in a social context shaped primarily by the demands and threats of men, even within the family. This perhaps stemmed from the anger and helplessness of her relationship with her stepmother. By doing so, she not only questioned the status quo but permitted me to undertake activities that require a secure sense of a separate and individualized self. A mother passes on the message of what is expected of a daughter in the given culture. In addition she communicates her personal experiences in terms of the wounds between and within generations of women. This immediately personal context has been called an 'underground' relationship that has much significance and is highly charged with emotion.[8]

There are four patterns of the mother-daughter relationship that emerge in this study:

1) A positive experience is the supportive, loving, nurturing, and caring attitude of the mother which, perhaps, the daughter unconsciously wants to imbibe.
2) In a negative experience, the daughter tends to resist the inhibiting, discouraging, invasive, competitive, and dismissive attitude of the mother.
3) The mixed, realistic model of mothering is most prevalent. Here the mother is intermittently and situationally stern and / or supportive.
4) The indifferent mother typically remains non-supportive and absent, or she neglects the children to suit her whims and fancies. Many women find their mothers indifferent at some stage or the other in their lives even though their relationship may otherwise be satisfactory.

Obviously, one's experience may not fall directly within these constructs. Nevertheless, women do seem to yearn for the perfect mother or even for the absent mother to be present, and for the negative attitude of the mother to be transformed into a positive one. The dilemma of the perfect mother has been described quite adequately in the following quotation:

'The culture of mother blaming creates a psychological prison for mothers of daughters. Whether or not a mother is conscious of these forces within the culture, the desire to do right, to provide a daughter with new opportunities, makes mothering incredibly pressured. Messages about 'good' mothering and the necessities of providing for children often conflict, leaving mothers guilty and torn. The enormous responsibility without full authority, the impossible ideals and required sacrifices, the self-doubt and confusion, all lead to powerlessness and a deep, vague sense of loss. Mothers can't afford to fail; failure would damage their daughters. But being set up by impossible expectations, mothers are doomed to fail.'[9]

When the idealized 'perfect' mother proves to be a myth, in the light of the mother-daughter relationship that inevitably is experienced as imperfect, daughters invariably feel unloved and abandoned. There are many instances of women having a deep wish to be different from their mothers and also a great fear that eventually they will turn out to be almost like their mothers. This is especially true when a woman becomes a mother herself or after she has lost her mother. It is also interesting to note that elimination of the man—brother, father, son, husband or a lover—becomes a prerequisite for improving the troubled relationship with the mother. On the other hand a sad and stormy relationship with the father often improves after a woman relates to a man, especially her husband or a lover. In the former case, the emotional structure of a triad is reduced to a dyad; in the latter, the dyad develops into a triad.

Today, a separate identity consciousness, autonomy, and personal achievement can avert the danger of mother and daughter becoming fused personalities, covertly or overtly. Previously, women distinguished themselves from each other through their relationships with men. Much awareness and care is required if mothers are to stop living vicariously through their daughters. Also, an over-identification with the daughter will not necessarily result in repairing their broken inner selves or eradicating their childhood suffering.

Another significant bond is the relationship between sisters. Examining the relationship with the literal sister, surrogate sister, and the archetypal sister will prove to be transformative in an ongoing journey of the feminine.[10] As revealed in the stories of the housewife, the freedom fighter, and the singer, envious, cruel, and callous sisters may ultimately serve an important function in the search for one's identity and in expediting the process of soul searching.

The relationship between sisters contains ample space for likeness and difference, for challenge, protection, domination, and disappointment. It can be as demanding, painful or satisfying as any other deep bond, but it also encompasses the polarity and complementarity script. The unalterable otherness of the sister creates the most permanent tie and moments of devastation and celebration strengthen this bond.

Although their relationship is marked by a remarkable degree of tolerance, protection, and admiration, the grit of hierarchy tensions of sibling the possibility of their estrangement and aggression. As Downing rightly maintains, the objective is not patching-up, correction, or resolution; the task is re-imagining, questioning, going deeper.[11] Also, this relationship requires constant revision for it keeps reappearing in women's lives.

Feminine transformation is thus the spiritual imperative that can bring about a profound modification in family relationships, as moderate bonding help one to minimize undesirable family hatred, and otherwise reduce the friction between family members. One needs to outgrow family attachments rather than destroy one's family relationships to avoid placing strong family ties in conflict with individual and social development.

## Sexuality

The domain of sexuality has generated substantial and noisy debates in the print and electronic media. Language itself inscribes structures by which the silence of the 'feminine' makes women feel alienated, repressed and burdened. Something of my subjects' 'sacred' or 'profane' experience in this sphere was stilled into silence when I requested them to articulate their desires. A conspiracy of silence and lack of proper communication in this nearly unknown, unrepresentable and interiorized sexuality seem to be at the centre of women's experiences. Few of the educated urban women studied felt comfortable with their experiences, and the expression of this sensitive, forbidden area was frightening for many.

My earlier work substantiates this point. Although I had anticipated a certain level of non-response, a surprising forty per cent of the two hundred respondents felt uninhibited when it came to speaking about their sexuality, while twenty per cent spoke in monosyllables and visibly withheld information. Also, women who willingly discussed this subject would periodically pause or lower their tone and even talk in whispers. Maybe women become suspect even by engaging in an enthusiastic discussion of sexuality. The educated, upper-class women were more articulate than the uneducated lower and middle-class women who were guarded in their comments. The educated middle-class women turned out to be the most inhibited and cautious about discussing their sexuality.[12] If a direct, conscious expression of their sexuality is a transgression and socially punishable, even a conversation on the subject can prove dangerous and damaging. Women probably protect their conventional self-image of being 'good' and 'pure' by remaining silent or lowering their voices. It is also possible that some of these women are still so emotionally involved that it prevents them from reasoning calmly, or that they take their revenge on the world by carrying their sexual sadness, pain, and anguish deep within themselves, while projecting a persona of indifference.

In his last work, Foucault questioned the standard view that the nineteenth century was an age of repression when sex was never discussed, while the twentieth century has been an age of emancipation in which it is freely discussed. Scientific investigation of sex only started the process of bringing sexuality under control by defining a norm. Thus the frequency of sex as a topic today, far from being a sign of liberation, has become a ubiquitous exercise of power to produce and maintain the norm of heterosexuality. However, Foucault's investigation of sexuality also introduced the theme of 'subjectification,' 'or the way a human being turns himself or herself into a subject'.[13] These are processes of self-formation in which the individual is not a passive object of constraint and manipulation by others but takes an active part. So, discourse on sexuality can be transformatory and emancipatory so long as it is open to all voices and is not a powergame. It is only through dialogue, not polemics, that the subject will survive and will ultimately arrive at some difficult truth. In the urban Indian context, I would hypothesize that male talk about sexuality is usually a result of sexual deprivation. This can at times lead to increased interest in other activities such as politics. Female sexual discourse, on the other hand, is generally a consequence of sexual indulgence or gratification.

The focus in this section, however, is admittedly limited. It does not deal with the emergence of sexual discourse or even the history of sexuality; sexual ideas, beliefs, and shifts in behaviour, or any connection between them; sexual orientation and individual/social rights as a citizen in different political systems; stigmatized sexual realities; sexual fantasies; sexual identity—ascribed or achieved—but with urban women's experience of desire and sexuality and its relationship to their spiritual development.

Discovering one's sexual mode of being is like dreaming in another language. Thinking back through one's mother is but natural and it at once becomes therapeutic and refreshing because, closely connected with the mother-daughter relationship is the notion of woman's sexual identity, which it refers to woman's identity as a biological female and the comfort level associated with one's body and its sexuality. Various studies have pointed out that a mother's confusing, vague, negative or ambivalent relationship to her sexuality quite often discourages the daughter's development of sexual identity.[14] Also, the male tendency to split sexuality into love and lust is a means to control female sexuality. The prevalent structures of dominance prove to be coercive and rarely permit women to express a difference in experience or view. Either the woman has been an object of male gaze or a mirror in which the male is reflected. The woman is occasionally allowed to utter her own alternative, otherwise she only receives and confirms the male. Hence, such dichotomies as male presence and female absence, male word and female verbal object, and male centre and female periphery perpetuate women's marginalization and expropriation of their decisional power.

It is generally believed, for example, that women's experiences have been systematically repressed in Western thought. For instance, the four French critics, Julia Kristeva, Luce Irigaray, Helene Cexous and Monique Wittig, find

Western culture fundamentally oppressive and phallogocentric. Man (white, European, and ruling class) as the unified, self-controlled centre of the universe defines the rest of the world as the other, and asserts that it has meaning only in relation to him as man/father. This claim to centrality is supported by religion, philosophy, and even language. Thus, writing and speaking from such a position is to appropriate the world and objectify it. These French women agree that resistance to institutions and signifying practices (speech, writing, images, myths, and rituals) of such cultures takes place in the form of jouissance, that is, in the direct re-experience of the physical pleasures of infancy and of later sexuality, repressed but not obliterated by masculine privilege or power.[15] Therefore, it is most essential that they express and understand their libidinal differences with regard to men.

That desires, sexuality, and expectations are acquired in a social context is a well-established fact. Yet, the body can be examined as a source of self-knowledge. Women can experience their bodies purely or essentially, transcending, at times, the acculturation process. Some urban Indian women today are involved in creating their subjectivities and space for change. Sexuality is one area of inner disturbance in which they desire to effect changes. Patterns of sexuality, as indicated in this study, cannot be reduced to compact suggestive statements because this field of human concern is saturated with self-deception, evasion, and anxiety (especially in this age of AIDS), usually leading to ironies, inconsistencies and incongruities in the social sphere. So, the question here is whether an absolute distinction between sex and gender is valid. If minds are never disembodied, then the body must have some part to play in the process of understanding.

Feminists have emphasized that the root of woman's power lies in the acknowledgement of her desire. As my subjects expressed it, desire is not just about sex. It is, as poet Audre Lorde has written, about the power of self-knowledge and of a self-love that moves outward to others. She speaks of the erotic as an assertion of the life-force of women; of that creative energy empowered, the knowledge and use of which we are now reclaiming in our language, our history, our dancing, our loving, our work, and our lives.[16] Thus, production of knowledge itself becomes a political intervention as false claims to objectivity have been debunked by showing how they masked masculine privilege and self-interest.

Studies show that a woman experiences her sexuality, often circumscribed, as a child, through the cultural definitions of the feminine. This process continues up through menstruation—i.e., through puberty, through her adult years marked by the repetition of cycles, and their cessation at menopause. In heterosexual or homosexual relationships, pregnancy, childbirth and child-care, she repeatedly experiences the life of her body. Our stories reveal the external dangers, the internal difficulties, and restrictions faced in this field and create ample room for narratives of regret and sadness; of humour; of fears banished or never let go; and of aspirations retained or dashed. However, one cannot have a monolithic conception of sexual experience or knowledge. Some of the subjects felt that a long-standing relationship leads to either greater compatibility or estrangement. Thus, long term continuity often underlies qualitative leaps and neither rationality nor the passionate impulse, as they characterize sexual behaviour, reveal anything of its ethical dimension.

Rural and urban women in India have contrasting experiences of sexuality. Rural women may be poor in knowledge and comprehension of the subject, but their attitude to sexuality is usually less problematic. Urban women, on the other hand, are more articulate and knowledgable, though differences based on class and educational backgrounds are more palpable here.[17] Also, if their sexuality is anchored in marriage, it becomes less contested because marriage tends to exclude the uncertainties and uneasiness relating to this subject.

The institution of marriage seems to take women's sexuality for granted, as evidenced by the celebration of sexuality in songs, music, dance, jokes and dresses that surround a wedding. Marriage allows the glorification of sex(uality), going so far as to give it a divine complexion. It has, therefore, been suggested that such initial and conventional contexts deposit residues of exegetical cliches and stock phrases, so that thinking afresh about issues of sexual difference and knowledge is deadlocked'.[18]

It is difficult to miss the particularity and uniqueness of each libidinal voice, yet reference to universal elements is equally manifest. Discovering the differences between procreative and communicative sexuality; its moral and aesthetic dimension; and sexual experience being a matter, not of frequency and variety, but of quality, intensity and motivation, have become significant to women's libidinal strivings and heightened their expectations about choices. While listening to my interviewees I was forced to pay attention to my own sexual consciousness because it not only sent me a message—'You have no right to look into our lives unless you examine your own world'—but questioned me as well.

Sexual awareness unfolded for the first time in my early childhood. I identified totally with the opposite sex. Discovering and playing with others' bodies, whether a boy or girl, was a mutual and secretive act. Childhood for me was marked by privacy. I never had to feel ashamed about it, because parents and other adults in the family were always kept in the dark. As a child I found adults rather frightening, but they also helped me to distinguish between the good and the bad touch. I remember feeling protective towards one passive and reluctant newly wedded woman who I thought was being harassed by her husband. Men responsible for producing phallic dread in me did not actually realize that it automatically led to my withdrawal and made me defensive. When the threat was external I sought shelter at home, whereas an internal threat made me disappear from home. In cities, since the parents are usually busy or are working, children are often left by themselves or with the servants. The counsellor, teacher and doctor mention the danger children and teenagers are exposed to in this context.

The normal growth spurt of adolescence is one of the many biological surprises in store for women. Everything changes for a girl as she develops physically, hormonally, and emotionally, during puberty. The subjects in my study reveal how mothers disapprove of the daughter's body or fail to notice their daughter's menses and how such disregard leaves the girls hurt and abandoned. In my case I was very excited to have come of age. I ran to my mother and announced cheerfully, 'You did not tell me but I know what all this is about.' My mother just smiled at me. Perhaps, at this stage, the eternal triangle comes into play as the daughter begins to separate herself from her parents. It seems that discussing these developments is easier with friends; both mother and daughter feel shy and embarrassed about sharing bodily and emotional changes taking place during adolescence. Some women, however, are now conciously changing in order to emotionally support their daughters.

I learnt about human physiology and biology in my science class. While returning home in our school bus, we would share our notions and ideas about the procreative potential and the method of tapping it. I had a scientific explanation for the coital act, whereas my childhood friend described the sexual act as one resembling the crucifixion of Jesus Christ. My adolescence, however, was marked by evolving strategies for protection, and any violation of my sexual integrity enraged me and produced resentment against offenders. As my subjects also relate, growing up with sexual harassment and learning to cope with it independently comes naturally to girls. Yet, this does not rule out the possibility of young girls being harmed.

It was during my twenties that I started to explore the nuances of love, in and outside the context of marriage. Ideas of purity and pollution sounded absolutely false, hollow and fabricated when it came to actual experience. A sense of discrimination and discretion developed in terms of continence, eros, casual sex, romance, surplus desire, and emotional involvements. The sexual path also led to the experience of disillusionment, crisis of faith, and a feeling of death, loss, and emptiness.

Many of my subjects have had to resolve the dilemmas of a negative image of femaleness and sexuality, probably inherited from their mothers. They value male attention and support because it validates their positive self-image. Nonetheless, sexual intercourse per se does not interest them as much as the act of being together, touching and maintaining tender contact.

For most of them it constitutes a marital duty, and they participate passively, remaining recumbent. Many women experience the sexual act with their husbands as 'unpleasant', 'dirty', 'distasteful', 'dangerous', 'painful', and 'disgusting', and they refuse to discuss their sexuality with them. They also tend to see sex exclusively in terms of reproduction. Non-procreative sexuality is only slowly gaining currency amongst a small section of urban women who are trying to expand their sexual flexibility.[19] Hence, openness and conservatism exist contextually and, at times, simultaneously.

When it comes to arranging marriages in India, due consideration is given to caste and religious boundaries, though prestige and wealth are equally important criteria. Sexual compatibility is almost never taken into account. Thus, in anticipation of an arranged marriage it becomes a social imperative to control the sexuality of an unmarried woman.

It is relatively easier for men to deny their pre- and extra-marital relationships and to adopt a stance of nonchalance, whereas for women such liaisons prove far riskier. Since a woman's sexual reputation is seen as reflecting her family's reputation, her chastity is socially controlled before and after marriage, for there are dangerous implications associated with her reproductive capacity, and there exist enduring beliefs that female sexuality is potentially threatening to social institutions.[20]

Women's sexuality blossoms in myriad forms if their desire is not forced to lie dormant. Research has shown that male libido rarely equals female sexual capacity. Throughout history, man has seen woman as a sinister and mysterious being, particularly dangerous when she is menstruating. Men attempt to deal with this dread through denial and defence. They deny their dread by resorting to love and adoration, and defend themselves from it by conquering, debasing and diminishing a woman's self-respect.[21] Foucault's insight that sexuality is endowed with the greatest instrumentality and is amenable to the most varied strategies also helps us to understand the dynamics of human relationships.[22] Hence, having sexual and emotional access to women only on women's terms, coupled with women's indifference towards men, is perhaps what perturbs men the most. It is not a question of women's sexual appetites overwhelming and devouring them, nor the fear that women can be emotionally over-indulgent.[23]

This study reveals women's sexuality being manifest at physical, mental, emotional and spiritual levels. These different levels always have their own social configurations and are also contingent upon the concerned mates. Sexual mismatching is the most common catastrophe, and yet Indian marriages survive even if the social trend is towards coupling and uncoupling. Whether women have had a love marriage or an arranged marriage, deep down they yearn for the right partner, a soul mate who will supposedly provide happiness ever after, even though intimacy, mutuality, and the desire for emotional union present risks and can leave one injured and in conflict. Thus, female emotional vulnerability and male sexual fragility form the core of sexual problems.

The pervasive sexual suffering and violence women experience take the form of harassment, the performing-my-duty syndrome, painful menstruation and childbirth, distasteful sex, marriage or date rape, incest and battering. Also, they are at the receiving end of crude psychological assaults such as economic deprivation, domination, and confinement, in addition to the more subtle and enduring forms of psychological scarring that result from indifference, humiliation, abuse, and emotional imprisonment. Only a few women—for instance, the fashion designer, the writer and the singer—equate their sexuality with a celestial or spiritual dimension that, more than mere relief or release, opens the door to the divine. Love, however, remains a prerequisite for the attainment of such a state of bliss and ecstasy, though it still does not lead to the highest goal of complete awakening and a pure mind. The secret lies in using the mind of bliss or misery (depending on the nature of sexual experience) to meditate upon emptiness and enter the spiritual path. This requires guidance from a qualified teacher, as explained in many philosophical and religions texts.[24]

Otherwise, there seems to be an inverse relationship

between women's sexuality and spirituality, and discovering soul mates becomes an impossible enterprise. Although there is always space for "passionlessness" or permissiveness, women desire a balanced and spontaneous sexuality. Asceticism, however, becomes a way of asserting control in the sexual domain and the turbulent order of conflict is juxtaposed against the equanimity of transcendence. Even the men I interviewed believe that sublimation and transcendence of their sexuality and worldly attachment is conducive to their spiritual progress. Nevertheless, an optimum amount of otherness is required to experience one's sexuality in terms of self-transcendence. This ubiquitous demand for self-transcendence is also satisfied by one's soul mate who, for many, happens to be their guru.

**The Guru**

The notion of guru is a cultural component of the Sikh tradition in India. One's plight without the guru's presence has been portrayed well in the sacred text: 'Even the light of hundred moons and thousand suns cannot dispel the utter darkness caused by the absence of one's guru.' Since I belong to this community, the value of being a 'disciple' has been a part of my socialization process. However, I did not have a religious upbringing. In fact, my family encouraged me and my sisters to have a questioning mind and opt for the scientific, secular, and progressive path, which I think contained the spiritual impulse to address issues that plague humanity at large.

The proliferation of gurus, both in India and in the West, did not interest me during my university days. I was even dismissive of them because they possessed no power or wisdom that was not also inherent in others. At the same time, the guru-disciple relationship between Shri Ramakrishna and Swami Vivekananda had left an indelible mark on my mind. While doing my doctorate in the early '80s, many questions regarding the nature of mind cropped up and I could not deny some of my personal experiences in this realm. All this actually did not destroy my notions of the scientific/rational paradigm but rather added another dimension to reality that I had to contend with and comprehend. I read extensively on this subject and, unwittingly, it turned out to be a sort of preparation required in order to meet a master.

Although I agreed with J. Krishnamurti's assertion that masters are not indispensible as they inevitably become intoxicated with their powers and tend to enslave their students and followers, I nevertheless developed a readiness to doubt and accept, and be open to infinite possibilities. I never sought the guru phenomenon, and yet it happened to me. Perhaps it was a blessing and conditions were ripe for my teacher to show up. The first lesson learnt was that it is one's practice, and not merely voracious reading, that will prove useful in the ultimate analysis, and that spiritual evolution continues for aeons and aeons. The responsibility to examine the teacher from the beginning lies with us. They say, even if it takes twelve years, one should wait and watch before one takes on a teacher. It took four years from the time I first saw him before I met him. In the past decade, the impact of meeting such a highly evolved and revered teacher as His Holiness Tenzin Gyatso, the fourteenth Dalai Lama, is quite perceptible in my life.

Sacred and classical texts speak of the significance of the spiritual teacher in developing the highest potential in man. Relying solely on your own endeavour and ability cannot propel one to the ultimate stage of spiritual attainment. Therefore, once you have examined the teacher with care, you have to follow him/her and finally, emulate his/her realizations and actions. P. Rinpoche states that the teacher we follow should possess at least the following qualities:

'He should be pure. He should be learned, and not lacking in knowledge of the tantras, sutras and shastras. Towards the vast multitude of beings, his heart should be so suffused with compassion that he loves each one like his only child. He should be well versed in the practices. He should have actualized all the extraordinary qualities of liberation and realization in himself by experiencing the meaning of the teachings. He should be generous, his language should be pleasant, he should teach each individual according to that person's needs and he should act in conformity with what he teaches; these four ways of attracting beings enable him to gather fortunate disciples around him.'[25]

He adds: 'A courageous disciple armoured with the determination never to displease his teacher even at the cost of his life, stable-minded enough not to be shaken by immediate circumstances, who serves his teacher without caring about his own health or survival and obeys his every command without sparing himself at all—such a person will be liberated simply through his devotion to the teacher . . .

'When you are perfectly versed in how to follow your teacher, you should be like a swan gliding smoothly on an immaculate lake, delighting in its waters without making them muddy; or like a bee in a flower garden, taking the flowers' nectar without spoiling their colour or fragrance. Tirelessly doing whatever he says, be receptive to your teacher and through your faith and steadfastness let yourself be filled with his qualities of knowledge, reflection and meditation, like the contents of one perfect vessel being poured into another.'[26]

Just the presence of the guru is enough to change one's life. He is not merely a mirror who reflects strengths and shortcomings, he facilitates the process of self-awakening and one's spiritual progress. Swami Vivekananda writes: 'You instinctively know that the sun has already begun to shine. Truth stands on its own evidence, it does not require any other testimony to prove it.'[27]

At times, the teacher acts in the most unreasonable, unkind, unjust, and odd manner, and the disciple gets tested. The disciple must show faith, humility, patience, and veneration. Hazrat Inayat Khan observes that 'attributes of the disciple are reserve, thoughtfulness, consideration, balance and sincerity'[28] and that, during the time of discipleship, one should not become a teacher. A teacher, therefore, has to be a true disciple who is not merely well versed in the scriptures but also in its spirit.

When we want to understand reality, Dharmakirti tells us: 'We are seeking something better than what the world considers the best. You have to have seen it all and yet not be satisfied. As long as you have not seen it all, you will not have become mature enough to leave it. Your experience of life should bring you to an existential crisis. Why does everything exist? Why does it exist the way it is? It requires an acute intellect, a relentless spirit that does not stop midway. Some of us have seen wars and famines and great personal hardship, persecution and abuse, and still we have not turned away from it all. So mere experience of suffering in itself is not sufficient. There has to be a kind of spirit that is impelled by the experience of suffering to seek its nature.

'Normally this path begins with some deep experience of personal suffering or loss. Somebody whom you love very much dies suddenly. Or you suddenly lose all your wealth or property or you are driven out of your country and become a refugee. A deep sense of personal loss is usually the beginning of the spiritual quest. Or one day, you discover that life is too boring.'

Women feel that the spiritual experience brings them to the threshold of the ultimate experience, that which crashes through the barriers of one's being to produce a oneness in which no alienation occurs. So, what leads the disciple to search for the guru and get initiation in his/her cult? Karkar describes: 'Almost invariably the individual had gone through one or more experiences that had severely mauled his sense of self-worth, if not shattered it completely. In contrast to the rest of us, who must also deal with the painful feelings aroused by temporary depletions in self-esteem, it seems that those who went to gurus grappled with these feelings for a much longer time, sometimes for many years, without being able to change them appreciably. Unable to rid themselves of the feelings of 'I have lost everything and the world is empty,' or 'I have lost everything because I do not deserve anything,' they had been on the lookout for someone, somewhere, to restore the sense of self-worth and to counteract their hidden image of failing, depleted self—a search nonetheless desperate for its being mostly unconscious. This 'someone' eventually turned out to be the particular guru to whom the seekers were led by events—such as his vision—which in retrospect seemed miraculous.'[29]

Generally speaking, the guru has traditionally performed many functions such as imparting knowledge of scriptures and religious texts; initiating the process of enlightenment; counselling people and advising the political elite; solving business and family problems; healing the sick and ailing, and supporting the destitute and the lonely.[30]

Finding a real teacher is not an easy or an ordinary task. Some of my subjects are wary of dishonest gurus, but eventually it is the disciple's power and sincerity that brings one to the right teacher. Women's skepticism is justified because, not infrequently, the modern cult gurus have manipulated people for the attainment of power, money, and sex. In such cases, the student may end up feeling exploited, diminished, abandoned, or used as an object.

One cannot even wish not to respond to a genuine teacher for he offers to each seeker what he or she most wants and values. The teacher teaches in a uniquely eloquent and appealing manner and tunes one's mind and body in order that one can experience and express beauty, harmony, and compassion.

Leslie points out that women are not given more prestige and importance in religious roles because of the tension between asceticism and eroticism. Asceticism is possible for men because they can give up the world after being involved in procreation. A man can practice seminal retention whilst a woman cannot control her bodily secretions. Thus, the argument goes, men have greater spiritual or religious potential.[31] However, His Holiness the Dalai Lama expressed his views about women's potential and their rights as follows:

'Men and women have a different physical structure. So, if you will have only males, then you cannot have children—lots of problems (*laughs*). Nature has created that difference for procreation and accordingly, due to their physical differences, they have different positions. Except that, they are hundred per cent equal. There may also be some differences in the mental attitude of men and women because of the element of nature.

However, on the basis of that reality, men have created some kind of distinction and women are considered weaker or lower in some traditional systems.

'Women have the same spiritual potential, according to Buddhism. However, Buddha made more rules, created more restrictions for Bhikshunis because of great caution. Physically, rape of women by males is easier than that of men. The opposite happens but rarely. There may be some cases of very strong women, and weak males being raped is possible, but generally the rape of women is more common.

'One of the rules out of 250 rules for monks is that in the daytime you must keep your door locked. This is so because, once, a strong-bodied woman, a woodcutter, invaded the room of a weak monk. Later on the story reached Buddha's ears. So, out of precaution, he made this rule for monks, "You should not sleep in the afternoon and if you do, you should lock the door (*laughs*)." Generally speaking, the physical condition itself made it necessary to make some rules, but it does not mean that you have to undermine the spiritual potential of women or even make a distinction.

'In Buddhist tradition, the Bhikshunis had a lower position and the Bhikshus an upper one. Some feminists have raised that point and criticized it. That is fair. Actually Buddha made that kind of rule because of the general social system and conditions existing at that time. Otherwise, from the Buddhist viewpoint, there is not much of a problem, especially from the Maha-Annutara Yoga Tantrayana. The importance of equality is very clearly stressed and emphasized. For example, the fourteenth point of the tantric vow is that the practitioner should not look down upon women. Whereas, the contrary or the opposite is not mentioned. Sometimes when you practice the Maha-Annutara Yoga Tantrayana, one special commitment is that whenever you meet women, you must prostrate (if there is no complication), circumambulate also, and then beg from them *(gestures and laughs loudly)*.

'After prostration, you have to recite, "you are my mother", "give me compassion and kindness", and "lead me to Buddhahood". These are clear indications of the importance of women. The cause for their inferior position lies in the social system that has a tendency to look down upon them.

'In the history of Tibet, in the Karmapa Nyingma tradition, the first lineage incarnation was the female lineage. The Karmapa's lineage started simultaneously with the female lineage. As far as religion is concerned we do not make a distinction, but sometimes it becomes problematic. Actually, in 1959, a high female lama escaped to India, and then she returned. We heard that she remained a puppet in the hands of others—maybe because she was a female. No other reincarnated lama did that; she was the only case we had.

'In another instance I was told that in one reincarnated lama lineage in 1959, a female lama who passed away was the fourth incarnation. When I heard about this, I immediately said that you have to follow up on this female lama and find the fifth incarnation of her. Traditionally such things have existed, but politically it is essential to demonstrate it.

'The other day someone (some Tibetan woman with modern education and feminist inclinations) suggested to me that certain words which have a negative connotation for women should be dropped from the Tibetan vocabulary. Her desire was that on some occasion the Dalai Lama should announce publicly not to use words such as "*keymen*", which means "lower birth", and others which mean "slim body," "slim waisted", etc. I told them that traditionally such words exist; it is silly to change that.

'As far as my own effort, is concerned, when I first visited the nunnery here, I told them that nuns should not follow those temples and monastaries that have just prayer and no teaching. The women must study and eventually be scholars and ultimately teach, just like men do. Later, I established a nunnery in South India. There I emphasized that nuns must carry out their study in dialectics. Thus, women must use this opportunity and make the effort instead of complaining. The Western people make an effort themselves. In India and Tibet, there is a lack of initiative on the part of women; they are not assertive about their rights. Violence against women, dowry, etc., are awful. The traditional thinking in societies is partially responsible for aggression against women. Change must take place.'

Today, the metaphysical individuals and transcendental feminists are articulating their need to develop spiritual potential instead of the political one. Feminists also point to the experience of the divine within. They describe it as a sacred power within women and nature, thereby suggesting a connection between women's cycles—menstruation, birth, menopause—and the life and death cycles of the universe. In this context, religion fulfils deep psychic needs by providing symbols and rituals that enable women to cope with the 'limit' situations in human life (death, evil, suffering) and to pass through life's important transitions (birth, sexuality and death).[32] Tapping the spiritual-potential is accomplished by realizing the impermanence, fragility and feebleness, as well as the illusory and dream-like quality of one's body. This body, which is always subject to change, has been beautifully described in the poem 'Ambapali Speaks':

Once my hair was black like the colour of bees
Alive-curly
Now it is dry like bark fibres of hemp
I'm getting old
This is true, I tell you the truth
Covered with flowers, my head was fragrant
Like a perfumed box
Now, because of old age, it smells like dog's fur
Thick like a grove it used to be beautiful—
ends parted by comb and pin
Now it's thin, I'm telling the truth
This was a head with fine pins once,
Decorated with gold, plaited, so beautiful
Now bald
My eyebrows were like crescents
Exquisitely painted by artists
Now because of old age they droop down with wrinkles
Ah, I'm telling the truth
My eyes used to be shiny, brilliant as jewels

Now they don't look so good
My nose was like a delicate peak
Now it's a long pepper
This scarecrow is telling the truth
My earlobes once—can you believe it?
Were like well-fashioned bracelets
Now they're heavy with creases
Formerly my teeth were pearly white
Like the bud of a plantain
Now they're broken and yellow
Indeed, this is the truth
Sweet was my singing like the cuckoo in the grove
Now my voice cracks and falters
Hear it? These words are true
My neck used to be soft like a well-rubbed
conch shell
Now it bends, broken
My arms were round like crossbars
Now they're weak as the petali tree
My hands were gorgeous—they
used to be gorgeous—
Covered with signet rings, decorated with gold
Now they are like onions and radishes
This is true, I tell you
Formerly my breasts looked great—
round, swelling, close together, lofty
Now they hang down like waterless waterbags
My body used to be as shiny as a sheet of gold
Now it is covered with very fine wrinkles
Both thighs—and this was once considered a
compliment—
looked like elephants trunks—very interesting
I swear I'm telling the truth
Now they're like stalks of bamboo
My calves too, like stalks of sesame
My feet used to be elegant
like shoes of soft cotton wool
Now they are cracked & wrinkled

This hag speaks true
Once I had the body of a queen
Now it's lowly, decrepit, an old house
Plaster falling off
Sad, but true.[33]

Thus, haunted by impermanence, metaphysical feminists aspire to embark upon a spiritual journey marked by learning, wisdom, mental quiescence and transcendental analysis, in order to become enlightened.

Today, there is no dearth of material on the modes of meditation and various techniques for achieving inner transformation. Moreover, the rise of numerous religio-political organizations, cults and gurus has been widely recognized. Urban women, however, have learnt to detach spirituality from religion because of either disillusionment with organized religious life or its politicization and commodification. Nonetheless, they search for a soul mate because they feel the need for a satisfying relationship. This ideal helpmate and redeemer is sought in the ultimate relationship with a guru or gurus, who, in India, have widespread influence and relevance. The relationship with the guru is the ultimate relationship because it is he or she who reveals to you the ultimate reality and guides you in your search for enlightenment.

During the past century, the search for the guru has become a widespread phenomenon. For most of my subjects, the search for a guru is a meaningful activity, and the guru is primarily a crisis-cum-salvation friend. Their spiritual growth lies in the gradual development of their personality through this relationship with the guru. Satisfaction to a woman means, as it does to all human beings, successful self-transcendence. This she achieves, either through her family relationships or, in present times, even through her work. Her fulfilment within the institution of marriage is partial because of the inherent contradictions in it, such as the lack of choice and the compulsion to conform, whereas her relationship with her guru—her soul mate—is unstructured and chosen freely.

This enables a woman to offer herself entirely to a guru—a

person who is not easily accessible or is, at best, rare. At times her attachment is merely an infatuation, but it can take the form of a passionate attraction. However, it is generally easier for women rather than for men, to surrender and achieve a total identification with the guru; the guru then transforms the women in order to make ultimate peace and contentment possible for her. For men, seeking self-transcendence through renunciation, legitimacy, and spiritual authority in their relationship with their guru becomes more significant.

Only a few women in this study perceive their parents, mentors, or political/literary figures to be their gurus; inspiring them to tread the humanitarian and compassionate path. And some of them just deny the need for, or idea of, a guru even though the suffering of cyclic existence, death, unsatisfactory family relationships and the banality of worldly reality may be gnawing at them. Perhaps they are unaware of their own need. Or maybe, unlike the scientist, (See Chapter 7) they have not experienced any devastating personal crisis that has tried them to such an extent as to leave them open and ready for some guidance. It seems that when young people commit themselves to religious groups or gurus, usually they have been going through times of personal upheaval or are trying to uphold the convention of supporting family gurus. For others, as Roy mentions, it is a natural and developmental sequence in their life-cycle.[34] The social network of the guru usually helps women to expand their universe, to connect and communicate with the world outside the home.

Thus, the relationship with the guru is variously nuanced. Women can have filial and friendly feelings or attitudes of the devotee towards their respective male/female gurus, whether they are yogic, gyani, tantric, or brahmanishta.[35] The ultimate goal, however, is to be aware of an 'inner guru', an 'outer guru', and a 'secret guru'. The 'inner guru' refers to an innermost subtle consciousness (experienced when we faint or are dying) as explained by my teacher.[36] The guru and all other sentient beings possess it, but it is usually the guru who actually experiences it with awareness and transmutes it into wisdom. The task is not trivial when one has to realize it within oneself and establish the connection with the real teacher. The manifestation of this consciousness, perceived as human or divine, in the form of the human body—male, female or transcending gender—is called the outer guru. The 'secret guru' refers to the 'method' one adopts to become aware of this consciousness.

So, whether through the guru or through family relationships, sexuality or death, meditational practices or self-knowledge, ultimately spirituality boils down to correct motivation and identifying the right and reliable object of refuge that will facilitate the realization of pure mind. Our protagonists experience the worldly order of tension and evanescence, and bear the brunt of civilizational conflicts by drawing upon their spiritual strength. They tend to deny the gap between the mundane and the transcendental levels and try to achieve peace by going through their anguish-filled temporal task of inner growth. This is in contrast to the tendency in men, to seek a total identification of the immanent and the transcendental while being relatively more inclined towards renunciation.

# Chapter 7

## *Another Aspect of the Path: The Sage and the Scientist*

As mentioned in an earlier section, the true teacher provokes us to contact ourselves. He/she can show us how we can progress on the spiritual path. The responsibility for pursuing this path is entirely upon the individual. No saviour or divine grace is going to intervene or do it for us. There is yet another aspect of the spiritual struggle that interests me: Whether they are teachers or disciples, how do men proceed on this path? What sort of difficulties do they encounter? Here the Sage and the Scientist describe their inward journey to me.

**The Sage**

I met him ten years ago, but each time I meet my teacher the freshness and fullness of his whole being touches my heart directly. His simplicity, humility, childlike innocence, serenity, joyousness, and scholarship are equally captivating. A stage comes when the boundaries between the master and the pupil disappear, and they experience a deep and momentous spiritual union. This is exactly what I felt when I went to Dharamsala to interview His Holiness the Dalai Lama for this book.

*Q. Can you give me some details about the difficulties you faced in your spiritual struggle?*

A. (*Long silence*) . . . Actually, I do not know how to say this. You see, according to Buddhist practice, basically there are three stages or steps. The first step or the initial stage is to reduce attachment towards life. The second stage is the elimination of desire and attachment to this Samsara. Then in the third stage, there is the elimination of self-cherishing. During the 1960s, as a result of some sort of rigorous practice or analytical meditation about the negativeness of Samsara and attachment to Samsara, I felt there was a possibility of cessation, i.e. nirvana. Of course, theoretically, I got some sort of feeling and I think, the desire to achieve nirvana was quite properly developed. However, at that time, I found it very difficult to practise infinite altruism, and altruism seemed to me a beautiful ideal. Then, around 1967 I received Shantideva's teaching and went for further training and meditation. By the mid 1970s, somehow I was completely changed. Thus, I did not find it difficult to cultivate infinite altruism, which was a basic experience for me.

Further, at least intellectually, I got some understanding of shunyata, and that was a great help to realize the possibility of cessation. Although not true realization, that kind of feeling led me to develop the determination to achieve nirvana. Now, since the mid-70s, I feel that the only problem is the shortage of time, and my position. Otherwise, if I have the opportunity to go to a remote area, then I almost have the confidence that I can develop these practices. At the moment, however, I have no real experience.

Now, in the case of desire and regarding the control of anger, sometimes it is still difficult. Whereas, right from my childhood I had no difficulty in eliminating or weakening ill-feeling. Desire as attachment to good things, and fame, is not strong either. Then comes desire as sexuality. The path of practising celibacy is followed in order to achieve the cessation. The main obstacle or the main factor which holds Samsara is desire or attachment. There are different kinds of attachment—attachment towards life, attachment towards oneself, and the sexual attachment. Attachment to food involves taste, smell, and sight. In the case of sexuality the combination is more complex—i.e., of beauty, appearance, smelling, also kissing and then finally the touch. The scriptures usually say that sexuality is the strongest or the worst kind of desire or attachment. Therefore, in order to reduce attachment it is useful to be celibate. Thus, from the Buddhist perspective, spiritual practice means reducing attachment to this life and Samsara.

For the layman or the Upasikava, it is not necessary to control sexual desire, but at the same time you can purify your mind, and eventually reach nirvana without becoming a monk.

*Q. For whom is it more difficult?*

A. I think it depends on the circumstances. Much depends on the individual. In some special cases, suppose that in those practitioners who are actually well-equipped to practice Maha-Annutara Yoga Tantrayana, strong sexual desire exist along with a high intellectual potential. They first try to understand Shunya. Then, with the help of the realization of Shunya, sexual desire is transformed into extra energy which leads our mind into deeper clarity. In some other individual cases, neither is there strong sexual desire nor are they able to transform the desire. Thus, in such cases, according to different circumstances, different Tantrayana systems exist.

*Q. Why have you also mentioned that one should practice Hinayana externally, Mahayana internally, and Tantrayana secretly?*

A. Many scriptures say that being secret does not mean doing wrong things and keeping quiet. Here, tantric teachings are called the secret doctrine, and there are some reasons for it. Vinaya, which is external, can clearly be seen from outside, whereas Mahayana Bodhichitta cannot be seen outwardly. It is a mental attitude which is called the inner worldly practice of Mahayana. Then, in the secret doctrine of Tantrayana, you have to visualize a deity with his/her consort. A monk is very much concerned about conserving and controlling one's energy, but through visualization with a consort, you have to think about some sort of sexual activities and the energy comes and goes back. This is what we have to practice and do.

*Q. Do you undertake any exercises during deep sleep and in your dream state?*

A. Occasionally I need some effort, but not regularly. Sometimes I do realize it is a dream state and I want to control it.

*Q. How do you conduct an exercise in pure consciousness? If neither language nor everyday experience can really communicate the experience of pure mind, how do you establish its validity?*

A. Unless you have some experience as a result of intense meditation for a duration of a month or so, you cannot know. Once, in Ladakh, I stayed in a retreat for forty days. There, slowly my inner stillness increased. I thought that kind of experience was valuable when half my mind was watching the other half of the mind and knew whether it was still or whether it was about to run in any direction. So, that time, I developed the confidence that if given a chance to practice continuously, I can achieve a certain state of mind.

*Q. What sort of psychological change or transformation took place in you when you took the Kalachakra initiation?*

A. When I received the first Kalachakra initiation from my tutor in Potala, it was not a special one. In the end, I was made to go around the Mandala by my guru, make prostrations and then afterwards, the teacher offers his student to the deity. At that moment, my tutor Ling Rinpoche was very moved when he offered me to the deity. He lost his voice. I felt it was a special experience.

*Q. Besides being unhappy, how did separation from your family, especially your mother, affect your personality? How do you handle sadness in your life?*

A. When I was small I do not know. When I grew up, I do not know. But at the same time, when as a child I was separated from my mother, the feeling came up. Later on, during one summer festival in Norbulinka, my mother came to stay with me, was close to me. (She used to come every year.) After the festival she used to leave for her residence in Lhasa. That particular day when she was leaving, I felt very uncomfortable and very sad. Perhaps, there were some other reasons also. It was a complete holiday for five days—drama, parades, band, etc. It was a very happy moment. After it was over, I felt very sad. Everything put together probably produced that sadness (*laughs*).

Then, you know, later on when my mother actually passed away, and my senior tutor and also my guardian, a person who served me as a father-mother—when these three persons passed away, I was most sad.

Of course, in the Buddhist practice it is part of nature. Birth and death are there whether you like it or not. In all the three cases, they were in their eighties—quite old, and had lived for a sufficient time. However, when my tutor and mother passed away, I had heavier responsibility. Earlier I could rely on my tutor, and now it means more responsibility for me. I realized that giving in to sadness or worry would not help, because death is natural. Other teachings and practices related to suffering from the Buddhist point of view also helped me.

Then, perhaps, it seems I usually make some distinction between the emotional and intellectual levels. At the emotional level, I always take it lightly or take it easy even when some serious thing happens. So there is no emotional shock or sadness. But then as time passes, on the intellectual level I begin to worry and feel uncomfortable. After two or three weeks my thinking increases my worry.

In the early 1960s, one good practitioner was suddenly missing. After a few days we noticed that he had hanged himself. Later I understood the reason. A few days before that we had had a discussion about the practice. I had told him about some of the Maha-Annutara Yoga Tantra practices and said that this body was a very important factor. When you are young, physical energy is growing. So, if the practice starts early, it is very effective. After the age of fifty, physical energy starts declining and therefore the practice becomes difficult. It seems that I mentioned this and he felt discouraged. He had a firm determination to be reborn in a new life and carry on with the practice. So, if he was reborn quickly, now he must be around there. There is still some possibility of receiving some teaching from me. I did not realize his calculation. He also left a note. At that time, people around him respected him very much, and they were in deep shock. I was the only person then who said that it does not matter, it is alright, and was consoling everybody. After a few weeks, however, I became very uncomfortable. Something happened at the emotional level, I felt. One way to reduce sadness is not to take things seriously at an emotional level.

Further, there is no room to argue with oneself at the emotional level. Such argument is disturbing. Emotion is like stubbornness. At an intellectual level, however, you can recognize negative things and can reason through it. Ah, this is bad but there are some good points too. At an emotional level there is no such reasoning. So, maybe that is my technique.

Now let us take, for example, desire and attachment. At an emotional level, there is blind desire and attachment: I want this and I want that. When you are reasoning at an intellectual level, you understand. At an emotional level you also have the power to reason, but you remain stubborn. Intellectually, yes, I want sexual desire. Everyone is very happy about it, everyone is very excited about it (*laughs*). And poor monk, he has no such glorious opportunity (*laughs heartily*). So, then you judge what course is best, and remain a simple monk for the rest of your life and develop a mental state of calmness. Of course, after a few weeks, life without attachment looks less colourful, but it is very steady and stable. After twenty, thirty, forty, or fifty years, that fact of life is conducive for health and happiness.

His Holiness the Dalai Lama is not only the spiritual head of the Tibetan community, but is also shouldering the political responsibility of the Tibetan freedom struggle. One can derive strength from hearing and reading about his inner and outer struggles, experiences and triumphs. Difficulties have challenged His Holiness, and he is very sensitive to the sufferings of others. Undoubtedly, he has risen to meet the challenge of hard times, and in silence and stillness he continues to inspire us to maintain our spiritual strength and poise. He urges a life of appropriate self-discipline dictated by conscience, rather than a life of expediency dictated by society. All in all, pure, unselfish and all-inclusive love has been the hallmark which attracts his students. It is not his power that creates a sense of devotion in others, rather, it is his own devotedness, his compassion and his commitment to humanity at large that is the power.

**The Scientist**

I encountered him nearly four years ago when he came to Delhi to teach. He was very focused, serious and articulate—though at times dismissive of others. He projected the image of a spiritual seeker or warrior, an example for others to emulate in their academic life. This young and brilliant Sikh, in the robes of a monk, the 'Sikh Lama', aroused a deep sense of curiosity in me. How did he get the name Dharmakirti? What compelled him to give up worldly life? And what did it mean to follow a different and difficult path?

He is now in his mid-thirties and resides in the mountains. However, during his annual winter visits to Delhi, I have been able to hold discussions with him.

As he says, 'I can see a continuity which goes back to my childhood, perhaps even before my childhood, where the events that led to my pursuing the spiritual path were in the early stages. I myself had no understanding of the real process of what was going on. In that sense I was a passive entity, led by internal and external forces. I feel that I understand a lot more about this process now. That sense of a passive, helpless entity being swept along is now no longer there. In the past, for example, being passive was a source of great fear. Certain events caused me to take interest in the spiritual path. They were of a very traumatic nature. Now slowly this fear and anxiety have evaporated.

'Even as a child, when I started becoming aware of myself, I would feel that I was different from most of my peers—my cousins, my family, at school—and this feature became more and more an important part of my personality. I reached a kind of crisis. I was very different from others and I did not share their ideas of happiness and pleasure. But as a child I had a natural inclination for science, a particular interest in living things, and I had a very curious kind of precocious personality. My father was teaching in Pilani. I was about seven years of age. I used to go out often in the afternoon all by myself to the garbage dump outside the chemistry department, sift through the garbage and pick up all kind of test-tubes, chemicals, skulls, all those things. Along with this I had a collection of all kinds of animals, dead things, skeletons, birds' eggs, etc. My father had given me my own room which I had converted into my science club, and I had a few close friends who used to do all sorts of things.

'My parents of course encouraged me. They were of Sikh origin, but they were not at all religious. They were progressive, educated, from a western educational background. There wasn't any kind of religious or spiritual activity in my house. The emphasis was on study, knowledge, and expanding our talents. As a child I had access to a vast collection of books on all sorts of topics. I started painting very early. I got a great deal of inspiration from those books, seeing pictures, reading, etc.

'My father was the most powerful influence in my life. I was the only son of my parents, and I had two younger sisters. I had a very special connection with my father, and we had certain physical peculiarities which were in common. Like both of us were born with ears pierced. My mother tells me that when I was a few months old my father had to go to another city for work. Often I would get up in the night shouting my father's name. My mother would note down the time and my father would dream of me at that time and also note down the time. It was as if we had some kind of telepathic connection. So he encouraged me greatly in my curiosity. I was a voracious reader. I had very eclectic tastes and read a wide range of books. I feel as if my father led me through various stages of my life. He brought me to a clear understanding. He in fact was the person who showed me and encouraged me to realize that my whole intention was to lead a spiritual life and be different from others, which I thought was some kind of aberration. He eventually helped me to develop the ideal to become a sage.

'As a child my ambition was to be a scientist; that was my

ideal. He encouraged me to pursue that ideal. But he showed me in my adult years, just a few years before he died, that being a sage is far more difficult than being any sort of scientist. He did that largely from personal example. My father was only twenty-two years older than me. He and I were more like friends. Often he would treat me as an equal rather than as his son or someone junior. He encouraged me to study science. When I was in class tenth or eleventh I was going through some kind of identity crisis, and I realized that I had a very complex mind. It worked in very complex ways and the working of my own mind became a source of a fascination for me.

'He advised me to study science. I took that to mean the scientific paradigm that the mind is the brain, which is obvious. Of course, I concluded that the mind was indeed the brain and the best way to study the mind was to study the chemistry of the brain. That is how I became interested in bio-chemistry. After I entered college, my father would push me to formulate a world-view, the philosophical world-view.

'I was influenced by Marxist ideology and I was very, very attracted to it. As a scientist advocating scientific materialism, Marxism fitted completely into my scientific world view. My father would demonstrate all kinds of flaws in my philosophical views. I don't know why, but I would often get very angry with him because he forced me to commit myself to my own philosophical views and I would be unable to pin him down to any point of view. He would make me aware of the inconsistencies in my thinking without committing himself to any view at all. He did not give me any alternative. I was very annoyed because I had no chance to demolish his philosophy or pin him down to any philosophy.

'I understand my father much more now, when I look back. The deeper I go the greater is my communication with him. He was very wise. I later understood that this is the Prasanghika method of dialectical discussion. Actually he understood all this at a time when there was neither information nor general interest in this matter. Today as I progress I find my connections with him becoming stronger and stronger, deeper and deeper.

So this was one of his methods of influencing me. The other method was his own personal example.

'He was a secretary in the state government. He was a man of conviction, and everybody knew, even admitted, that he had a vision and philosophy unlike many other goverment officials. Also, he was known to be a very upright and honest man in a completely corrupt system. The situation became so bad that he was living with very high tension. His boss was bad, his subordinates were bad, and they wanted to get rid of him. Things became so tense for him that he suffered a very serious heart attack at the age of forty-nine and died. It was a turning point in my life. With his personal example, he exemplified an uncompromising honesty. He went to Sikkim at a time when it was a very remote region. Nobody knew about Sikkim. He joined as the principal of the Tibetan Refugee School and gave up his academic career. So from the beginning he showed that one should stick by one's convictions, and that there are more important things in life than money and social status.

'For the last three to four years of his life, he underwent a complete change. He had a big beard and he looked like a saint. Often I would observe that he was lost in thought. It always seemed that he was too preoccupied, as though his mind was all the time resting on some internal object. I didn't understand it until much later. I remember when he died it was the biggest funeral in Gangtok. People came from all over the state, causing a traffic jam almost twelve kilometres long.

'My mother was the stabilizing influence in our family. She is very down-to-earth and straightforward. She was a very necessary kind of presence to my father, who without her would have been lost. It was her influence that kept him cool, at home, and in proper health. I thank her for the physical form that I have today, and I thank my father for the mind that I have today.

'I realized that many scientists are technicians, not philosophers. They never think of the philosophical implications of what they are doing. As a result, I began having doubts that perhaps science is not as final, as comprehensive, and as persistent as I would like to believe. I began to realize slowly that in fact I was not a real scientist as much as a philosopher who had somehow found his way into science.

'So, by the time I was doing my master's degree I had already begun to run into some very serious philosophical problems regarding the relationship between mind and body. The more I researched scientific views on this matter, the more dissatisfied I became. I began to realize I was not actually understanding what I really wanted to, and still want to understand, which is consciousness—the fact that I am thinking, feeling, loving, weeping, and have all these powerful forces and emotions working in my mind. The molecule does not tell me what all this is. Through studying chemistry, I realized not what the mind is but what the mind is not. Doubts began to seep into my thoughts.

'In 1982 my father came to meet me. He was supposed to come in the evening and I was supposed to pick him up from the bus stand. I had a motorcycle. That very day a friend of mine and his mother had come from Delhi. I had met her and she had left her bag in my room. She had gone to stay with some relatives, so she said, "When you go in the evening to pick up your father, you come by and drop my bag". So we went in the evening with my friend to drop her bag.

'I walked into the drawing-room, and she was sitting there talking to an old man. And this old man was being very loud, very boorish, and he was drinking beer. Aunty made me sit down to have a cup of tea. This man ignored me and carried on his conversation with the lady. Just as I had finished my tea and was about to get up to leave, the man turned around and asked me to remain seated. I remember he was a remarkable looking man. He had no external mark of distinction. But he had very peculiar features. He had a very big face. He was completely bald. He had very small, very deep-set and piercing eyes. When you looked at him you somehow felt uncomfortable under his gaze.

'He had a strange appearance. Later I found that this is characteristic of the face of highly realized masters. He asked me about the grey bandage on my wrist. I said that I had fallen from my motorcycle and had slightly strained my wrist. He looked at me and said, "Son, when I look at you I feel like weeping." I asked why. He said, "What's now going to happen to you is something so bad that I feel like weeping." I was very perplexed. He was very emphatic in his manner and I said, "Look, I don't know you". He said, "You don't know me?" I looked at him and said, "You have never met me before." He picked up a black wooden ruler on the table in front of him and struck the table again and said, "Don't you know me?" I suddenly remembered that a week ago I had in fact had a very peculiar and strange dream.

'I dreamt that I was walking in the mountains of Sikkim with my father. It was before dawn, and I asked him where he was taking me. He said that he was taking me to teach me how to fly. So we walked along and we came to a plateau and I said, "OK, now teach me how to fly." He said, "First of all you have to get rid of all these heavy chains that you are wearing". I looked and said "what chains?" I was amazed to see that indeed all this time I was wearing all those very, very heavy chains. I was not at all aware of them, and I was shocked. My father said, "Be aware of them."

'When I became aware of the chains, they fell, and then I asked what I should do. He said, "You already know what, and you just remember what you did." I looked at him, and this time I knew exactly what to do. I started rising up in the air on my own and when I was high up, I looked at him and he said goodbye to me. I remember feeling sad, thinking that perhaps I would not see him again. That sadness was immediately overcome by the fact that I was actually not only flying, I seemed to have control over my moves. I also seemed to know that I had somewhere to go. I waved to my father, and immediately I took off over towns, villages, valleys and plains. As dawn was breaking and the sun was rising, I landed in a mountain valley, a very steep valley on the banks of a river. There was a group of young women in white saris waiting for me.

'They took my hands and took me into an igloo kind of a

hut. It had a long narrow tunnel entrance, and inside, it had a dome shape. I had no clothes on and I felt embarrassed being naked in front of these ladies. They were not embarrassed and seemed to be not at all aware of the fact that I was naked. Inside this hut an old man was sitting behind a square platform where he was performing some kind of a ritual. He was pleased to see me. These ladies sat down and the woman in front of him massaged my body with oil until it shone and glistened as though made of gold.

'I was so struck by the dream that I walked to my friend's room in the hostel where I stayed and woke him up. But I had completely forgotten about it until this man forced me to remember the details. It was what psychologists would call an incident of extreme cognitive dissonance. My direct experience did not fit with my understanding of it. So either I had to alter my understanding of the world or find a way to dismiss this occurrence.

'The man I met that day at first didn't talk to me, but then described to me in great detail what I had been eating, drinking and wearing in the past two days, and which hospital I had been to—facts that no person would have access to. I was by then very puzzled. He seemed to take a great interest and asked me to sit down. I said I wanted to leave as I had to pick up my father. But he said, "No, you won't leave." So he told my friend to go and pick up my father and take him to my hostel room, and then come back and pick me up. And the command of his voice and the imperativeness was so great that I had no choice except to obey. He told me, "Son, within a week or so you will have an accident that will alter all your views, and within two months your whole life will be uprooted."

'It was very shocking and frightening and I was completely perplexed. I just didn't know what to make of it. He behaved as though a great tragedy was going to occur, and he was showing great concern for me. But I could feel that he was trying to conceal his mirth. There was sense of comedy to the situation. I felt very strange. Perhaps this was a mischievous man who intended to harm me. In fact, that was the strongest feeling I have had, and it didn't go away for months. Then he let me go.

'Immediately I went to my room where my father was waiting, and I told him that I had met such a man. My father looked very grim. He said, "You have a philosophy of life, yes, a scientific world view. Can't it explain this?" I said that it couldn't. He said, "In that case, just dismiss this whole matter." I was very relieved. Then he got up and said, "Mind you, he has made two predictions and if those predictions come true what are you going to do about your scientific world?" We spent the whole night together, and he said, "I will answer your philosophical crisis. I cannot answer it at length, but I will answer it indirectly." He took me to my room and took out a new Tankha which he had bought that symbolized the Wheel of Life. He took out a bottle of rum and poured a drink for himself as well as for me. We sat the whole night and we finished the bottle of rum. He explained the Wheel of Life and what it means. He told me I was at a point where I should particularly meditate upon the fourth link of the twelve links of interdependence of the chain. The first is the link of Ignorance, second is the link of Karma, third is the link of Consciousness, fourth is the link of Mind and Body. My problem would be solved if I studied this in length, its nature, mind and body. I took his advice very seriously. The next morning he left. I was very shaken by this.

'About a week later I went on a holiday to Pinjore, outside Chandigarh, with a friend of mine. We spent the day there and in the evening at 9:30 p.m. we were driving back on my motorcycle. I struck a buffalo head-on at very high speed. I landed about ten feet away on my elbows and knees. My immediate concern was my friend, and I turned around and asked her if she was all right. She was not hurt at all, but was shocked and cried out. Not only were my clothes torn off my elbow, but my skin had come off and I was bleeding. I could see the bone in one elbow, and was in terrible pain. I collapsed. In such a situation one loses consciousness after some time. But strangely that day I didn't pass out. My mind became more clear. I experienced intense pain and was wishing I could pass out. My bike was smashed absolutely. That night I was on the road for two and a half hours. After some time shock set in, and I started feeling very cold.

'Soon after that I started hallucinating, and became delirious. I felt that I would die because of exposure and loss of blood. Many vehicles passed by that night, but nobody helped. They stopped, they looked, but they didn't help. Till then I had felt that the world was a known and secure place, especially for us who come from an upper-middle-class background. We know that if the car breaks down it can be fixed. If you are ill, the doctor heals you. You may have a problem, but usually somebody is there to look after you. But in this instance my sense of security and well-being evaporated, and I realized that this was going to be my day to die. Then, when I had given up all hope, a motorcycle stopped, went to Pinjore to get me water, and then actually took me to a small dispensary somewhere nearby where there was nothing but a blanket. I waited there while this fellow went all the way to Kalka to get a taxi. He put me in the taxi, took me to PGI, and went off. No bone was broken, but I was very seriously ill, more mentally than physically. Then immediately after that I went home. That was a very traumatic experience.

'We had a summer break. Certain things happened, and I got engaged to a lady and we got married. There is another aspect which I had left out, which I will go back to now. You see, after I finished my graduation, I came home. My father told me that there was no need to go straightaway for a master's degree. I could think it over and teach there. He gave me an ordinary teaching job in Gangtok where I was teaching biology and chemistry to class ten and twelve. I taught there for nearly a year, during which time I started thinking about my life. Then towards the end of the year the Dalai Lama came to Gangtok.

'This was in the fall of 1981. I remember there were banners, placards, arcades and arches erected all over Gangtok to welcome him. I was teaching my class when I saw his motorcade coming and, well, it did not mean very much. I had no interest in him. That day when I was going back home in the school bus with the children there was a massive traffic jam. So I went out and was horrified to see that there was a truck standing there which was unloading dismantled dead bodies like piles of wood. There was a heap of arms, legs, heads, and all kinds of horrifying sights of dead people. In the morning apparently a group of seventy-eighty people in the truck had died in an accident, and they had just been able to find pieces of the bodies here and there. An emergency morgue was constructed so that relatives could come and identify the dead.

'That pile of bodies had a very powerful impact on me; I could not eat or sleep. My mind became absolutely agitated and concerned about the matter of those dead. It struck me that I could die any time, my father could die. For the first time, the thought of mortality troubled me. The Dalai Lama came and stayed in a building just above our house. We could see him coming and going every day. He was giving a series of talks in the main compound there, in Tibetan, for about ten-fifteen days, after which he gave a small talk in English for government officials. We were all invited. My father asked me to come but I refused. I didn't want to go. But he said, "No, no, you must go and meet the Dalai Lama. After all, he is a world leader and a noble mind. You could learn something. Come along." He persuaded me and I went along with him.

'There was a special enclosure cordoned off for the government officials. Then there was a ground where the general public was gathered. Father of course had a seat in the enclosure, and my mother and sister sat there. But he and I went and stood in the crowd. I remember His Holiness the Dalai Lama coming and taking his seat. He tapped the microphone which promptly fell off, and he screwed it on again. He tapped it again and it again fell off. He laughed then, and said, "This microphone and my English are very similar; both are broken." He laughed and laughed and laughed over that. I was puzzled by this man. I basically thought of him as a politician. But now I saw that he was a very genuine person, he was free, and in his laughter I detected genuine and sincere joy, something which I had noticed almost nowhere. That got me thinking about the reasons he had to be so happy.

'Something about his joy touched my heart. At the end of that talk my father presented the question—what is the final antidote to anger? His Holiness spoke for the next forty minutes, during which he gave a complete summing up of the Buddhist path. Nothing made much sense to me.

'After that I forgot about it all and went back to do my master's degree. While leaving Gangtok to come down to the plains, the train passed through the Farrakka barrage. Great floods had occurred in Bihar and Bengal and sluice gates of the barrage were closed. There was a whole lot of debris collected at those sluice gates and I looked out of my train at bloated bodies of men, women, children and animals floating there. First that encounter with the heap of dead bodies in Gangtok, and now this—my mind became more and more preoccupied thinking about death. I was twenty-two. Soon after I joined a graduate programme, my grandfather, my mother's father, died of congestive heart failure in Chandigarh, and I saw him dying. I sat with him the whole night and witnessed the process of death. That tuned my mind even more towards the matter of death, and I started thinking about it a great deal. I started reading medical and scientific discussions of death. What I read made me deeply dissatisfied. The authors knew almost nothing about the process.

'In the meantime I got engaged to a young lady who was in the foreign service. Her father was a very senior diplomat. He was the same age as my father. Both of them were forty-nine years old, young and healthy, and very good men. My father-in-law didn't smoke, didn't drink. He was based in New York, where he suffered a heart attack. In the most advanced city on this earth, where he was in a senior position, in the best locality where all the amenities were immediately available to him, they could not save him. He died, and that really disturbed me. It hit me very hard. During that period I got married to this lady, and wondered whether she would find a father figure in my father.

'She was beginning to get a feeling that my father was very, very strange. It was as if he was not there most of the time. I remembered the next half of this man's prediction. I experienced a constant sense of dread because the first part had already come true. Those were the most terrible days of my life.

We went for a honeymoon to a hotel which my father had booked in Gangtok, a very beautiful spot. After four days of staying there, I felt like sitting cross-legged every evening, which I had never done before. I tried to submit to this instinct, and my wife was worried and surprised as to why I was drawn to methods of reflection and meditation. Secondly, after four days I felt an imperative need to come back home. So against the wishes of my wife, we returned home. I remember having dinner with my father that night and feeling very strongly that he was not well. My mother, a heart patient, had been very much against my marrying this particular lady, and those days she was unwell. So all our concern was for her. Early in the morning I heard a shout from my father's room, and I went running. I thought something had happened to my mother.

'As soon as I reached my father's room I saw my father standing, hand on his chest, breathing very heavily. I knew he was having a heart attack. I took him in my arms and we sent for a nearby doctor. Then I knew he was dying, and I told my mother, the doctor, and everybody to leave the room. I remember him telling me in some casual context some weeks before that when a warrior dies he should not be placed on a high place. The dead body should be put on the earth. Immediately I did so. I washed him, bathed him, cleaned him, put fresh clothes on him. It was devastating. Absolutely devastating. Many things changed.

'There is this arrogance, pride, and vanity that one has about one's social position. I think we were dropped by almost everybody. It was a very humbling experience. Suddenly my mother lost everything. We had to leave the house, we had to shift to a more modest accommodation. That was a great shock to me. I was completely devastated, to an extent my wife could not comprehend. She was also very close to her father, but I don't think the impact of death was the same. My father's death took away the earth from beneath my feet. The worst thing was that with his death my philosophical world-view completely collapsed. Suddenly the world became very weird, frightening, strange—it was a catastrophe for me.

'I went back to my studies in Chandigarh and I knew I had

to seek out that man. But I was very frightened of him. I thought in some way he was responsible for my devastation. One day I built up the courage and went with a friend to meet him. This man was very gentle with me, unlike that first day. I broke down and I wept and blamed him. He told me that the worst had happened, things would be alright now, and he would help me.

'He told me that soon somebody would offer me a job, and that I should accept whatever was offered. Soon enough I was offered a job as an accounts executive in an advertising agency. I took up this job, coming out of the cocoon of a bio-chemical lab to a mad corporate world. For me it was turning suddenly from a white-collar job to a blue-collared job. Anyway, it was a very educative period of intense spiritual awakening in my life. I wanted answers. I was visiting this man regularly and my fears were slowly evaporating. He evoked a very direct Zen master kind of manner, a makeshift kind of world view which, in retrospect, I realize is very similar to the world view in Buddhism called Chittamaatra—The Mind Only school. It is an idealistic kind of school and very similar to Hindu Vedanta. He restored a little bit of my self-confidence. It was very remarkable.

'Strange phenomena would occur. A passing conversation between strangers on the street would have meaning for me. I would feel a sudden crystallization in my mind. He taught me the idea of what you call "Faqir aadmi", someone who is a typical sufi saint. He is one who cares for nothing, who has nothing of his own. Such a man cannot be defeated by anyone because he has nothing to lose.

'By then my wife and I had separated and lived apart—I in India, she in New York. She wanted me to go to New York, but I had no wish to leave, because slowly I was getting the hang of advertising and I felt a lack of connection with her. She was staying with her mother, who was at that time forced to come back to India to deal with some official matters. She met me and persuaded me to go to New York, if not permanently, than just for a month to try and revive my marriage. That man advised me strongly to go. The day I was leaving for New York I asked this man if he was my Guru. He laughed and told me that he was not my Guru. He told me to go to Bodhgaya, and I did. It was then I saw the inevitability of my following a spiritual path, but at that time I still didn't want to do it. For me it meant renunciation, which meant leaving behind everything, which I was not prepared to do. I loved this world too much. I enjoyed it too much. I didn't want to leave it behind. I had very passionate involvements. I couldn't bring myself to accept the idea that I had to leave it. So I thought that by going to New York I could somehow make my marriage work, be happy, and stay there. Then I would forget about this whole matter.

'I went there and joined my wife. But again the world would not let me get away. The first few months of marital life with my wife were very good, but after some time I realized that we were basically very different people. We diverged. We had very different kinds of views, very different values, and we could not find a common meeting ground. Moreover, we both were very headstrong people, and we were not ready to compromise for each other. I was twenty-four years old at that time and she was about two and a half years older than me. We had major conflicts. When she became pregnant, our problems became even more complicated. At that time I simply detested and hated New York.

'I just couldn't bear the American way of life. Firstly, I had never lived in a city all my life; I had lived in the Himalayas. To go away and live with people who were absorbed in such busy, purposeless, pointless lives—I found this utterly stupid. At that time the stark possibility of getting into this nine-to-five routine was staring me in the face. I thought, well, if you are do it now, you will do it the rest of your life. You are finished. Things became so bad between me and my wife that we had to leave. I compelled her to leave New York. She was very unhappy about this. It was an unthinkable thing; people in the foreign service queue up for a long time to get a posting to New York. That's when you make money, buy things, and come back. I had a five-year diplomatic visa to stay there, but it didn't work.

'Anyway, it finally was in New York, just before I left, that through very strange circumstances I encountered the book *Meditation on Emptiness*. Right from the beginning I had a very intense connection with the book. I had all kinds of dreams and visions when I brought it. When I looked through the line drawings, I felt as if I knew all those people. It was as if I had returned home and found my long-lost friends.

'As soon as I arrived in India I got a good job in an office at Connaught Place. It was an air-conditioned office, and I had long periods of no work. It was as if I was given a special environment to sit and absorb the book. I read it for three months, during which time my son was born. My marriage fell apart, and after the second reading of the book I realized that now I was free—that I had to go and find a man who could authenticate the validity of what was within the book, and with whom I could test my understanding and methods of achieving spiritual realization in this life. I could think of only one person, a friend of my father in Sikkim. I went to him. He read the book and told me that my lineage was the Gelukpa lineage, and that I would have to find a Gelukpa monk.

'He helped me find a monk with whom I debated over a period of two weeks. We spent about two hours every day, during which I deepened my understanding through debate. They both advised me that I should now leave and try to meet the Dalai Lama. I thought, what a ridiculous thing. Why should the Dalai Lama meet me? During that time I got involved in a relationship with a Sikkimese lady.

'She was actually a very old family friend of ours and in fact had been a friend and admirer of my father; she was much older, maybe ten years older than me. I desperately needed some affirmation, some empathy, which I did not find at all in my wife. She felt that I was becoming slightly insane. At one point I thought that perhaps, yes, I was. Of course, my wife was the closest person to me, and I should have expected empathy. I found none at all from my mother and sisters either, and I had not too many friends. In a sense, perhaps, this Sikkimese lady saw what I needed. We had a very meaningful and very fruitful relationship for two years, and she groomed me, guided me in Tibetan culture.

'For me it was a massive culture shock because I had grown up with the idea that Tibetans are very backward, barbaric, barely civilized people, who require all kinds of help. I found that those people whom I had always regarded with a mild sort of contempt possessed the most marvellous qualities and were people who deserved reverence and respect. She really helped me to tackle the cultural shock and gave me the utmost respect from the very beginning. She treated me as though I was a Buddha, and by treating me in that manner she added to my confidence and confirmed the value of my pursuit. She herself was interested in pursuing the path, and had been dabbling in it for some time.

'After I left Sikkim, I found my way to Dharamsala. I just went to the residence of His Holiness. I had no contact there and announced that I had come to meet the Dalai Lama. First they thought I was a foreigner, an Iranian. They were slightly sceptical, but then the security chief came up and interviewed me. He found me safe enough to be interviewed for about half an hour. He asked me what I had read. He refused to believe that I could have actually read such books. I had an interview with His Holiness the Dalai Lama within two days, and I had till that moment not decided what I was going to do.

'I had no idea how to behave, what to do when you first meet the Dalai Lama of Tibet. When I first entered the room he was standing up, and the moment I saw him, without any hesitation, I prostrated myself before him. I had never prostrated myself like that in my life, and I was about to make three prostrations. He picked me up after the first prostration and told me not to do it any more. Then we sat down and he questioned me on the state of my mind. He asked me, "Who taught you to meditate?" I told him that I had never formally learned meditation. Then he asked me if I was aware that right now I was in a state of absorption. I was, for the first time in my life, focused and calm, in what Buddhists technically describe as a meditative state. He immediately told me that our connection with each other was not new, that we had known each other in many past lives, that he was greatly delighted to see me. He told me various things about my path and my practice, which I cannot reveal to anybody. Then he asked me what I would like to do. I said I think it's now time, I don't know, that I should become a monk.

He said it was time for me to become a monk, and to meet him at Sarnath within so many days, where he would ordain me. Then he called his secretary and organized things for me.

'It was a very emotional situation. The moment I was leaving, he clasped my hand and he said, "Welcome, welcome Sardarji monk, welcome Sardarji monk!" He laughed. Oh, I was laughing and I was also crying. Then he also asked me: "What do you intend to do after you became a monk?" I told him that I intend to go back to Sikkim and teach the underprivileged children, where I could not earn a salary but just get an honorarium. He told me that teaching is a very good thing, but it's better you stay here and teach my monks. I was surprised and said, "What can I teach your monks?" He said, "No, no, you stay in the Dialectic School and teach my monks, teach them what you know." He gave me board and lodging. I had given up everything. So, I had free room, free food, and Rs 100 per month from him to buy soap, toothpaste, toothbrush, and so on. I lived like that for more than one and a half years, and I taught the monks my understanding of science.

'When I met His Holiness, he asked me to recite a mantra six hundred thousand times, along with a certain very special kind of practice called Guru Yoga. After I completed it, I reported to him. He asked me if I would follow his instructions explicitly. I said, "Of course." He said, "Will you do hundred thousand prostrations on the floor in front of the temple in the winter?" I said, "Certainly, without any hesitation." He laughed and said, "Fine, go ahead and do that." I, proud scientist, and highly educated person, found myself in front of the temple there with ten or fifteen illiterate, backward Tibetan women, doing prostrations. I thought, am I like them, does my guru think no better of me?

'I started doing the prostrations. It was very hard, very difficult, specially for a man like me who had never in his whole life been interested in sports or any other physical activity of any kind except walking (*laughing*)—and that too only when necessary. So I started doing them, and when I had done about 12,000, I kept thinking—"I am no better than these illiterate Tibetan women". I went on doing prostrations, I did 30,000, and with each prostration I thought more and more about the matter until I became physically and mentally ill. I became paralysed, I developed a very serious chest problem, I developed sinus problems, and I could not breathe. I reached a state where I could not feel comfortable sitting up or lying down or standing or walking about, and I stopped my prostrations.

'That night I had a wonderful dream. I can't tell you what the dream was but it was very powerful. It forecast events of the future clearly, and I somehow resolved the crisis in my mind. Next morning I was back in the monastery—I had not been there for a week—and I started my prostrations again. I found myself surrounded by the Tibetan crowds who were doing the New Year's prayers. In fact, I had no space to do prostrations. I started anyway.

'Suddenly the crowd disappeared. I looked around and saw that they were clearing the whole place. I saw them lining up in front of His Holiness's gate, and I suddenly realized that His Holiness was coming. Immediately all the other prostrators vanished, and I thought I should also run away. Then I thought, why should I run away? I am doing what he has told me to do. The security man came and told me to leave, but I continued. Then His Holiness came over. I was very foolish, now that I think of it from the Tibetan point of view. I should have dressed properly, but I was just doing prostrations—a sweaty, tired monk, you know. He asked me, "How many have you done?" I told him that I had done about 30,000. He said "Did you have some problem?" I said that I've had many problems. He just patted my cheek. Of all the human beings who have ever treated me as a child, not even my father dared to pat my cheek. Truly I felt wonderful to be treated like a child by some human being, some being in this world who could actually dare to treat me as a child. I didn't even give that authority to my parents. Do you understand? Ha!

'In fact, I can sum up my entire relationship with my Guru as the only being alive in whose presence I can feel like a child. And I have met in my life academics, industrialists, scientists, rich people, scholars—people who are arrogant in one way or the other. I tell you, they are all immature people. Anyway, he told me that from now on things were going to be OK and that I should finish doing my prostrations. I immediately knew that it was going to be so. Then he asked me to do 100,000 repetitions of a hundred-syllable Sanskrit mantra. I'd never done such things, chanting such nonsensical syllables wasn't my way of having fun, you know. But I did all that he asked me to do. Then he told me that it was time for me to go into retreat. "I will build a house for you and you will stay alone in the mountains," he said.

'So that's what I've been doing—living in the jungle for the past five years. I come down to deal with society when it is necessary. Otherwise, I basically think I have to carry this on to its completion, and after that what I have to do is extremely different. I don't have to stay in jungles to prove anything to anybody, or because I am trying to behave like a holy man, or because my Guru is trying to make me someone like that, but because the task has to be completed. It's like developing a very sophisticated computer that requires very specialized care, and with the kindness of my Guru apparently all this is happening. I hope this continues and I am able to develop abilities that I need to perform the function that I have to in my life.

'My sole aim is to benefit as many people as I can through making them understand why the Buddha Dharma is a final and complete doctrine. I have the task of re-establishing the Buddha Dharma in the country where it originated, and from which it completely vanished for 1500 years. I can say confidently I don't know even one Indian who knows anything at all about the Buddha Dharma. They know bits and pieces, fragmentary knowledge. I know nobody who has a complete understanding of it.

'I do not feel any cultural conflict because Sikhs are very pious and spiritual people, and this is a very pious and spiritual path. Sikhs have a long tradition of devotion to the gurus. I find it natural and that's why the level at which I am practising this entire path is total, complete devotion towards the Guru. It is not surrender; warriors surrender to nobody. I would say that there is a man who knows everything about something that I need to know. It is a very dangerous task that I have to do. He can guide me. He is the only person I trust in this matter. I actually laid my life in his hands, and he's returned it to me after making sure that I am wise enough, careful enough, responsible enough to take care of it. That's what I am doing now by being a humble practitioner. I know I've got a long, long way to go. The path is very difficult. There is too much to be done and too little time. The time of death cannot be predicted, and within that context I'd like to do my very best.

'I've faced many physical hardships on the path—I broke my back getting twenty litres of water every day for six months up and down a kilometre-high hill—but I am not at all afraid of facing these hardships. The greatest hardship was in my family, leaving the life that I loved so much. Then going into the forest, living a solitary life, and learning to cook for myself. What I basically learned there was to take complete responsibility for my life. Normally we live with this illusion that there are doctors, servants, fathers, mothers, brothers, sisters, society, jobs—things that give you security. I've learned to live in the jungle alone. I can survive there. So, to get that knowledge, great hardship had to be undergone, and it's no sacrifice.

'If a poor man has to give up his little roadside teashop in order to inherit a billionaire's fortune, you think giving that up and going through whatever hardship is any sacrifice? Ah! So from a certain point of view, it's pretty wonderful.'

*

Exchanging hearts is a deep mystery. The scientist has gone through a lot and given up a great deal. Certain conditions were created and he was drawn to his spiritual master. The teacher's indefinable attentiveness transported him to another level of consciousness, and he made a certain contact with himself. He was given tasks which enabled him finally to recognize his mission for what it was.

When we feel the difficulty of our situation, or as Needleman puts it, 'when life seems shallow and contradictory, when all our assumptions are challenged, our hearts are broken, and our hopes for happiness seem to be fading away: all those things which make up the disappointments of life. This is a first stage, surface-eros, and it is important not to confuse it with the deeper one. We touch the deeper eros in moments of great shock and grief, or extraordinary joy.'[1] So, in our age of chaos and uncertainty, one's spiritual inclination can be seen as a search for enlightenment and meaning. With the world pressing on us, obviously there is work to be done.

The Sage and the Scientist have shown us how with the help of a detached view and philosophical understanding, we can see through the illusion of inherent existence. Enlightenment is entirely based on the wisdom of emptiness and this acts as an antidote to delusions. Also, in order to practise tantra one must have a solid grounding in altruism, and the wisdom that comes from understanding concepts of emptiness. A constant familiarization with this philosophic path finally requires aeons to attain some realizations through one's practice. In order to receive an unbroken lineal transmission, and for developing one's practice, one needs the guidance and blessings of the guru.

Self-examination, alertness and meditative antidotes enable one to recognize luminosity and knowing as the nature of mind, and help to eliminate its adventitious and temporary defilements. To fight the inner enemy of ignorance, aversion and attachment, and bring about inner transformation, is most difficult, yet a worthwhile goal to aspire for. It seems that men are very focused once they take to this path while women approach it through simultaneity. However, it does not exclude the possibility of men and women adopting each other's ways, and even synthesizing them.

**Concluding Thoughts**

It is widely believed that if you know the beginning, you will know the end as well, but if the beginning is beginningless, then the end will be endless. This book is part of the beginning. Through describing secular experiences in the lives of contemporary urban Indian women I have tried to show how they attempt to synthesize their worldly lives with their desire to transcend it. The spirituality of women in these turbulent times remains a relatively unexplored terrain. Only recently has it been taken up as a subject of study in the fields of gender and religion.

The term spirituality has been trapped between religion and philosophy. It is a wise choice to give up the temptation to define it. Various connotations of spirituality can be deciphered, but they by no means exhaust all its roots. From meanings range from religious affiliations, rituals and prayer to knowledge, devotion, meditation and yoga; from self-exploration to ethical conduct; from community outreach to political activism; from divine inspiration to healing; from worldly preoccupations to attaining enlightenment; from nature to art, music and literature; from understanding the essence and power of mind to developing wisdom and compassion; from experiencing human suffering to experiencing human bliss; and humanstic philosophy informs us about the richness and diversity of the spiritual landscape.

In the midst of increasingly complex technology, ecological awareness, and socio-economic changes, religion remains a constant source of consolation in women's lives. Engagement with one's spiritual development, it seems, allows people to withstand the corrosive influence of modernity and its concomitant disenchantments. Also, this micro-level excercise has repercussions for the macro-reality. In this age of materialism, meditation transmutes one's distress and dissatisfaction into contentment and tranquillity and will perhaps put an end to the pervasive cultural aggression and conflict, the violence and chaos.

None of us has the whole truth or the same piece of it. Even though women will keep drawing their spiritual strength from religious discipline, they apparently find no contradiction between their secular and spiritual aspirations. Women's daily struggles subsume their spiritual quest, as is clear from their individual life-stories. So, the spiritual quest does not necessarily involve renunciation. The humane element is inexhaustive in the feminine spiritual paradigm as it contains the toil and tears of the here and now rather than the masculine infinite and abstract ascent. Thus, feminine transformation in family relationships, especially in the mother-daughter bond; achieving intellectual asceticism through their education and work; emotional blossoming in their journey from sexual mismatching to sexual compatibility; evolution from mates to soulmates; accessing the privileges of the Guru connection—all these indicate women's desire to possess a pure and positive mind (their inner protector).

Irrespective of their class background, the enormous spiritual stature of women—like the familiar metaphor of muddy water that, when allowed to stand, becomes clear—arises from everyday life and prepares women to walk in receptive silence. While they endeavour to find a permanent remedy for their 'dukkha' (suffering), women's spiritual aspirations carry them upwards on the wings of hope and peace.

# Notes

Introductior

1. United Nations Population Fund: *The State of World Population, 1994. Choices and Responsibilities*. Introduction.
2. See *Towards Equality—Report of the Committee on Status of Women in India*, 1974. ICSSR, Department of Human Welfare, New Delhi.
3. King, Ursula (ed.) 1995. *Religion and Gender*, Oxford: Blackwell Publications. *Introduction.*
4. Leslie, J. 1991. *Roles and Rituals for Hindu Women*, London: Pinter Publishers.
5. McNay, Lois 1992. *Foucault and Feminism*, Cambridge: Polity Press. pg. 1.
6. Berry, P. & Wernick, A. (eds.) 1992. *Shadow of Spirit: Postmodernism and Religion*, London: Routledge. pg. 205.
7. Raschke, C. 1992. 'Fires and Roses' in Berry, P. & Wernick, A. 1992. *Shadow of Spirit*. ibid. pg. 94.
8. Taylor, M.C. 1992. 'Reframing Postmodernisms' in *Shadow of Spirit*. ibid. pg. 11.
9. Berry, P. & Wernick, A. (eds.) 1992. op. cit. pg. 3.
10. Wernick, A. 1992. 'Post-Marx: Theological Themes' in *Baudrillard's America*. ibid. pg. 57.
11. Wyschogrod, E. 1990. *Saints and Postmodernism*, Chicago: University of Chicago Press.

12. Finn, G. 1992. 'Politics of Spirituality' in Berry, P. & Wernick, A. (eds.) *Shadow of Spirit*. op. cit. pg. 120.
13. Panjwani, N. & Sehgal, R. 1996. 'Sects and the New Indian' in *Times of India*, November 10, 1996. New Delhi.
14. Bem, Sandra Lipsitz 1993. *The Lenses of Gender: Transforming the Debate on Sexual Inequality*, New Haven and London: Yale University Press.
15. Johnson, Patricia Altenbernd & Kalven, Janet (eds.) 1988. *With Both Eyes Open: Seeing Beyond Gender*, New York: Pilgrim Press.
    Van Leeuwen, Mary Stewart et. al. (eds.) 1993. *After Eden: Facing the Challenge of Gender Reconciliation*, Grand Rapids, MI: William B. Eerdmans Publishing Company, and Carlisle: The Paternoster Press.
16. King, Ursula (ed.) 1995. op. cit. pg. 1.
17. Buchanan, Constance H. 1987. 'Women's Studies' in M. Eliade (ed.) *The Encyclopedia of Religion*, New York: Macmillan; London: Collier Macmillan, vol. 15. pp. 433-40.
18. Ruether, Rosemary Radford 1983. *Sexism and God-Talk: Toward a Feminist Theology*, Boston: Beacon Press. Whitmont, E.C. 1987: *Return of the Goddess*, London: Arkana.
19. O'Connor, June 1989. 'Rereading, Reconceiving and Reconstructing Traditions: Feminist Research in Religion' in *Women's Studies*, 17, 1. pp. 101-23.
20. King, Ursula (ed.) 1995. op.cit. pg. 16.
21. ibid.
22. Gross, Rita M. 1993. *Buddhism after Patriarchy: A Feminist History, Analysis, and Reconstruction of Buddhism*, Albany NY: State University of New York Press.
    Young, Serenity (ed.) 1993. *Sacred Writings By and About Women: A Universal Anthology*, London: Pandora, and New York: Crossroad.
23. King, Ursula 1993. *Women and Spirituality: Voices of Protest and Promise*, London: Macmillan, and University Park, PA: Penn State Press.
24. Martin, Judith G. 1993. 'Why Women Need a Feminist

Spirituality' in *Women's Studies Quarterly*, XXI, 1 & 2, pp. 106-20.

25. Christ, Carol P. and Plaskow, Judith (eds.) 1992. *Woman Spirit Rising, A Feminist Reader in Religion*, San Francisco: Harper & Row.
26. Harris, Maria 1991. *Dance of Spirit*, New York: Bantam Books.
27. Singh, Renuka 1990. *The Womb of Mind*, New Delhi: Vikas.
28. Madan T. N. (ed.) 1991. *Religions in India*, New Delhi: Oxford University Press. Introduction.
29. ibid.
30. Chatterjee, M. 1989. *The Concept of Spirituality*, New Delhi: Allied Publishers Pvt. Ltd. Preface.
31. Berry, P. & Wernick, A. (eds.) 1992. op. cit. pp. 4-5.
32. Bannet, E.T. 1992. *Marx, God and Praxis*. ibid. Chpt. nine.
33. Ling, T. 1980. *Karl Marx and Religion*, New York: Barnes & Noble.
34. Lyotard, J.F. 1984. *The Postmodern Condition: A Report on Knowledge*, Manchester University Press.
35. Sen, Amratya: *Indian Express*, March 1995. New Delhi.
36. Clarke, J.J. 1995. *C. G. Jung: Jung on the East*, London: Routledge. pg. 50.
37. Lash, Scott 1990. *Sociology of Postmodernism*, London: Routledge. pp. 12-13.
38. ibid. pg. 14.
39. Yamane David & Polzer Megan. 'Ways of Seeing Ecstasy in Modern Society: Experiential-Expressive and Cultural—Linguistic Views' in *Sociology of Religion*: in Vol. 55-No I. Spring 1994.
40. Otto, Rudolf 1958. *The Idea of the Holy*, London: Oxford University Press.
41. Eliade, Mercia 1959. *The Sacred and the Profane*, San Diego: Harcourt Brace Jovanovich.
42. Leeuv, Vander G. 1986. *Religion in Essence and Manifestation*, Princeton, NJ: Princeton University Press.
43. Luckmann, T. 1967. *The Invisible Religion*, New York: Macmillan.

44. Berger, P. 1979. *The Heretical Imperative*, Garden City, New York: Doubleday/Anchor.
45. Bellah, Robert 1970. *Beyond Belief*, New York: Harper & Row.
46. Singh, Renuka, op. cit. Introduction.
47. Merton, R. K. 'Some Thoughts on the Concept of Sociological Autobiography, in *Sociological Lives* (ed.) Riley, M.W. 1988. California: Sage. pg. 18.
48. Smith, S. 1987. *A Poetics of Women's Autobiography*, Bloomington and Indianapolis: Indiana University Press.
49. Oakley, J. and Callaway, H. (eds.) 1992. *Anthropology and Autobiography*, London: Routledge. Chpts. I & II.

Chapter 6: Self-Reflections

1. Narayan, Dhirendra (ed.) 1975. *Explorations in the Family and other Essays*, Bombay: Thacker and Co.
   Gore, M.S. 1968. *Urbanization and Family Change*, Bombay: Popular Prakashan.
   Goode, W.J. 1963. *World Revolution and Family Patterns*, London: The Free Press of Glencoe.
   Ross, Aileen D. 1961. *The Hindu Family in its Urban Setting*, Canada: University of Toronto Press.
   Uberoi, P. (ed.) 1993. *Family, Kinship and Marriage in India*, Delhi: Oxford University Press.
2. Singh, Renuka 1990. *The Womb of Mind*, Delhi: Vikas. pp. 107-12.
3. ibid. pg. 108.
4. Hammer, S. 1976. *Daughters and Mothers, Mothers and Daughters*, London: Hutchinson.
   Lannoy, R. 1971. *The Speaking Tree: A Study of Indian Culture and Society*. New York: Oxford University Press.
5. Sobti, Krishna. 1994. *Eh Ladki*, New Delhi: Raj Kamal.
6. Pandey, Mrinal. 1993. *Daughter's Daughter*, New Delhi: Penguin.
7. Debold Elizabeth et. al. 1993. *Mother Daughter Revolution*, New York: Bantam Books.
8. Hammer. op. cit. pg. xiii.

9. Debold Elizabeth et. al. op. cit. pg. 31.
10. Downing, Christine. 1990. *Psyche's Sisters*, New York: Continuum. pg. 13.
11. ibid. pg. 9.
12. Singh, Renuka. op. cit. pg. 196.
13. Foucault, Michel. 1978. *The History of Sexuality*, Vol. I translated by Robert Hurely, New York: Pantheon Books.
14. Friday, Nancy. 1977. *My Mother My Self*, USA Fontana/Collins and Hammer, op. cit. Chpt. III.
15. Jones, R. Ann. 1986. *Writing the Body in the New Feminist Criticism* (ed.) Elaine Showalter, London: Virago.
16. Lorde, Audre. 1982. *Zami: A New Spelling of My Name*, Freedom, California: The Crossing Press and 1984. *Sister Outsider*, Freedom, California: The Crossing Press.
17. Singh, Renuka. op. cit. Chpt. Seven.
18. Brennan Teresa (ed.) 1989. *Between Feminism and Psychoanalysis*, London: Routledge. Introduction.
19. Singh, Renuka. op. cit. pp. 198-99.
20. ibid. pg. 156.
21. Horney, Karen. 1967. *Feminine Psychology*, New York: W.W. Norton. Chpt. 'The Dread of Woman'.
22. Foucault, Michel. op. cit. & Gutting Gary 1994. *The Cambridge Companion to Foucault*, Cambridge: Cambridge University Press.
23. Singh Renuka. op. cit. pg. 203.
24. Yeshe, Lama Thubten. 1987. *Introduction to Tantra: A Vision of Totality*, Compiled and edited by Jonathan Landaw, Boston: Wisdom Publications.

    Zopa Rinpoche, Lama Thubten 1994. *The Door to Satisfaction*, Boston: Wisdom Publications.
25. Rinpoche, P. 1994. *The Words of My Perfect Teacher*, Delhi: Harper Collins Publishers India. pg. 138.
26. ibid. pp. 144-149.
27. Vivekananda, Swami. 1992. *The Complete Works of Swami Vivekananda*. Calcutta: Advaita Ashram. Vols. 3, 5 & 7.
28. Khan, Hazrat Inayat. 1990. *Sufi Mysticism*. Vol. X. Delhi: Motilal Banarsidass Pvt. Ltd. pp. 57-114.

29. Kakar, S. 1991. *The Analyst and the Mystic*, New Delhi: Viking. pp. 47-48.
30. Mitchiner, John. 1992. *Guru*, New Delhi: Viking. Chpt. I.
31. Lesile, J. 1985. 'Essence and Existence: Women and Religion in Ancient India' in *Women's Religious Experiences* (ed.) Pat Holden, NY: Croom Helm.
32. Singh, Renuka. 1990. *The Womb of Mind*, Delhi: Vikas. pg. 159.
33. Poem extracted from 'Tricycle'.
34. Roy, Manisha. 1975. *Bengali Women*, Chicago: University of Chicago Press.
35. Saraswati, Swami Satyananda. 1984. *Light on the Guru Disciple Relationship*, Munger, Bihar: Bihar School of Yoga. pp. 29-42: A yogic guru is one who has mastered and perfected the science of yoga through long and arduous practice. The *gyani* guru is a very learned person who has a thorough knowledge of scriptural lore. The tantric guru is a synthesis of a yogi, a *gyani* and a tantric. After the initiation, their knowledge is transformed into experience and then they become tantric gurus. A brahmanishta guru is one who is established in supreme consciousness. He is a jivanmukta, 'liberated while living'. He is totally immersed in his knowledge and experience of the absolute, and that is where he dwells.
36. Dalai Lama. 1988. *Bodhgaya Interviews*. ed. by Cabezon, Jose Ignacio, Ithaca, New York: Snow Lion Publications. pp. 44-46.

Chapter 7
Another Aspect of the path: The Sage and the Scientist

1. Needleman, J. 'Between Heaven and Earth' in *Parabola*, Winter 1995. Vol. XX, No. 4. pp. 12-13.

# *Bibliography*


Achterberg, J. 1990. *Woman as Healer*, London: Rider.

Adams, Carol J. (ed.) 1993. *Ecofeminism and the Sacred*, New York: Continuum.

Appiquanesi, L. 1973. *Femininity and the Creative Imagination*, London: Vision Publishers.

Archer, J. & Llyod, B. 1982. *Sex and Gender*, Harmondsworth: Penguin.

Ardener, E. 1989. *The Voice of Prophecy*, Oxford: Basil Blackwell.

Ardener, S. (ed.) 1978. *Defining Females*, London: Croom-Helm.

Aries, P. & Bejin, A. (eds.) 1985. *Western Sexuality*, Oxford: Basil Blackwell.

Aron, R. 1968. *Progress and Disillusion*, Harmondsworth: Penguin.

Babb, Lawrence A. 1975. *The Divine Hierarchy: Popular Hinduism in Central India*. New York: Columbia University Press.

Barker, P. 1972. *A Sociological Portrait*, England: New Society.

Bateson, M.C. 1984. *With a Daughter's Eye*, New York: William Morrow.

Baudrillard, J. 1983. 'The Ecstasy of Communication' in H. Foster (ed.) *Postmodern Culture*, London: Pluto Press.

Beebe, J.(ed.) 1989. C.G. Jung: *Aspects of the Masculine*, London: Ark Paperbacks.

Belenky, Mary F. et. al. 1986. *Women's Ways of Knowing*, USA: Basic Books.

Bellah, R. 1970. *Beyond Belief*, New York: Harper & Row.

Bellah, Robert N. et. al. 1989. *Habits of the Heart*, New Delhi: Tata McGraw-Hill Publishing Co. Ltd.

Bem, Sandra L. 1993. *The Lenses of Gender: Transforming the Debate on Sexual Inequality*, New Haven & London: Yale University Press.

Berger, P. 1979. *The Heretical Imperative*, Garden City, New York: Doubleday / Anchor.

Bernard, J. 1981. *The Female World*, New York: The Free Press.

Bhattacharyya, N.N. 1995. *Religious Culture of North-Eastern India*, New Delhi: Manohar.

Block, M. & Parry, J. (eds.) 1982. *Death and the Regeneration of Life*, USA: Cambridge University Press.

Bott, E. 1964. *Family and Social Network*; London: Tavistock.

Bourdieu, P. 1990. *In Other Words: Essays Towards a Reflexive Sociology*, Cambridge: Polity.

Brennan, T. (ed.) 1989. *Between Feminism and Psychoanalysis*, London: Routledge.

Buber, M. 1985. *Ecstatic Confessions*, San Francisco: Harper & Row.

Buchanan, Constance H. 1987. 'Women's Studies' in M. Elaide (ed.) *The Encyclopedia of Religion*, New York: Macmillan; London: Collier Macmillan.

Buckley, T. & Gottlieb, A. (ed.) 1988. *Blood Magic*, Berkeley: University of California Press.

Burguiere, A. Zuber, Klapish C. et. al. (eds.) 1996. *A History of the Family*, Vol. I. Cambridge: Polity Press.

Caplan, P. (ed.) 1987. *The Cultural Construction of Sexuality*, London: Tavistock Publications.

Carroll, Theodora F. 1983. *Women, Religion and Development in Third World*, New York: Praeger.

Chatterjee, M. 1989. *The Concept of Spirituality*, New Delhi: Allied Publishers Pvt. Ltd.

Chodorow, N. 1978. *The Reproduction of Mothering*, Berkeley: University of California Press.

Christ, Carol P. 1983. 'Symbols of Goddess and God' in Carl Olson (ed.). *The Book of Goddess: Past and Present*, New York: Crossroad.

Christ, Carol P. and Plaskow, J. (eds.) 1979. *Woman Spirit Rising. A Feminist Reader in Religion.* New York: Harper & Row, (1992 edition: Harper San Francisco).

Cixous, H. & Clement, C. 1986: *The Newly Born Woman.* Trs. Betsy Wing. Minneapolis: University of Minnesota Press.

Cohler, B. & Grunnebaum H. 1981. *Mothers, Grandmothers and Daughters,* New York: Wiley and Sons.

Craib, I. 1976. *Existentialism and Sociology,* London: Cambridge University Press.

Crowley, H. & Himmelweit, S. 1992. *Knowing Women: Feminism and Knowledge,* Oxford: Polity Press.

Debold, E. et. al. 1993. *Mother Daughter Revolution,* New York: Bantam Books.

Deutsch, H. 1944. *The Psychology of Women,* New York: Green and Stacton.

Downing, C. 1984. *The Goddess: Mythological Representations of the Feminine,* New York: Crossroad.

——— 1990. *Psyche's Sisters,* New York: Continuum.

Dumont, L. 1970. *Religion, Politics and History in India,* Paris: Mouton Publishers.

During, S. 1992. *Foucault and Literature,* London: Routledge.

Durkheim, E. 1961. *The Elementary Forms of the Religious Life,* New York: Collins.

——— 1975. *Durkheim on Religion,* London: Routledge & Kegan Paul.

Eliade, M. 1959. *The Sacred and the Profane,* San Diego: Harcourt Brace Jovanovich.

——— 1963. *Patterns in Comparative Religions,* New York: Meridian Books.

Elster, J. 1986. *The Multiple Self,* New York: Cambridge University Press.

Embree, A. T. 1991. *Sources of Indian Tradition,* Vol. I & II. New Delhi: Penguin.

Estes, C.P. 1992. *Women Who Run With the Wolves,* London: Rider.

Evans, D.T. 1993. *Sexual Citizenship,* London: Routledge.

Evola, J. 1969. *The Metaphysics of Sex,* London: East-West Publications.

Faludi, S. 1991. *Backlash,* New York: Crown Publishers, Inc.
Fawcett, J.T., Khoo, S. E. and Smith, P.C. 1984. *Women in the Cities of Asia,* Colorado: West View Press.
Foster, H. (ed.) 1985. *Postmodern Culture,* London: Pluto Press.
Foucault, M. 1978. *The History of Sexuality,* Trs. by Robert Hurely, New York: Pantheon Books.
Freud, S. 1953-74. *The Standard Edition of the Complete Psychological Works of Sigmund Freud.* 24 vols. Ed. James Strachey. London: Hogarth Press.
——— 1972. *Civilization and its Discontents,* London: Hogarth Press.
——— 1973. *The Future of an Illusion,* London: Hogarth Press.
Friday, N. 1977. *My Mother My Self,* USA: Fontana/Collins.
Fromm, E. 1961. *Marx's Concept of Man,* New York: Fredrich Ungar Publishing Co.
Gane, M. 1993. *Harmless Lovers?,* London: Routledge.
Gellner, E. 1985. *The Psychoanalytic Movement,* London: Paladin.
Gilligan, C. 1982. *In a Different Voice: Psychological Theory and Women's Development,* Cambridge, MA: Harvard University Press.
Gluck, S.B. & Patai, D. (eds.) 1991. *Women's Words,* London: Routledge.
Goldenberg, Naomi R. 1993. *Resurrecting the Body: Feminism, Religion and Psychoanalysis,* New York: Crossroad.
Golombok, S. & Fivush, R. 1994. *Gender Development,* New York: Cambridge University Press.
Goode, W.J. 1963. *World Revolution and Family Pattern,* London: The Free Press of Glencoe.
Gore, M.S. 1968. *Urbanization and Family Change,* Bombay: Popular Prakashan.
Government of India, 1974. *Report of the Committee on Status of Women in India,* New Delhi.
Govinda, L. A. 1977. *Creative Meditation and Multi-Dimensional Consciousness,* Delhi: Vikas.
Griffin, S. 1978. *Woman and Nature.* New York: Harper & Row.
Gross, Rita M. 1993. *Buddhism after Patriarchy. A Feminist History, Analysis, and Reconstruction of Buddhism,* Albany NY: State University of New York Press.

Gunew, S. (ed.) 1991. *A Reader in Feminist Knowledge*, London: Routledge.

Gutting, G. (ed.) 1994. *The Cambridge Companion to Foucault*, USA: Cambridge University Press.

Gyatso, Y.K. 1982. *Clear Light of Bliss*, London: Wisdom Publications.

Hammer, S. 1976. *Daughters and Mothers, Mothers and Daughters*, London: Hutchinson.

Harding, S. 1986. *The Science Question in Feminism*, Ithaca: Cornell University Press.

Hardy, F. 1995. *The Religious Culture of India*, New Delhi: Foundation Books for Cambridge University Press.

Harris, M. 1991. *Dance of Spirit*, New York: Bantam Books.

Haug, F. 1993. *Female Sexualization*, London: Verso.

Herrera, N. C. 1992. *Beyond Gurus*, New Delhi: Rupa & Co.

Hewlett, S. A. 1987. *Lesser Life*, New York: Warner Books.

Hill, R. & Koning, R. (eds.) 1970. *Families in East and West*, The Hague: Mouton.

Hochschild, A. 1990. *The Second Shift*, New York: Avon Books.

Holden, P. (ed.) 1983. *Women's Religious Experiences*, USA: Croom-Helm.

Homans, G. C. 1967. *The Nature of Social Science*, New York: Harbinger Book Harcourt.

Horney, K. 1942. *Self-Analysis*, New York: W. W. Norton.

——— 1945. *Feminine Psychology*, USA: W. W. Norton.

Jacobus, M. (ed.) 1979. *Women Writing and Writing about Women*, London: Croom-Helm.

Janeway, E. 1980. *Powers of the Weak*, New York: Knopf.

Jeffrys, S. (ed.) 1987. *The Sexuality Debates*, London: Routledge & Kegan Paul.

Jenkins, R. 1992. *Pierre Bourdieu*, London: Routledge.

Johnson, P.A. & Kalven, J. (eds.) 1988. *With Both Eyes Open: Seeing Beyond Gender*, New York: Pilgrim Press.

Jones, R.R. 1992. *The Empowered Woman*, New York: S.P.I. Books.

Jung, C.G. 1957. *The Undiscovered Self*, Mentor Books.

——— 1986. *Aspects of the Feminine*, London: Ark Paperbacks.

——— 1995. *Jung on the East*, ed. by Clarke, J.J., London: Routledge.

Kakar, S. 1991. *The Analyst and the Mystic*, New Delhi: Viking.
Kenter, R.M. 1977. *Men and Women of the Corporation*, New York: Basic Books, Inc. Pub.
Kapadia, K.M. 1981. *Marriage and Family in India*, Calcutta: Oxford University Press.
Kapoor, P. 1973. *Love, Marriage and Sex*, Delhi: Vikas.
Khan, Hazrat I. 1990. *Sufi Mysticism*, Delhi: Motilal Banarsidass Pvt. Ltd.
King, U. 1993. *Women and Spirituality. Voices of Protest and Promise*, second edn. London: Macmillan; University Park, PA: Penn State Press.
King, U. (ed.) 1995. *Religion and Gender*, Oxford: Blackwell Publishers.
Knott, K. 1987. 'Men and Women, or devotees? Krishna Consciousness and the role of Women', in U.King (ed.), *Women in the World's Religions, Past and Present*. New York: Pargon Hourse.
Lama, D. 1988. *Bodhgaya Interviews*, ed. by Cabezpn, J.I. Ithaca, New York: Snow Lion Publications.
Lannoy, R. 1971. *The Speaking Tree*, New York: Oxford University Press.
Lash, S. 1990. *Sociology of Postmodernism*, London: Routledge.
Lee, C.P., Stewart, R.S. (eds.) 1976. *Sex Differences*, New York: Urizen Books.
Leeuv, V.G. 1986. *Religion in Essence and Manifestation*, Princeton, NJ: Princeton University Press.
Lerner, H. G. 1985. *The Dance of Anger*, New York: Harper & Row.
——— 1989. *The Dance of Intimacy*, New York: Harper & Row.
——— 1993. *The Dance of Deception: Pretending and Truth Telling in Women's Lives*, New York: Harper Collins.
Leslie, J. 1992. *Roles and Rituals for Hindu Women*, Delhi: Motilal Banarsidass Publishers Pvt. Ltd.
Lorde, A. 1982. *Zami: A New Spelling of My Name*, Freedom, California: The Crossing Press.
——— 1984. *Sister Outsider*, Freedom, California: The Crossing Press.
Luckmann. T. 1967. *The Invisible Religion*, New York: Macmillan.

Lyotard, J.F. 1984. *The Postmodern Condition: A Report on Knowledge*, Manchester University Press.

Madan T. N. (ed.) 1991. *Religions in India*, New Delhi: Oxford University Press.

Martin, Judith G. 1993. 'Why Women Need a Feminist Spirituality' in *Women's Studies Quarterly*, XXI. 1 & 2.

Mattoon. M. A. 981. *Jungian Psychology in Perspective*, New York: The Free Press.

McDougall, J. 1982. *Theatres of the Mind*, London: Free Association Books.

——— 1991. *Theatres of the Body*, London: Free Association Books.

McNay, L. 1992. *Foucault and Feminism*, Cambridge: Polity Press.

Miller, D. 1994. *Women Who Hurt Themselves*, New York: Basic Books.

Miller, J. B. (ed.) 1973. *Psychoanalysis and Women*, London: Penguin.

Millet, K. 1971. *Sexual Politics*, London: Hart Davis.

Mitchell, J. (ed.) 1986. *The Selected Melanie Klein*, London: Penguin.

Mitchiner, J. 1992. *Guru*, New Delhi: Penguin.

Moi, T. 1987. *French Feminist Thought*, Oxford: Basil Blackwell.

Mol, H. (ed.) 1978. *Identity and Religion*, New York: Basil Blackwell.

Moore, J. 1980. *Sexuality and Spirituality*, New York: Harper and Row.

——— 1989. *And What About Men?*, Bath: Ashgrove Press.

Morinis, E.A. 1984. *Pilgrimage in the Hindu Tradition*, New Delhi: Oxford University Press.

Mullin G. H. 1986. *Death and Dying*, Boston: Arkana.

Nakamura, H. 1992. *A Comparative History of Ideas*, Delhi: Motilal Banarsidass.

Narain, D. (ed.) 1975. *Exploration in the Family and Other Essays*, Bombay: Thacker and Co. Ltd.

Narayan, K. 1992. *Storytellers, Saints and Scoundrels*, Delhi: Motilal Banarsidas.

Negroponte, N. 1996. *Being Digital*, London: Hodder and Stoughton.

Neu, J. (ed.) 1991. *The Cambridge Companion to Freud*, New York: Cambridge University Press.

Neumann, E. 1974. *The Great Mother*, Trs. by Manheim, R. Princeton, NJ: Princeton University Press.

O'Connor, June 1989. 'Rereading, Reconceiving and Reconstructing Traditions: Feminist Research in Religion' in *Women's Studies*, 17,1.

Okakley, A. 1971. 'Interviewing Women: A Contradiction in Terms' in H. Roberts (ed.) *Doing Feminist Research*, London: Routledge and Kegan Paul.

Oakley, A. 1972. *Sex, Gender and Society*, London: Temple Smith.

Oakley, J. & Callaway, H. (eds.) 1992. *Anthropology and Autobiography*, London: Routledge.

Otto, R. 1958. *The Idea of the Holy*, London: Oxford University Press.

Paglia, C. 1991. *Sexual Personae*, New York: Vintage Books.

——— 1994. *Vamps and Tramps*, New York: Vintage Books.

Pandey, M. 1993. *Daughter's Daughter*, New Delhi: Penguin.

Plaskow, J. and Christ, Carol P. (eds.) 1989. *Weaving the Visions: New Patterns in Feminist Spirituality*, San Francisco: Harper and Row.

Pons, V. & Fancis, R. (eds.) 1983. *Urban Social Research: Problems and Prospects*, London: Routledge and Kegan Paul.

Postman, N. 1986. *Amusing Ourselves to Death*, New York: Penguin.

Preston, James J. (ed.) 1982. *Mother Worship*, USA: The University of North Carolina Press.

Radha Krishnan, S. & Raju, P.T. 1992. *The Concept of Man*, Delhi: Motilal Banarsidass.

Rao, V.V.P. & Rao V. 1982. *Marriage, the Family and Women in India*, New Delhi: Heritage Publishers.

Redfield, J. 1993. *The Celestine Prophecy*, New York: Warner Books.

Reich, W. 1945. *The Sexual Revolution: Toward A Self Governing Character Structure*, New York: Organe Institute Press.

Reinharz, S. 1992. *Feminist Methods in Social Research*, Oxford: Oxford University Press.

Rhodes, C. 1972. *The Necessity for Love: The History of Interpersonal Relations*, London: Constable.
Rich, A. 1979. *On Lies, Secrets and Silence*, New York: Norton.
Riley, M. W. (ed.) 1988. *Sociological Lives*, California: Sage.
Rinpoche, S. 1993. *The Tibetan Book of Living and Dying*, New Delhi: Rupa & Co.
Robertson, R. 1970. *The Sociological Interpretation of Religion*, Oxford: Basil Blackwell.
Rosenberg, M. 1979. *Conceiving the Self*, New York: Basic Books.
Ross, A.D. 1961. *The Hindu Family in its Urban Setting*, Canada: University of Toronto Press.
Roy, M. 1975. *Bengali Women*, Chicago: University of Chicago Press.
Ruether, R. Radford 1983. *Sexism and God-Talk: Toward a Feminist Theology*, Boston: Beacon Press.
Ruth, S. 1990. *Issues in Feminism*, California: Mayfield Pub.
Saraswati, S. S. 1984. *Light on the Guru Disciple Relationship*, Munger, Bihar: Bihar School of Yoga.
Sharma, A. (ed.) 1987. *Women in World Religions*, Albany: State University of New York Press.
Singh, R. 1990. *The Womb of Mind*, New Delhi: Vikas.
Singh, Y. 1977. *Modernization of Indian Tradition*, Faridabad: Thomson Press, Publication Division (India) Limited.
Smart, N. 1969. *The Religious Experience of Mankind*, New York: Collins.
Smith, S. 1987. *A Poetics of Women's Autobiography*, Bloomington and Indianapolis: Indiana University Press.
Sobti, K. 1994. *Eh Ladki*, New Delhi: Raj Kamal.
Sommers, C. H. 1994. *Who Stole Feminism*, New York: Simon & Schuster.
Spencer, R. F. 1971. *Religion and Change in Contemporary Asian Society*, Minneapolis: University of Minnesota Press.
Spender, Dale (ed.) 1981. *Men's Studies Modified: The Impact of Feminism on the Academic Disciplines*, Oxford: Pergamon.
Srinivas, M.N., Shah, A.M. and Ramaswamy, E.A. 1971. *The Fieldworker and the Field: Problems and Challenges in Sociological Investigation*, Delhi: Oxford University Press.

Stimpson, Catherine R. and Person, Ethel S. 1980. *Women: Sex and Sexuality*, Chicago: The University of Chicago Press.

Tambiah, S.J. 1985. *Culture, Thought and Social Action*, Cambridge, MA.: Harvard University Press.

Tiwari, K.N. 1986. *Suffering: Indian Perspectives*, Delhi: Motilal Banarsidass.

Toffler, A. 1981. *The Third Wave*, USA: Bantam Books.

Uberoi, P. (ed.) 1993. *Family, Kinship and Marriage in India*, Delhi: Oxford University Press.

United Nations Population Fund: *The State of World Population, 1994: Choices and Responsibilities.*

Van, L., Stewart, M. et. al. (eds.) 1993. *After Eden: Facing the Challenge of Gender Reconciliation*, Grand Rapids, MI: William B. Eerdmans Publishing Company, and Carlisle: The Paternoster Press.

Vivekanana, S. 1992. *The Complete Works of Swami Vivekananda*, Calcutta: Advaita Ashram.

Walsh, Mary R. (ed.) 1987. *The Psychology of Women*, New Haven: Yale University Press.

Weber, M. 1965. *The Protestant Ethic*, London: Unwin.

——— 1967. *The Religion of India*, New York: The Free Press.

Whitmont, E.C. 1987. *Return of the Goddess*, London: Arkana.

Wilson, E. 1986. *Hidden Agendas*, London: Tavistock Publications.

Wittgenstein, L. 1989. *Lectures and Conversations on Aesthetics, Psychology and Religious Belief*, Oxford: Basil Blackwell.

Wright, G. Von. 1971. *Explanation and Understanding*, London: Routledge & Kegan Paul.

Yeshe, Lama T. 1987. *Introduction to Tantra, A Vision of Totality*, ed. by Jonathan Landaw, Boston: Wisdom Publications.

Young, S. (ed.) 1993. *Sacred Writings By and About Women: A Universal Anthology*, London: Pandora, and New York: Crossroad.

Zaechner, R. C. 1961. *Mysticism: Sacred and Profane*, Oxford: Oxford University Press.

Zimmer, H. 1956. *Philosophies of India*, New York: Meridian Books.

Zimmerman, D.H. & West, C. 1975. 'Sex Roles, Interruptions,

and Silences in Conversation' in B. Thorn & N. Henley (eds.), *Language and Sex: Difference and Dominance*, Rowley, MA: Newbury House.

Zopa Rinpoche, L. T. 1994. *The Door to Satisfaction*, Boston: Wisdom Publications.

Zukav, G. 1979. *The Dancing Wu Li Masters*, USA: Bantam Books.

# READ MORE IN PENGUIN

In every corner of the world, on every subject under the sun, Penguin represents quality and variety – the very best in publishing today.

For complete information about books available from Penguin – including Puffins, Penguin Classics and Arkana – and how to order them, write to us at the appropriate address below. Please note that for copyright reasons the selection of books varies from country to country.

**In India:** Please write to *Penguin Books India Pvt Ltd, 706 Eros Apartments, 56 Nehru Place, New Delhi, 110019*

**In the United Kingdom:** Please write to *Dept. JC, Penguin Books Ltd, Bath Road, Harmondsworth, West Drayton, Middlesex, UB7 ODA, UK*

**In the United States:** Please write to *Penguin USA Inc., 375 Hudson Street, New York, NY 10014*

**In Canada:** Please write to *Penguin Books Canada Ltd, 10 Alcorn Avenue, Suite 300, Toronto, Ontario M4V 3B2*

**In Australia:** Please write to *Penguin Books Australia Ltd, 487 Maroondah Highway, Ring Wood, Victoria 3134*

**In New Zealand:** Please write to *Penguin Books (NZ) Ltd, 182–190 Wairau Road, Private Bag, Takapuna, Auckland 9*

**In the Netherlands:** Please write to *Penguin Books Netherlands B.V., Keizersgracht 231 NL–1016 DV Amsterdam*

**In Germany :** Please write to *Penguin Books Deutschland GmbH, Metzlerstrasse 26, 60595 Frankfurt am Main, Germany*

**In Spain:** Please write to *Penguin Books S. A., Bravo Murillo, 19-1' B, E-28015 Madrid, Spain*

**In Italy:** Please write to *Penguin Italia s.r.l., Via Felice Casati 20, I–20124 Milano*

**In France:** Please write to *Penguin France S. A., 17 rue Lejeune, F–31000 Toulouse*

**In Japan:** Please write to *Penguin Books Japan, Ishikiribashi Building, 2-5-4, Suido, Tokyo 112*

**In Greece:** Please write to *Penguin Hellas Ltd, Dimocritou 3, GR–106 71 Athens*

**In South Africa:** Please write to *Longman Penguin Southern Africa (Pty) Ltd, Private Bag X08, Bertsham 2013*

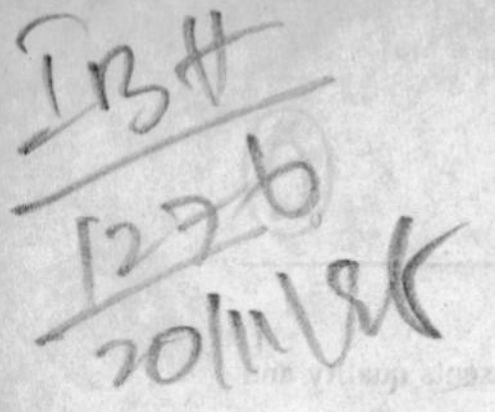


# READ MORE IN PENGUIN

In every corner of the world, on every subject under the sun, Penguin represents quality and variety – the very best in publishing today.

For complete information about books available from Penguin – including Puffins, Penguin Classics and Arkana – and how to order them, write to us at the appropriate address below. Please note that for copyright reasons the selection of books varies from country to country.

**In India:** Please write to *Penguin Books India Pvt Ltd, 706 Eros Apartments, 56 Nehru Place, New Delhi 110 019*

**In the United Kingdom:** Please write to *Dept. JC, Penguin Books Ltd, Bath Road, Harmondsworth, West Drayton, Middlesex, UB7 0DA, UK*

**In the United States:** Please write to *Penguin USA Inc., 375 Hudson Street, New York, NY 10014*

**In Canada:** Please write to *Penguin Books Canada Ltd, 10 Alcorn Avenue, Suite 300, Toronto, Ontario M4V 3B2*

**In Australia:** Please write to *Penguin Books Australia Ltd, 487 Maroondah Highway, Ringwood, Victoria 3134*

**In New Zealand:** Please write to *Penguin Books (NZ) Ltd, 182–190 Wairau Road, Private Bag, Takapuna, Auckland 9*

**In the Netherlands:** Please write to *Penguin Books Netherlands B.V., Keizersgracht 231 NL-1016 DV Amsterdam*

**In Germany:** Please write to *Penguin Books Deutschland GmbH, Metzlerstrasse 26, 60594 Frankfurt am Main, Germany*

**In Spain:** Please write to *Penguin Books S. A., Bravo Murillo, 19 1° B, E-28015 Madrid, Spain*

**In Italy:** Please write to *Penguin Italia s.r.l., Via Felice Casati 20, I-20124 Milano*

**In France:** Please write to *Penguin France S. A., 17 rue Lejeune, F-31000 Toulouse*

**In Japan:** Please write to *Penguin Books Japan, Ishikiribashi Building, 2–5–4, Suido, Tokyo 112*

**In Greece:** Please write to *Penguin Hellas Ltd, Dimocritou 3, GR-106 71 Athens*

**In South Africa:** Please write to *Longman Penguin Southern Africa (Pty) Ltd, Private Bag X08, Bertsham 2013*